教育学专业英语

ENGLISH FOR PEDAGOGY

董晓波 主编

叶霞 边君 副主编

李傲然 蒋菲 参编
邵筱芳 张玉梅

北京大学出版社
PEKING UNIVERSITY PRESS

图书在版编目(CIP)数据

教育学专业英语 / 董晓波主编. -- 北京：北京大学出版社，2024.8. -- ISBN 978-7-301-35190-1

I. G40

中国国家版本馆 CIP 数据核字第 2024WP8333 号

书　　名	教育学专业英语 JIAOYUXUE ZHUANYE YINGYU
著作责任者	董晓波　主编
责任编辑	吴宇森
标准书号	ISBN 978-7-301-35190-1
出版发行	北京大学出版社
地　　址	北京市海淀区成府路 205 号　100871
网　　址	http://www.pup.cn　新浪微博：@北京大学出版社
电子邮箱	编辑部 pupwaiwen@pup.cn　总编室 zpup@pup.cn
电　　话	邮购部 010-62752015　发行部 010-62750672　编辑部 010-62759634
印刷者	三河市北燕印装有限公司
经销者	新华书店
	787 毫米 ×1092 毫米　16 开本　17 印张　471 千字 2024 年 8 月第 1 版　2024 年 8 月第 1 次印刷
定　　价	68.00 元

未经许可，不得以任何方式复制或抄袭本书之部分或全部内容。
版权所有，侵权必究
举报电话：010-62752024　电子邮箱：fd@pup.cn
图书如有印装质量问题，请与出版部联系，电话：010-62756370

Preface
前　言

教育专业英语教学助力中国式教育现代化

　　中国式教育现代化是中国共产党领导、造福于全体人民的中国特色社会主义教育现代化。党的二十大擘画了"中国式现代化"的宏伟蓝图。二十大报告把教育、科技、人才作为"全面建设社会主义现代化国家的基础性、战略性支撑"（习近平，2022）。科技创新和人才培养，都必须依靠教育。教育是基础。这是对新中国成立以来现代化推进历史的规律性总结。一切现代化的本质都是人的现代化，中国要实现现代化，必须充分发挥人才这个第一资源的作用，坚持把科技作为第一生产力，把创新作为第一动力。

　　对于中国式教育现代化而言，没有教师的教育是不成立的；没有高质量的现代化教师队伍，教育现代化也是不可能的。教师是国家价值与权威的代言人，是青少年、儿童健康成长和全面发展的人生导师。正如习近平总书记所言："一个人遇到好老师是人生的幸运，一个学校拥有好老师是学校的光荣，一个民族源源不断涌现出一批又一批好老师则是民族的希望。"（霍小光、吴晶、施雨岑，2016）建设高质量的现代化教师队伍，既是中国式教育现代化的内涵建设，同时也是中国式教育现代化的动力蓄能。要培养现代化的高素质人才、塑造新时代中国公民，就必须首先具备现代化的高素质教师队伍；要培养担当民族复兴大任的时代新人，就必须首先具备具有民族担当和民族精神的教师队伍。因此，近年来，我国政府十分重视教师队伍建设。中共中央、国务院颁布了《中共中央　国务院关于全面深化新时代教师队伍建设改革的意见》，教育部等五部门印发了《教师教育振兴行动计划（2018—2022年）》，教育部等八部门印发了《新时代基础教育强师计划》，各省市也陆续发布了相关政策，为中国式教师队伍现代化提供了政策指引。这些政策立足国家或地方全局，从实际问题出发，坚持系统观念，积极推动新时代教师教育守正创新。尽管如此，我国教师教育发展仍然存在不少挑战，比如不同地区教师供需和师资配给依旧不均衡、不充分，教师职业吸引力和发展后劲不足，职前教师人才培养理念与社会发展需求未能有效衔接，入职和职后教师培训质量不尽如人意，政府、高等院校、中小学校及家庭协同育人机制不健全等。因此，在学习贯彻党的二十大精神过程中，我们应该充分认识到，建设教育强国、实现教育高质量发展，以中国式教育现代化助推中华民族伟大复兴，离不开一支师德高尚、业务精湛、结构合理、充满生机活力的高素质专业化创新型教师队伍。

中国式教师队伍现代化首先是教师素质的中国式现代化，根本上是要突出师德的建设与发展。教师是人类灵魂的工程师，是人类文明的传承者，承载着传播知识、传播思想、传播真理、塑造灵魂、塑造生命、塑造新人的时代重任。在推进中国式现代化的历史进程中，教师素质无论是从师德角度还是专业角度，都应立足于巨大规模受教育人口、全体人民共同富裕、物质文明和精神文明相协调、人与自然和谐共生以及世界和平发展等中国式现代化基本内涵，核心是"明确教师的使命是为党育人、为国育才"。中国式教师现代化具有国外教师现代化的特征，也需要把立德树人融入思想道德教育、文化知识教育、社会实践教育各环节，贯穿基础教育、职业教育、高等教育各领域；要立足于中国式现代化的教育实际，推动教师从固化的教育思维习惯转向不定式思维方式，坚持终身学习和跨专业学习，并在构建教师间合作网络中构筑教师自主知识体系，形成中国式的教育风格。

中国式教师队伍现代化其次强调的是教师队伍结构的中国式现代化。中国式现代化是社会各领域全方位而均衡的现代化，而中国式教育现代化作为中国式现代化的重要组成部分或衍生概念，自然也绝对不是碎片式的、点状的、单独某一类教育的中国式现代化。全面推进中国式教育现代化必须坚持统筹兼顾和全面协调，促进各级各类教育中国式现代化的均衡发展与齐头并进。这意味着教师队伍建设必须以中国式教育现代化的价值目标、基本内涵和本质要求为总体依据，对新时代中国教师队伍进行整体性重塑和结构化培养，始终保持国家教师队伍、区域教师队伍、学校教师队伍在多种维度上的结构合理性。一是根据新型城镇化战略、乡村振兴战略的总体部署，适应以县城为重要载体的城镇化建设和城乡融合发展的需求，优化教师队伍建设整体布局，将素质提升、结构优化摆在教师队伍建设的优先位置，推动教师队伍建设由规模扩展走向质量提升。二是加强乡村教师队伍建设，补齐教师队伍薄弱短板。深入落实《关于加强新时代乡村教师队伍建设的意见》，在乡村教师培养培训、职称、待遇、表彰宣传等各方面给予政策支持，为乡村学校打造"下得去、教得好、留得住"的教师队伍。三是面向基础教育，建设培养卓越之师的教师教育体系。推动师范教育发展，将办好师范教育作为第一职责，实施好师范教育协同提质计划，强化区域教师发展机构建设，加快健全以师范院校为主体、高水平大学参与，本科和硕博士一体化培养的中国特色教师教育体系。四是面向职业教育，发展培养高质量工匠之师的教师教育体系。优化职业教育类型定位，推进职普融通、产教融合、科教融汇。其一，支持高水平理工科大学、行业企业、职业院校等多主体共同参与职业院校教师培养培训。其二，支持高水平学校和大中型企业共建"双师型"教师培养培训基地和企业实践基地，启动实施职业学校教师学历提升行动、名师（名匠）名校长培养计划。其三，突出"双师型"导向的教师考核评价改革，优化职业院校教师队伍结构。五是推进高校教师队伍改革，打造高素质专业化创新型教师队伍。高等学校的教师队伍是我国教师队伍中学历水平和职称等级最高的部分，但是相对于创新驱动发展战略所需的创新型教师还有很大距离。因此，深化高校人事管理及教师考核评价改革，激发教师队伍创新活力，加强校级教师发展机构建设和院系教师发展共同体建设，支持高校教师教育教学创新和专业素质能力提升尤为重要。

再次，中国式教师队伍现代化，教师教育体系现代化是基础，创新人才培养机制是关键。我国高等教育整体水平进入了世界第一方阵，但仍存在着人才培养模式相对陈旧、评价标准相对单一、学生培养同构化发展、创新创造能力不足等较为严重的问题和短板。《中华人民共和国国民经济和社会发展第十四个五年规划和2035年远景目标纲要》提出，要深化教育改革，建立高水平现代教师教育体系。《新时代基础教育强师计划》提出，到2035年，适应教育现代化和建成教育强国要求，构建开放、协同、联动的高水平教师教育体系。因此，在中国式教育现代化进程中，我们需要进一步从体系化、特色化和专业化中加快推进高水平教师教育体系建构，打造服务国家和地方社会发展的多主体、多层级和多功能的中国特色教师教育新体系。一是强化师范院校在教师教育体系中的主体性地位；二是以教育硕士和教育博士等教师学历提升策略为突破，推进教师专业发展的系统性与连贯性，实现教师教育职前职后的一体化发展；三是以教师教育学科体系建设为关键，促进教师教育师资队伍、课程资源、学术科研等方面专业化，推动教师教育体系内部结构要素全面实现优化升级。

从次，中国高校应准确把握好"中国特色"和"世界一流"之间的辩证关系，紧跟世界发展趋势。在体现国际共性和可比性的同时，绝不能把以美国为代表的西方国家高等教育发展模式奉为圭臬，而是要扎根中国大地，体现中国自主，坚持自己的制度特色、文化特点和价值特性，遵循教育规律和人才成长规律，顺应科技革命、产业革命和世界高等教育格局的深刻变化，打破壁垒和路径依赖，加快中国高等教育的国际化、数字化战略，以"四新"（新工科、新医科、新农科、新文科）建设，创新人才培养机制，不断提升中国高等教育对国家经济、社会、科技文化的服务力、支撑力、引领力、感召力、塑造力和国际影响力，力争在新领域、新赛道作出更大的全局性、先导性贡献。

最后，中国式教师队伍现代化要加快推进教师队伍数字素养现代化，大力提升教师信息、数字教育综合能力。当前，中国式教育现代化正处在一个教育数字化转型的时代。教育数字化转型成为中国式教育现代化的实践新样态，并为教育高质量发展全面赋能。党的二十大报告首次对教育、科技、人才进行"三位一体"统筹安排、一体部署，并首次将"推进教育数字化"写入报告，赋予了教育在全面建设社会主义现代化国家中新的使命任务，明确了教育数字化未来发展的行动纲领，具有重大意义。教育数字化转型是一种划时代的系统性教育创变过程，有利于打破教育空间与教育资源的壁垒，通过教育技术变革实现教育领域的融合式、整体式和联通式发展，创建崭新教育样态。教师是改革的实施者，要加强数字时代教师队伍数字素养现代化建设，多层次开展教师数字化能力培训工作，积极应对教育信息化、数字化挑战，大力提升教师信息、数字素养与综合能力，主动应用教育数字化、智能化工具，创新教育教学方法与实践，为教师职业发展赋能，为教学改革升级。

《教育学专业英语》将学习英语与了解教育领域内一些常见学科理论以及教学实践有机结合，目的是向高等院校教育学专业的本科生和研究生通俗、系统地介绍教育学学科理论和教学实践知识体系，提升解决实际教育问题的能力，即让学生在学习英语的同时，系统地了解教育学科学理论、专业知识和教学实践；在认识、走进教育领域的同时，学习和了解教育学科中一些常见的教育理论、观点（包括专业词汇、术语等）的英语表达，在巩固一般语言知识和运用能力的基础上进一步扩展学生的语言知识，提高学生的语言应用能力，将语言教学和专业教育融会贯通，以期提升一线教师以及师范生的综合素质，并在此基础上推进我国教师教育国际化发展进程，助力中国式教育现代化。

本教程选材广泛，信息量大，基本涵盖了当代教育学的主要方面。此外，文字浅显，结构严谨，行文流畅，语言地道也是本教程的显著特点。所有的文章均由英语国家教育学专业人士写作。在编选时，除极少数文章因技术需要略作删节外，力求保持原文风貌，避免一些同类教材用汉语材料译成英语的语言生硬的翻译痕迹，让读者享受纯正的教育学专业英语。在编排体例方面，为了便于读者提高阅读能力，本书增加了文章背景知识介绍，言简意赅地介绍文章基本线索，方便读者快速阅读和理解文章主旨；注释力求简单明了，方便读者了解教育学知识。词汇接近大学英语四、六级难度，主要汇集教育学专业词汇，以降低阅读难度。本教程另附有练习答案（请联系责任编辑索取），便于读者自学，自测学习效果。

本教程除适合高等院校师范英语专业本科生、研究生使用外，也可供各级各类教育学院教育学、教育心理学、英语教学法等专业的本科生、研究生学习教育学专业英语之用。此外，对于大、中、小学教师了解教育学理论知识、提高教育学专业英语水平也是难得的参考书。

在整个编写过程中，我们力求臻于完美，但是限于水平及一些不可避免的因素，定不乏偏颇和疏漏，恳请广大读者朋友和同行不吝指正。

董晓波
2024年2月于南京仙林

Contents

Unit 1 Origin & History of Education ·· 1
    Text A   The History of Compulsory Education in Europe ················ 1
    Text B   A History of American Higher Education ························ 6
    Supplementary Reading: The Origins of Distance Education ············ 12

Unit 2 Educational Objective ··· 15
    Text A   Aims and Objectives of Education ······························· 15
    Text B   Education, Basics of Education and Educational Objectives ······· 24
    Supplementary Reading: Knowing Your Learning Target ··················· 31

Unit 3 Teacher & Student ·· 37
    Text A   The Teacher, the Student and the Classroom ····················· 37
    Text B   Teacher-Student Attachment and Teachers' Attitudes Towards Work ············· 46
    Supplementary Reading: Teacher Effectiveness: What Do Students and
        Instructors Say? ·· 56

Unit 4 Teaching Methods ·· 61
    Text A   Refuting Misconceptions about Classroom Discussion ············ 61
    Text B   Brainstorming: A Creative Way to Learn ························ 68
    Supplementary Reading: Learning Styles and Teaching Styles ············ 75

Unit 5 Materials & Test ·· 83
    Text A   Materials and Media ·· 83
    Text B   Test Anxiety and Academic Performance ························ 90
    Supplementary Reading: Using Examinations and Testing to Improve
        Educational Quality ··· 95

Unit 6 Educational Evaluation ·· 104
Text A Integration of Technology and Educational Assessment 104
Text B Sustainable Assessment and Evaluation Strategies for Open and
Distance Learning 111
Supplementary Reading: Online Diagnostic Assessment in Support of Personalized Teaching
and Learning: The eDia System 118

Unit 7 School Management ·· 120
Text A What Is School-based Management? 120
Text B Data-informed Decision Making and Transformational Leadership 128
Supplementary Reading: Evaluating School-based Management 133

Unit 8 School & Family ·· 140
Text A School and Family Cooperation Models for Reducing Social Problems 140
Text B School-Family Partnership in Hong Kong, China 149
Supplementary Reading: Parent-Teacher Communication: Tips for Creating a Strong
Parent-Teacher Relationship 156

Unit 9 Extra-curricular Activities ·· 160
Text A Extra-curricular Activity and the Transition from Higher
Education to Work 160
Text B Extra-curricular Physical Activity and Socioeconomic Status in Italian
Adolescents 165
Supplementary Reading: Discussion and Conclusion of Correspondence Hypothesis ... 170

Unit 10 Moral Education ·· 174
Text A Education as a Moral Enterprise 174
Text B Moral Education of Youth in the Information Age 179
Supplementary Reading: The Role of Moral Education in Students' Value
Development 184

Unit 11 Education & People's Overall Development ·· 187
Text A Importance of Early Childhood Education 187

Contents

    Text B   Social Skills Development in Primary Education 191

    Supplementary Reading: Importance of Education in Human Development 198

Unit 12   Education & Social Development 201

    Text A   Open and Distance Education: A Better Way of Competence

                  Building and Sustainable Development 201

    Text B   Higher Education Within a Knowledge-based Society 207

    Supplementary Reading: The Global "Imagined Community"—

                  International Education 214

Unit 13   Educational Justice 217

    Text A   Educational Justice in Schools... 217

    Text B   Efficiency and Equity of Education... 222

    Supplementary Reading: Educational Policy, Housing Policy and Social Justice......... 228

Unit 14   Educational System & Educational Law 230

    Text A   E-learning in Modern Educational System 230

    Text B   Legislation and Equality in Basic Education 234

    Supplementary Reading: Major Continuities and Changes in the *Compulsory Education*

                  Law 240

Unit 15   Educator & Educational Thoughts 242

    Text A   Disciples of Confucius... 242

    Text B   Educational Thought and Teaching 246

    Supplementary Reading: Frederick James Gould: Education Inspired by

                  Humanity's Story 252

References 254

Unit 1　Origin & History of Education

Text A　The History of Compulsory Education in Europe

> **导读**：义务教育，是根据法律规定，适龄儿童和青少年都必须接受的，国家、社会、家庭必须予以保证的国民教育。其实质是指政府有义务运用公共资源保障所有适龄儿童接受的教育。义务教育又称强迫教育或免费义务教育。义务教育具有强制性、免费性、普及性的特点。凡是适龄儿童都应接受教育，并且教育对象没有阶级或是出身的限制，此外还必须是免纳学费的。1717年，普鲁士王国开始实施义务国民教育，是全世界第一个实施义务教育的国家。《世界人权宣言》第26条第一款指出："人人都有受教育的权利，教育应当免费，至少在初级和基本阶段应如此。初级教育应属义务性质。"现在多数的国家和地区都在实施义务教育，但年数和成效不一。

In the past few years, there has been a high-profile anti-truancy publicity campaign aiming to send out a clear and tough message to the community, particularly the parents of truants—that truancy will not be tolerated. Thousands of press releases from LEAs have been fed to the national and local press generating adverse news and stories about the fining and jailing of truants' parents, who are regarded as shamefully irresponsible by failing to stop their children from truanting.

Picking up any local newspaper, one would easily find the headlines that slam the "irresponsible parents" whose children are skipping school. These press headlines on truancy have undoubtedly reinforced the fear that truancy levels have reached a crisis point. They have also given people the impression that the perceived newly-emerged "irresponsible parents" are one of the modern days' social phenomenon that is seriously threatening our compulsory education system.

However, nearly 500 years ago, Luther (1967) was already able to observe three equivalent groups of "irresponsible parents" who were most likely to neglect their parental duties in sending their children to school. Most "irresponsible parents" at that time were those who might not understand what Luther thought as their God-given responsibility, others might not be suited for the duty, "...for they themselves have learned nothing but how to care for their bellies".

The third group of parents was the ones who did not have the opportunity or the means to educate their children. Luther observed that these parents placed their children's material comfort above their spiritual needs. He argued in his address to the lawmakers that the civil authorities are under obligation to compel the people to send their children to school:

Dear rulers...if the government can compel such citizens as are fit for military service to bear spear and rifle, to mount ramparts, and perform other material duties in time of war, how much more has it a right to compel the people to send their children to school, because in this case we are warring with the devil, whose objective it is secretly to exhaust our cities and principalities of their strong men.

(Luther, 2018)

One of the hallmarks of the Renaissance movement, which was reaching northern Europe in the sixteenth century, was the rebirth of learning. The Christian Reformation activists tirelessly advocated universal education as an important means of producing responsible citizens. In his open letter to the councilmen, Luther (2018) urged them to have a vested interest in education for a city's best and greatest welfare, safety and strength consist rather in its having many able, learned, wise, honorable, and well-educated citizens than in mighty walls and magnificent buildings.

However, in the early sixteenth century, there was no state education system and most education activities were conducted in monasteries, cloisters and other religious institutions run by the Roman Catholic Church. These institutions very often lacked minimal resources and did not enjoy parents' trust because of the corruption and abuse among the clergy. Many parents were increasingly reluctant to send their children to the training institutions run by the Catholic Church.

Luther (1967) therefore wrote an open letter to the parents to convince his "beloved Germans" that the spiritual well-being of their children was more important than their physical comfort. Luther based his arguments for parental responsibility firmly on the *Bible*, citing several texts as proof.

In Geneva another Protestant reformer, John Calvin (1995), was similarly making a case for compulsory schooling where all children were to be instructed in the "true faith" and "in the languages and worldly sciences" which served as a necessary preliminary for such instruction.

Like Luther, Calvin was supremely confident that his possession of "the truth" gave him a warrant to override the wishes and desires of parents who did not share his beliefs.

As a result of a Protestant reformers' campaign in the state of Gotha, the world's first primitive form of state schooling was established in 1524. It soon spread to Thuringia, Saxony, Wurttemberg and other German Protestant states. In 1559, the duchy of Wurttemberg ordered the introduction of a school attendance register and for the first time in educational history, levied fines on the parents whose children truanted.

However, the elaborate version of compulsory education as we see today did not emerge until the beginning of the nineteenth century when the Kings of Prussia established a system of state-controlled compulsory schooling and forcefully discouraged voluntary education. A minister of the interior was appointed to supervise the running of state schools. In 1810, state certifications of teachers were instituted and in 1812 children were prohibited from leaving school until they had passed a compulsory examination.

Regarded as a successful way of making every citizen useful to the state, the Prussian schooling system soon spread to most Western countries in the nineteenth century, including the USA and the UK.

Notes:

1. **LEA = Local Education Authority (英国地方教育局)**: It is a local authority in England and Wales that has responsibility for education within its jurisdiction. Since the *Children Act 2004* each local education authority is also a children's services authority and the responsibility for both functions is held by the director of children's services.

2. **Luther— Martin Luther (马丁·路德)**: Luther was a German priest and professor of theology who initiated the Protestant Reformation. He strongly disputed the claim that freedom from God's punishment of sin could be purchased with money. His theology challenged the authority of the pope of the Roman Catholic Church by teaching that the *Bible* is the only source of divinely revealed knowledge and opposed sacerdotalism（祭司制度，僧侣政治）by considering all baptized Christians to be a holy priesthood. Those who identify with Luther's teachings are called Lutherans.

3. **John Calvin (约翰·加尔文)**: Calvin was an influential French theologian and pastor during the Protestant Reformation. He was a principal figure in the development of the system of Christian theology later called Calvinism. His writing and preaching provided the seeds for the

branch of theology that bears his name. The Reformed and Presbyterian churches, which look to Calvin as a chief expositor of their beliefs, have spread throughout the world.

4. **Prussia (普鲁士):** Prussia was a German kingdom and historic state originating out of the Duchy of Prussia and the Margraviate of Brandenburg. For centuries, the House of Hohenzollern ruled Prussia, successfully expanding its size by way of an unusually well-organized and effective army. Prussia shaped the history of Germany, with its capital in Berlin after 1451. After 1871, Prussia was increasingly merged into Germany, losing its distinctive identity. It was effectively abolished in 1932, and officially abolished in 1947.

New Words and Expressions:

1. compulsory [kəm'pʌlsəri]	adj.	强制的；义务的	
2. truancy ['truːənsi]	n.	逃学；旷课	
3. slam [slæm]	v.	砰地关上；用力一放；猛烈攻击	
	n.	猛关；猛摔的声音	
4. rampart ['ræmpɑːt]	n.	壁垒；城墙	
5. principality [ˌprinsi'pæləti]	n.	公国；侯国	
6. hallmark ['hɔːlmɑːk]	n.	金银纯度标记；标志；特征	
7. monastery ['mɒnəstri]	n.	修道院；寺院	
8. cloister ['klɔistə]	n.	（教堂、修院或寺院的）回廊；修院（或寺院）的生活	
9. clergy ['klɜːdʒi]	n.	[统称]神职人员	
10. reluctant [ri'lʌktənt]	adj.	不情愿的；勉强的	
11. preliminary [pri'liminəri]	adj.	初步的；预备性的	
	n.	初步行动；准备；初步措施	

Exercises:

I. Vocabulary.

Fill in the blanks with the most suitable words. Change the form when necessary.

reluctant	compulsory	preliminary	slam	principality
hallmark	rampart	truancy	monastery	

1. The plan has all the _____ of being a total failure.

Unit 1　Origin & History of Education

2. A _____ is a building or collection of buildings in which monks live.
3. He closed the door with a _____.
4. The schools were fighting endlessly to combat _____.
5. Ministers have shown extreme _____ to explain their position to the media.
6. Perhaps the tower is part of the _____ of the city.
7. A _____ talk on the future of the bases began yesterday.
8. Attendance at evening prayers is not _____.
9. I've been to the _____ of Monaco.

II. Translate the following words and phrases into English.

义务教育　　　　　　_____
说服，使信服　　　　_____
物质享受　　　　　　_____
精神需求　　　　　　_____
监督，管理，指导　　_____

III. Comprehension of the text.

Decide whether the following statements are true (T) or false (F) according to the passage.

1. National and local press have generated adverse news and stories about the fining and jailing of truants, who are regarded as shamefully irresponsible. (　)
2. A third group of parents placed their children's material comfort below their spiritual needs. (　)
3. In the early sixteenth century, there was only one state education system and most education activities were conducted in monasteries, cloisters and other religious institutions run by the Roman Catholic Church. (　)
4. As many parents were reluctant to send their children to the training institutions run by the Catholic Church, Luther wrote an open letter to them to convince the importance of the spiritual well-being of their children. (　)
5. The elaborate version of compulsory education as we see today emerged at the beginning of the nineteenth century when the Kings of Prussia established a system of state-controlled compulsory schooling. (　)

Text B A History of American Higher Education

> **导读**：高等教育（Higher Education）广义上是指一切建立在中等教育基础上的专业教育，是培养高级专门人才的社会活动。高等教育是大学、文理学院、理工学院和师范学院等机构所提供的各种类型的教育，包括专科教育、本科教育和研究生教育，其基本入学条件为完成中等教育，学完课程后授予学位、文凭或证书，作为完成高等学业的证明。高等教育的发展历史可以追溯到中世纪的大学，后来历经发展，主要是英国、德国、美国的大学的不断转型，形成了高等教育的三项职能，即培养专门人才；科学研究；服务社会。美国高等教育发展肇始于17世纪初的殖民地时期，继承了自中世纪以来的欧洲大学传统，尤其是直接继承了英国的高等教育传统，主要表现为哈佛学院（1636）、威廉玛丽学院（1693）、耶鲁学院（1701）、新泽西学院（1746）、国王学院（1754）、费城学院（1755）、罗得岛学院（1764）、王后学院（1766）和达特茅斯学院（1769）等九所学院的设立，从而开启了发展高等教育的历程。

Higher education in the United States has been molded and influenced by a variety of historical forces. On one hand, there are the patterns and traditions of higher learning which have been brought over form Western Europe. On the other hand, we find the native American conditions which have affected and modified the development of these transplanted institutions. Out of the interaction of these two essential elements and, most importantly, out of the growth of democracy in every area of American life, America has developed a truly unique system of higher education.

English Influences

Oxford and Cambridge furnished the original model which the colonial colleges sought to copy. The prototype for the first English-American college was Emmanuel College, Cambridge University. As we read the explicit statements left by Harvard's founders, we find that the earliest Harvard College statutes were taken directly from the Elizabethan statutes of the University of Cambridge; that the phrase *pro modo Academiarum in Anglia* ("according to the manner of universities in England") is to be found in the first Harvard degree formula; that early Harvard, like Elizabethan Cambridge, welcomed "fellow commoners" as well as serious degree students, "gentlemen" who paid double tuition for the privilege of residing in the college and dining with the Fellows; that even the names of the four college classes—freshmen, sophomore, junior sophister, and senior sophister—were borrowed directly from England. In other points involving student discipline, curriculum, administrative regulations, and degree requirements, Harvard followed English college precedents as closely and faithfully as she could; and Harvard, in turn, became the great prototype for all the later colleges of English-America.

As late as the middle of the eighteenth century, President Clap of Yale prepared himself for his administrative duties by borrowing histories of Oxford and Cambridge and seeking information from Americans who had secured English college degrees. When Clap waged his campaign of 1745 to secure a new Yale charter, he based it on a careful and detailed study of administrative practices at Oxford and Cambridge.

Even at William and Mary, English influence soon challenged an earlier Scottish trend. From 1729 to 1757, eight of thirteen faculty members were Oxford men, and of these eight, Queens College. After 1757, a battle raged almost continuously between this Oxford-bred faculty and the native Virginian Board of Visitors. By 1766 the Visitors "had rid the college of the last of that band of able Oxford graduates, ministers all of them, whose chief fault had been that their ties with English were too close, that they looked too blindly to their homeland."

In almost every case, however, the English colonists eventually found that the unique conditions of the American physical and social environment produced unexpected changes and modifications in their academic institutions. Some of these were destined to be of great importance for the later development of higher education in the United States.

It was soon discovered that it would be impossible to erect in English-America any great university collection of colleges such as existed at Oxford or Cambridge. For one thing, it was doubtful that the Crown would ever grant the required royal charter for such an American university. Besides, the land was too vast and the people too poor. The narrow fringe of British settlements which faced the broad Atlantic on one side and trackless forests on the other represented what for that time was the far western frontier of English civilization. All that could be done under these circumstances was to establish several scattered, widely separated degree-granting colleges, thus diffusing educational effort.

After a time, still another colonial divergence from the English norm made an appearance. Because of the heterogeneity of the American population, collegiate boards of control were established which were interdenominational in make-up and at least one of which was completely secular. Nothing like this had yet been seen in the home country, although the University of Leyden in the Netherlands already followed this pattern.

Scottish Influence

Other modifications were due mainly to Scottish influence. The post-Reformation Scottish university, unlike Oxford or Cambridge, was nonresidential, professionally oriented, and under the control, not of the faculty, but of prominent lay representatives of the community. At the College of William and Mary, some of these Scottish ideas seem to have been influential from the very founding. Commissary James Blair, founder and first president, was a graduate of Marischal College, Aberdeen, and the University of Edinburgh. Reverend William Smith, graduate of Aberdeen, exercised a great influence, as we shall see, over the curricular planning of both King's College in New York, later Columbia, and the College of Philadelphia. John Witherspoon, Scotch theologian who came to the New World in 1768 to become president of the College of New Jersey, later Princeton, exerted an important influence over American higher education.

Although even Harvard was not immune to Scottish university influence, it was at William and Mary that it was felt most directly. The charter Blair obtained for the Virginia school resembled that of a Scottish "unicollege" institution. Like Aberdeen, Glasgow, King's, and Marischal, it incorporated both a university and a degree-granting college by a single letter-parent. At the same time, a governing board was created, made up of members of the nonacademic community; this was, in characteristic Scottish fashion, to have real administrative authority over the college. Even William and Mary's architecture reflected Scottish influence, as did Blair's early plans for a course of study.

Spanish and French Influence

As an afterthought on how different the development of higher education in the United States might have been if Continental rather than English precedents had been dominant, we might look for a moment at the institutions of higher learning founded by the Spanish and French in America. Originally, the English and Continental European universities had a somewhat similar type of organization. Nevertheless, Oxford and Cambridge very early began to follow a largely independent line of development. By the time of the Renaissance, these English universities were changing into loosely federated associations of residential colleges. The Continental universities, on the other hand, were becoming nonresident graduate schools providing specific types of post-baccalaureate training.

The French and Spanish universities in America represented the later Continental type of university. When Charles V of Spain in 1551 founded "the Royal and Pontifical University" of Mexico and the University of San Marcos in Lima, Peru, he accorded them all "the privileges, exemptions, and limitations of the University of Salamanca." This meant that they were definitely to follow the Continental model, because Salamanca was essentially a collection of graduate faculties in arts, theology, law, and medicine. Besides Mexico and Lima, eight other universities were chartered and opened for instruction before a single college appeared in English-America. In all, the Spanish-Americans established twenty-three such institutions.

In contrast, higher education in New France developed more slowly. It was not until the 1660s that Bishop Laval developed at Quebec a "great seminary" for advanced theological training. Although modern Laval University developed from this nucleus, in colonial times the Quebec institution never covered as broad a field as had the Spanish-American universities.

Notes:

1. **Oxford (牛津大学):** It is a public university in Oxford, United Kingdom. It is the second-oldest surviving university in the world and the oldest in the English-speaking world. Although the exact date of foundation remains unclear, there is evidence of teaching there as far back as the 11th century. The University grew rapidly from 1167 when Henry II banned English students from attending the University of Paris. In post-nominals, the University of Oxford was historically abbreviated as *Oxon.* (from the Latin *Oxoniensis*), although Oxf is nowadays used in official University publications.

2. **Cambridge (剑桥大学):** It is a public, research university located in Cambridge, United Kingdom. It is the second-oldest university in both England and the English-speaking world and the seventh-oldest globally. In post-nominals the university's name is abbreviated as *Cantab*, a shortened form of *Cantabrigiensis* (an adjective derived from *Cantabrigia*, the Latinised form of Cambridge).

3. **Harvard (哈佛大学):** It is a private Ivy League university located in Cambridge, Massachusetts, United States, established in 1636 by the Massachusetts legislature. Harvard is the oldest institution of higher learning in the United States and the first corporation (officially *The President and Fellows of Harvard College*) chartered in the country. Harvard's history, influence, and wealth have made it one of the most prestigious universities in the world.

4. **Yale (耶鲁大学):** It is a private Ivy League university located in New Haven, Connecticut, United States of America. Founded in 1701 in the Colony of Connecticut, the university is the third-oldest institution of higher education in the United States. Yale is widely considered one of the most prestigious and selective universities in the world.

5. **Renaissance (文艺复兴):** It was a cultural movement that profoundly affected European

intellectual life in the early modern period. Beginning in Italy, and spreading to the rest of Europe by the 16th century, its influence affected literature, philosophy, art, politics, science, religion, and other aspects of intellectual inquiry. Renaissance scholars employed the humanist method in study, and searched for realism and human emotion in art.

6. **Quebec (魁北克)**: It is a province in east-central Canada. It is the only Canadian province with a predominantly French-speaking population and the only one whose sole official language is French at the provincial level. Quebec is Canada's largest province by area and its second-largest administrative division.

New Words and Expressions:

1.	prototype ['prəʊtətaɪp]	n.	原型；雏形
2.	explicit [ɪk'splɪsɪt]	adj.	明确的；清晰的；清楚的；露骨的
3.	formula ['fɔːmjələ]	n.	配方；公式；配方奶
4.	commoner ['kɒmənə]	n.	平民
5.	erect [ɪ'rekt]	v.	竖立；建立；建造
		adj.	直立的；竖立的；笔直的
6.	fringe [frɪndʒ]	n.	流苏；边缘；次要部分
		v.	形成……的边缘
7.	heterogeneity [ˌhetərədʒə'niːəti]	n.	多相性；异质性
8.	interdenominational [ˈɪntədɪˌnɒmɪ'neɪʃənl]	adj.	各教派间共有的
9.	secular ['sekjələ]	adj.	世俗的；现世的；非宗教的
10.	commissary ['kɒmɪsəri]	n.	（军事基地、监狱等出售食品的）杂货商店；（大型机构，尤指电影制片厂的）员工餐厅
11.	baccalaureate [ˌbækə'lɔːriət]	n.	（法国等国家的）中学毕业会考；宗教礼仪
12.	exemption [ɪg'zempʃn]	n.	免除；（指部分收入）免税

Unit 1   Origin & History of Education

Exercises:

I. Vocabulary.

Match the word in Column A to the correct definition in Column B.

Column A	Column B
1. commissary	A. standing/ sitting straight up
2. erect	B. an original model on which sth. is patterned
3. exemption	C. of or relating to the worldly or temporal
4. secular	D. a particular method of doing or achieving sth.
5. explicit	E. a shop that provides food and equipment
6. commoner	F. clear and easy to understand
7. formula	G. shared by different religious groups
8. prototype	H. official permission not to pay sth.
9. interdenominational	I. a person without noble rank or title
10. baccalaureate	J. the last secondary school exam in France

II. Translate the following words and phrases into English.

（大学）新生，一年级学生　　_____

（大学）二年级学生　　　　　_____

（大学）三年级学生　　　　　_____

（大学）四年级学生　　　　　_____

学术机构，学院，研究所　　　_____

行政规章　　　　　　　　　　_____

未预料到的变化　　　　　　　_____

注定的，注定要　　　　　　　_____

不受……影响，对……有免疫力　_____

寄宿制大学，寄宿学院　　　　_____

III. Comprehension of the text.

Decide whether the following statements are true (T) or false (F) according to the passage.

1. The earliest Harvard College statutes were taken indirectly from the Elizabethan statutes of the University of Cambridge. (　)
2. Harvard followed English college precedents closely and faithfully in terms of student

discipline, curriculum, administrative regulations, and degree requirements, and in turn, it became the great prototype for all the later colleges of English-America. (   )

3. At William and Mary, from 1729 to 1757, eight of thirteen faculty members were Oxford men, from Queens College. (   )

4. Only in some cases, the English colonists found that the unique conditions of the American physical and social environment produced unexpected changes and modifications in their academic institutions. (   )

5. It is impossible to erect in English-America any great university collection of colleges such as existed at Oxford or Cambridge and there are two reasons mentioned in the article. (   )

6. The post-Reformation Scottish university was professionally oriented, and under the control of prominent lay representatives of the community, which resembled the system of Oxford or Cambridge. (   )

7. In characteristic Scottish fashion, it was possible to have real administrative authority over the college. (   )

8. Originally speaking, there were somewhat slightly different types of organization in the English and Continental European universities. (   )

9. The Spanish-Americans established twenty-three institutions which were chartered and opened for instruction before a single college appeared in English-America. (   )

10. It was not until 1660 that Bishop Laval developed at Quebec a "great seminary" for advanced theological training. (   )

Supplementary Reading: The Origins of Distance Education

Distance education, also called distance learning, is the education of students who may not always be physically present at a school. Customarily, this usually involved correspondence courses wherein the student corresponded with the school via mail. Today, it involves online education. A distance learning program can be completely distance learning, or a combination of distance learning and traditional classroom instruction (called hybrid or blended). It provides extraordinary opportunities to transform the when, where and how of what we learn. Distance education built around new technology offers one way of meeting the need for a more flexible system, allowing people to dip in and out of education and update their knowledge periodically. The awareness of the possibilities of open and distance learning in education is increasing,

Unit 1 Origin & History of Education

and the use of new technologies to foster lifelong learning becomes increasingly attractive and appropriate.

Origins

The first distance education course in the modern sense was provided by Sir Isaac Pitman in the 1840s, who taught a system of shorthand by mailing texts transcribed into shorthand on postcards and receiving transcriptions from his students in return for correction. The element of student feedback was a crucial innovation in Pitman's system. His concept was so hot that within a few years he was corresponding with a legion of far-flung learners. Within a few decades, regular, and in some cases, extensive programs were available in the United Kingdom, Germany, the United States and Japan. The University of London was the first university to offer distance learning degrees, establishing its External Programme in 1858. By the 1900s, the first department of correspondence teaching was established at the University of Chicago. In Australia, the University of Queensland established a Department of External Studies in 1911. Before 1969, distance teaching had developed into an important sector of higher education in quite a few countries.

The Open University revolutionized the scope of the correspondence program and helped to create a respectable learning alternative to the traditional form of education. The founding of United Kingdom's Open University (OU) in 1969 marked a significant development of the second phase of distance learning, with its mixed-media approach to teaching. By mail the OU sent students learning materials which included carefully constructed texts and audio and video materials. These were supplemented with conventional broadcast radio and television. Every student was assigned a tutor available for tutoring over the telephone and in group sessions in the evenings or at weekends. The OU pioneered distance education on a massive scale. The OU and other open universities played a remarkable role in raising the profile of distance education, effectively bringing distance teaching closer to the center stage of higher education from the margins.

Meanwhile, as the founding of the OU, satellites were moving into commercial use. PEACENET in the Pacific Basin was founded in 1971 and used in the first ever application of satellites in distance education.

Growth

In the two decades following the opening of the OU in 1969 in the UK, four open universities were established in Europe, and over 20 were established in countries around the world.

There was considerable growth over the ensuing decades. In the United States, more than 300,000 students were enrolled in university-taught distance education courses by the mid-1980s.

In Canada, some 19 conventional universities were active in distance teaching. In Australia, by the late 1960s, the University of Queensland initiative had grown to some 3,000 students. By the mid-1980s, some 40 institutions had an enrollment of external students equivalent to approximately 12% of higher education students. In the Soviet Union, where distance teaching was adopted in the late 1920s, all 61 universities eventually offered education by correspondence, and it is reported in the German Democratic Republic that roughly 25% of the university and technical college graduates attained their qualification via distance education. It is clear that distance education had developed into a substantive sector of higher education in quite a few countries.

In many cases, particular open universities have a student population that is bigger than that of the median-size university in the same country, and in a few cases bigger than the largest traditional university. Some open universities have grown to become mega-universities, a term coined to denote institutions with more than 100,000 students. The widening over time of the range of distance learning programs provided and the kinds of student populations served has, in both cases, reinforced the trend toward further growth.

In modern times, internet technology has enabled many forms of distance learning through open educational resources and facilities such as e-learning and MOOCs. Massive open online courses (MOOCs), offering large-scale interactive participation and open access through the World Wide Web or other network technologies, are recent educational modes in distance education. Many other terms (distributed learning, e-learning, m-learning, online learning, virtual classroom, etc.) are used roughly synonymously with distance education.

Distance education is first and foremost a movement that seeks not so much to challenge or change the structure of higher learning, but to extend the traditional universities and to overcome its inherent problems of scarcity and exclusivity. It deals with the problem of too many students in a single physical space. The university can, in effect, reach out, offering not seats, but the opportunity to learn.

Unit 2　Educational Objective

Text A　Aims and Objectives of Education

> 导读：教育目的是一个国家教育精神的集中体现，是根据一定社会的政治、经济、生产、文化、科学技术发展的要求和受教育者身心发展的状况确定的。它反映了一定社会对受教育者的要求，是教育工作的出发点和最终目标，也是确定教育内容、选择教育方法、检查和评价教育效果的根据。目的不明确的教育就像一艘无舵的船。以下这篇出自印度教育研究与发展组织的文章对此做了阐释。

1. Introduction

The importance of the aims and objectives of education is recognized by all the educational, professional, political, nonpolitical and religious associations, organizations and groups at various levels in their memoranda, letters and brochures. It is said that education without clear-cut aims is like a rudderless ship. The following comparisons emphasize this point fully well.

Every pilot has a route chart and set timing of landing at the predetermined destination. There is the constitution or set of principles and traditions through which a country is governed. Similarly, there should be properly defined and declared principles, aims and objectives of education or the basis of which policies and programs of education have to be formulated to achieve the set goals without wasting scarce energies and resources in chasing the wild goose.

It is generally felt that our educational system has not followed the desired aims as a result that it does not produce ideal citizens in the country. It has followed rather a narrow aim of preparing individuals for livelihood, as mentioned in one of the documents received from an organization.

The main reason for the failure of the educational system is that it basically stands on pre-independence system. The main objective of its products was how to take a degree and to earn money and to be a careerist without consideration of ethical values and national spirit. It has also been pointed out that it is unreasonable to criticize the educational system alone because it is based on the other subsystems accepted by us.

On the one hand, we are developing and cultivating the British given economy, judicial system and system of administration and parliament. And on the other, we are decrying and criticizing the education system which merely fulfills the needs of the British systems that we are propagating.

As pointed out in a memorandum of an association, "the main defect of the old education policy is that it had completely ignored the Indian culture and the interest of the masses of India and has left them economically too backward and socially too fragmented to articulate their miseries..."

The aims and objectives of education, suggested in the documents, include individual as well as social aids, with emphasis of social transformation aiming at reconstructing society to make it a modernized, productive, participative, and value-oriented nation committed to its constitutional obligations.

2. Individual Development

The development of an individual—physically, mentally and spiritually—is well-known as the aim of education. Objectives related to this aim of individual development have been expressed in various ways in the memoranda:

Developing physical and mental faculties

—Acquiring the capacities of understanding, appreciation and expression through word and act, are the fundamental aims of education;

—Aim of education should be to make children self-confident and self-dependent, and to make them strong physically and mentally;

—Education is meant to develop every child's character, personality and culture and as much knowledge as the child can assimilate, not merely memorize.

The policy should be directed to the aim of enlightenment of head and heart; illumination of consciousness for all-round development of individual personality. Education should enable a human being to attain the greatest possible harmony, internal and external, spiritual and material, for the fullest possible development of human potentialities and

Unit 2 Educational Objective

capacities.

3. Social and National Development

The social aim of education is equally important because an individual lives in society and has his obligations towards his nation. There is a realization that, "The present education system does not yield required results mainly because it is divorced from the real social content and social goals".

It has, therefore, been suggested that education should be able, to discharge its natural functions and must correspond to its structure, goals and content in the interest of national development and social progress. It has also been suggested in this connection that students from a young age should be made aware of the social responsibility cast on them.

At the same time, there are certain constitutional commitments, which are intimately related to this aim. We as the citizens of the republic are constitutionally committed to democracy, social justice, equality of opportunity, secularism and above all to a welfare state. It has, therefore, been suggested that, "Educational policy and educational program should clearly reflect these commitments".

The objectives of developing a sense of national identity, unity and patriotism are advocated by many associations. It is pointed out that the national objectives of planning and programs and development with special emphasis on popular participation and the national problems that we face in different fields should be taught at relevant stages.

Individual and social aims of education are not contrary to one another. In fact, they are complementary to one another. The following view strikes a balance between individual and social aims of education.

The purpose of education should be the development of the fullest possible capacities and potentialities physical and spiritual of a "total man". It should make a man capable of earning his livelihood reasonably well to enjoy a happy and secure life while making effective contributions to the society and national effort of making India strongly advanced and prosperous.

4. Social Transformation

Education should not merely equip an individual to adjust with society to its customs and conventions, but it should enable him to bring desirable changes in society. It has been, therefore, suggested that, "Every educational institution from secondary school to university and college should be developed to become an agency of change..."

However, it is essential that we should be quite clear about the purpose of change. It is, therefore, natural to ask the question, "Reform and change to achieve what?" What type of society do we aim at and what type of citizens do we wish to produce? The following ideas give an indication of the kind of changes education is expected to bring about.

4.1 Modernization

Modernization of society in terms of scientific and technological advancement is a view which seems to be quite popular. It is thought that education should enable us to move with the times and attain excellence in science and technology.

Scientific and technological advances are gaining momentum, and conscious efforts are being made to incorporate them into the development sectors. This calls for the modernization of education in order to make it in conformity with modern times and to keep pace, with the advances in the world.

Modernization, however, is not interpreted and equated with westernization. In fact, a lot of emphasis is given to "Indianness" while talking about modernization. One of the suggestions explicitly points out that, hour education should integrate and unite the people of India, and modernize society while preserving what is authentically Indian in our cultural and spiritual heritage.

This suggestion beautifully reconciles the twin objectives of modern technical sophistication and ancient spirituality: "New education policy of India should be built on the foundation of ancient spirituality and modern culture and technical sophistication. It should develop scientific temper and spirit of enquiry in the students."

4.2 Productivity

Some documents have insisted on linking education with productivity and thus making individuals productive citizens to build a productive society. One of the suggestions, in a memorandum, for example, says: "It should bring about a social transformation, and enhance greater efficiency and productivity in all sectors: agricultural, industrial and service." It is in this context that Mahatma Gandhi's system of basic education is still considered a basically sound system and a suggestion has been made that with necessary modification elements of basic education may form part of education not only at the primary stage but at all stages in our national system of education. These elements are:

(i) Productive activity in education;

(ii) Correlation of the curriculum with productive activity and physical and social environment;

(iii) Intimate contact between the school and the local community.

4.3 Community Participation

In a democracy education without community participation is barren. This aim of education is therefore voiced by several groups and organizations. The change that is envisaged on this front is that of integrating education with community in all respects. To quote a suggestion in this regard:

> The education system in all its branches and sectors should get itself involved in activities related to problems of local community life and shall thus endeavor through the desirable community participation and involvement in the educational field to bring all education of its rightful place in community life.

5. Acquisition of Values

Moral, cultural and spiritual values in education have been given immense importance in the memoranda documents. One of the expressions emphatically point out that "certain basic values as respect for others, responsibility, solidarity, creativity and integrity must be fostered in our children."

It is interesting that several specific values have been suggested in the documents. The values which are considered important are mentioned below:

> Emphasis should be given to cultivate good qualities like cooperation, goodwill, forgiveness, tolerance, honesty, patience, etc. in order to encourage universal brotherhood and to prepare students as worthy citizens of the country.
>
> Values of optimism and secularism, and service to the poor should be stressed in the young minds.

6. Summing Up

It is worth reproducing what the document mentions about the aims of education:

The aim of education is two-fold: development of the individual in society and consequent development of society. The aim of education in relation to an individual may be spelt out as follows:

(i) to produce a full human personality with courage, conviction, vitality, sensitivity and intelligence so that men and women may live in harmony with the universe;

(ii) to bring out the fullest potential of a child and prepare him for life and its varied situations so that he becomes a cultured and responsible citizen dedicated to the service of the community.

In relation to society, the aim of education is to create:

(i) a sane and learning society where made-of-material production will be such that no section of the society remains unemployed. In the Indian context such a made of production will be necessarily based on a decentralized economy utilizing all available manpower;

(ii) a society where the conditions of work and the general environment will offer psychic satisfaction and effective motivations to its members;

(iii) a society reconciling technological and scientific advancement with the general well-being and security of its members, enhancing the joy of life and eliminating all forms of exploitation.

The broad objective of education should, therefore, be to look beyond the existing society and to develop men and women amenable to the advent of a sane and healthier society of tomorrow.

While summing up, it may be pointed out that various dimensions of individual and social development, social transformation, value acquisition, etc. have been well identified in the memoranda documents. The following words briefly summarize the various dimensions which are considered important indeed in the 21st century:

We are of the opinion that Indian education should aim at producing men and women of knowledge, character and cultural values and trained skills to achieve excellence in their careers and life. Let us make it clear that we wish to prepare youth in the 21st century on the ideals of truth and non-violence as shown to us by our great leaders.

Notes:

1. **Memorandum (备忘录):** A memorandum or memo is a document or other communication that helps the memory by recording events or observations on a topic, such as one that used in a business office. The plural form is either memoranda or memorandums.

2. **Ethical value (伦理价值):** In ethics, value is a property of objects, including physical objects as well as abstract objects (e.g. actions), representing their degree of importance. Ethic value denotes something's degree of importance, with the aim of determining what action or life is best to do or live, or at least attempting to describe the value of different actions. It may be described as treating actions themselves as abstract objects, putting value on them. It deals with right conduct and good life, in the sense that a highly, or at least relatively highly, valuable action may be regarded as ethically "good" (adjective sense); and an action of low, or at least

relatively low, the value may be regarded as "bad".

3. **Judicial system (司法制度):** Judicial system is the system of courts that interprets and applies the law in the name of the state. It also provides a mechanism for the resolution of disputes. It generally does not make law (that is, in a plenary fashion, which is the responsibility of the legislature) or enforce law (which is the responsibility of the executive), but rather interprets law and applies it to the facts of each case.

4. **Social transformation (社会转变):** One definition of social transformation is the process by which an individual alters the socially ascribed social status of their parents into a socially achieved status for themselves. However, another definition refers to large-scale social change as in cultural reforms or transformations. The first occurs with the individual, and the second with the social system.

5. **Modernization (现代化):** In the social sciences, modernization refers to a model of an evolutionary transition from a "pre-modern" or "traditional" to a "modern" society. The teleology of modernization is described in social evolutionism theories, existing as a template that has been generally followed by societies that have achieved modernity.

New Words and Expressions:

1. objective [əb'dʒektiv]	*adj.*	客观的；目标的；宾格的
	n.	目的；目标
2. association [ə,səusi'eiʃən, ə,səuʃi'ei-]	*n.*	协会，联盟，社团；联合；联想
3. rudderless ['rʌdəlis]	*adj.*	无舵的；无指导者的
4. chase [tʃeis]	*v.*	追逐；追捕；试图赢得；雕镂
5. propagate ['prɔpəgeit]	*v.*	传播；传送；繁殖；宣传
6. fragment ['frægmənt]	*n.*	碎片；片段或不完整部分
	v.	使成碎片
7. assimilate [ə'simileit]	*v.*	吸收；使同化；把……比作；使相似
8. enlightenment [in'laitənmənt]	*n.*	启迪；启蒙运动；教化
9. external [ik'stə:nəl]	*adj.*	外部的；表面的；[药] 外用的；外国的；外面的
10. discharge [dis'tʃɑ:dʒ]	*v.*	解雇；卸下；放出；免除
	n.	排放；卸货；解雇

11. intimately ['intimitli]		adv.	熟悉地；亲切地；私下地
12. patriotism ['pætriətizəm]		n.	爱国主义；爱国精神
13. relevant ['reləvənt]		adj.	有关的；中肯的；有重大作用的
14. prosperous ['prɔspərəs]		adj.	繁荣的；兴旺的
15. convention [kən'venʃən]		n.	大会；[法] 惯例；[计] 约定；[法] 协定；习俗
16. desirable [di'zaiərəbl]		adj.	令人满意的；值得要的
		n.	合意的人或事物
17. essential [i'senʃəl]		adj.	基本的；必要的；本质的
		n.	本质；要素；要点；必需品
18. indication [ˌindi'keiʃən]		n.	指示；迹象；象征
19. incorporate [in'kɔ:pəreit, in'kɔ:pərət]		v.	包含；吸收；体现；把……合并
		adj.	合并的；一体化的；组成公司的
20. equate [i'kweit]		v.	使相等；视为平等
21. heritage ['heritidʒ]		n.	遗产；传统；继承物；继承权
22. sophistication [səˌfisti'keiʃən]		n.	复杂；诡辩；老于世故；有教养
23. barren ['bærən]		adj.	贫瘠的；不生育的；无益的；沉闷无趣的；空洞的
		n.	荒地
24. envisage [in'vizidʒ]		v.	面对；想象
25. acquisition [ˌækwi'ziʃən]		n.	获得物；获得
26. sane [sein]		adj.	健全的；理智的；[临床] 神志正常的
27. decentralized [ˌdi:'sentrəlaizd]		adj.	分散的；分散管理的；去中心化的
28. reconcile ['rekənsail]		v.	使一致；使和解；调停，调解；使顺从
29. amenable [ə'mi:nəbl]		adj.	应服从的；有义务的；经得起检验的
30. dimension [di'menʃən, dai-]		n.	[数] 维；尺寸；次元；容积
		v.	标出尺寸
		adj.	规格的

Unit 2　Educational Objective

Exercises:

I. Vocabulary.

Match the word in Column A to the correct definition in Column B.

Column A	Column B
1. objective	A. in a close manner
2. relevant	B. not influenced by personal feelings or opinions
3. convention	C. bring into consonance or accord
4. reconcile	D. having a bearing on or connection with the subject at issue
5. intimately	E. something regarded as a normative example

II. Comprehension of the text.

Decide whether the following statements are true (T) or false (F) according to the passage.

1. Our educational system has followed the desired aims and it produces ideal citizens in the country. ( )
2. The aims and objectives of education, suggested a memorandum of an association, include individual as well as social aids. ( )
3. Individual and social aims of education are contrary to one another and are complementary to one another. ( )
4. Education should not merely equip an individual to adjust with society to its customs and conventions, but it should enable him to bring desirable changes in the society. ( )
5. Modernization is actually interpreted and equated with westernization. ( )

III. Try to fill in the space with suitable words.

1. The main reason of failure of educational system is that it basically stands on _____ _____.
2. Acquiring the capacities of understanding, appreciation and _____, are the fundamental aims of education.
3. The present education system does riot yield required results mainly because it is divorced from the real _____.
4. Values of _____, and service to the poor should be stressed on the young minds.
5. The aim of education is two-fold: development of _____ and consequent

development of _____.

Text B　Education, Basics of Education and Educational Objectives

> **导读**：教育是培养新生一代准备从事社会生活的整个过程，也是人类社会生产经验得以继承发扬的关键环节。教育目的是根据一定社会的政治、经济、生产、文化科学技术发展的要求和受教育者身心发展的状况确定的。它反映了一定社会对受教育者的要求，是教育工作的出发点和最终目标，也是确定教育内容、选择教育方法、检查和评价教育效果的根据。

Definition of Education

Education can be defined as a continuous process that aims at bringing about desirable changes in the behaviour of learners on a relatively permanent basis and which are evident by way of acquisition of knowledge, proficiency of skills and development of values.

History of the Taxonomy of Educational Objectives

For a long time, organised educational system is facing difficulties with student evaluation. A group of educational psychologists took up the challenge of infusing transparency in teaching and evaluation. Thus, at the convention of American Psychological Association in 1948, a

group of teachers decided to adapt the model of taxonomy used in biology for educational practices. They described this classification as Taxonomy of Educational Objectives. This informal group consisted of Benjamin Bloom, Max D. Englehart, Edward J. Furst, Walker H. Hill, David Krathwohl and Bertran B. Masic among others.

Their findings were published in the book—*Taxonomy of Educational Objectives: The Classification of Educational Goals, Handbook 1: Cognitive Domain* in the year 1956. This group of psychologists identified that most educational objectives can be grouped under three headings—cognitive, affective and psychomotor. The cognitive domain, according to this book includes such educational objectives as dealing with recall or recognition of knowledge and development of intellectual abilities and skills. The educational objectives in affective domain are concerned with "changes in the interest, attitudes and values, and the development of appreciations and adequate adjustments." The educational objectives belonging to psychomotor domain refer to "the manipulative or motor skill area."

Further, this book explained the various levels of cognitive domain. The hierarchy of objectives in affective domain was explained in *Taxonomy of Educational Objectives: The Classification of Educational Goals, Handbook 2: Affective Domain* that was published in the year 1964.

This group did not explore the hierarchy of educational objectives in psychomotor domain. Many others attempted to develop this hierarchy and in the year 1972, Elizabeth Simpson presented the levels of objectives psychomotor domain. The taxonomy marked an important milestone in the field of higher education. Since learners in higher education are adults, and seek reasons and purposes for their learning, educational objectives and their hierarchy provide a useful benchmark.

Aims and Objectives

Definition of Aim

Aim can be defined as a broad statement of educational activity, e.g. to understand disease. It describes what one intends to achieve at the end of an educational activity.

Definition of Objective

Objective is a precise point in the direction of aim, e.g. identify uncommon symptoms. It can be defined as a statement of intent in an educational context. Other terms that are synonymous with educational objectives are: teaching objectives, learning objectives, intended learning objectives, enabling objectives, instructional objectives, curriculum objectives, terminal objectives, operational objectives, performance objectives, outcomes, competencies, etc. Of these, the terms performance objectives and competencies refer more specifically to objectives in psychomotor domain.

Educational objective can be defined as a statement of intent in an educational context, which is demonstrable and measurable on predetermined parameters. Thus, educational objective is a statement that clarifies the complete range of activity and expected performance outcomes.

Functions of Objectives

Purpose for Teaching
- Direction to teaching
- Teaching made easy
- Structure for teaching

The sequencing of objectives not only makes it easy to teach, but also provides a comprehensive structure to teaching.

- **Layers** *of educational objectives—core, intermediate, peripheral*

Educational objectives determine learning contents. Because educational objectives determine what has to be learnt, it becomes necessary to know how much has to be taught/learnt. This classification of learning is made under three headings—must know, desirable to know and nice to know. This classification is equally applicable to each of the three domains of learning. The "must know" segment consists of educational objectives that represent the core competences of the discipline. The learner must acquire the knowledge, skill and attitude listed in this category, if he/she has to be certified as competent/successful. These comprise 70% of the total statements of educational objectives in the discipline. The other category is "desirable to know", which constitutes 20% of educational objectives. This includes statements, which are not core competences, but something beyond it. These objectives complement the core competences and may become core objectives in higher levels of learning. "Nice to know" consists of objectives that are of "general knowledge" interest. The significance of "must know" category is to ensure that the student passing out with a health sciences degree must have the basic and necessary competences to practice and provide health services competently and comprehensively. The purpose of including desirable and nice-to-know components is to differentiate the exceptional learner from the average ones for awarding grades in certifying exams.

- **Levels** *of educational objectives—institutional, departmental and specific learning*

Educational objectives can also be classified at three different levels. The statements in this classification are more in the form of goals than objectives, as explained earlier to differentiate goal/aim and objectives.

The broadest and most general form of goals are said to be institutional or course goals. These list the competences that a graduate has to acquire at the end of the course of study. These are mainly drawn from the national health policy and the strengths of the health sciences discipline for which the course is being prepared. While listing these goals, not only the current health needs, but also the future needs of the community have to be kept in mind, so that the course does not become obsolete and lose its relevance to society.

Departmental goals refer to the statements made for the subject/department in the context of the course. For example, anatomy is taught for various health sciences disciplines like medical, dental, nursing, physiotherapy, etc. But the teaching of anatomy in each of these disciplines is determined by the course goals. There are situations, where the goals of two or more departments

Unit 2 Educational Objective

within a course may overlap or complement each other. For example, the departments of Community Medicine and Paediatrics may share the goal of immunisation. Or the departments of Community Medicine and OBG may share the goals for Family Planning. Speaking of the homeopathic course, the departments of Community Medicine and Homeopathic Philosophy may share the goals of prevention of epidemics. The statements, which express these shared goals, are known as interdepartmental goals. These are at the same level as departmental goals.

Specific learning goals are the same as instructional objectives. These are the specific statements, which are written for each departmental goal. These explain the precise performance that is expected of the learner in the department at the end of a specified educational activity.

SLOs, or Educational Objectives as they are more conventionally known, are explained in three different domains: cognitive, affective and psychomotor. The significance of knowing domains of learning is the possibility to plan the educational activity in an accountable manner. Such a planned educational activity provides space to think, understand and justify teaching/learning. In the absence of planning, the entire exercise may become vague, opinion based and dogmatic. As the saying goes, "if you fail to plan, you plan to fail."

Domains of Education

Educational activity is broadly classified into three domains: cognitive, affective or psychomotor, depending on the type of intended learning objectives—whether it is the acquisition of knowledge, development of attitude or proficiency of skill.

- Cognitive domain is about learning the behaviours that involve thinking, understanding or explaining. It ranges from simple recalling of facts to implementation and justification of ideas and concepts.
- Affective domain includes the learning behaviour that involves demonstration of feelings/values towards facts or concepts. It ranges from receptivity for people or events to automated empathy for them.
- Psychomotor domain includes all the skill-based performances like eye–hand / foot coordination.

Characteristics of Educational Objectives

Relevant: It is already noted that while stating educational objectives we have to keep in mind the national health needs. Any effort made towards realising such health needs adds relevance. It can therefore be said that relevance of educational objectives depends on the extent to which these statements conform to the national health needs. Relevance of educational objectives is a three-tier process—first determine course goals, second the departmental ones and finally the specific learning goals. Thus, educational objectives that are written can be said to be relevant.

Valid: It is the degree to which the statement conforms to the domain to which it belongs.

Clear: The words must be precise and sentences clear. The idea is that message has to reach clear and correct. There should be no room for confusion, misinterpretation or vagueness. The major ingredient of any educational objectives statement is an active verb. The entire statement revolves around explanation for the verb, which must be unambiguous.

Feasible: The statement has to tell what is possible to do, both in terms of human capacity and resources/infrastructure available.

Observable: The very definition of learning is a change in learner behaviour. Thus, to know whether learning has taken place, it is necessary to observe the changes that have taken place. Therefore, educational objectives have to be stated in terms that are observable.

Measurable: Measurability does not mean that learning has always been quantitative. But to know whether learning has taken place, one has to measure the extent of change. Learning a skill could be qualitative, but the time taken to perform the skill before and after a learning session could be used as a benchmark to measure qualitative change.

Elements of Educational Objectives

Act—What the learner will be able "to do" at the end of a learning session. This could be in any of the three domains. Depending on the domain, the appropriate verb has to be identified to state the act.

Content—It is the performance that learner is expected to demonstrate.

Condition—The conditions under which the performance is done. It includes the enabling and restraining factors. It also denotes the range of manoeuvrability.

Act, Content and Condition together constitute the *Task*.

Criterion—This is the degree of freedom allowed for performance.

Notes:

1. **American Psychological Association (美国心理学协会):** The American Psychological Association (abbreviated APA) is the largest scientific and professional organization of psychologists in the United States. It is the world's largest association of psychologists with around 150,000 members including scientists, educators, clinicians, consultants and students. The APA has an annual budget of around $115 million.

2. **Elizabeth Simpson (伊丽莎白·辛普森)**: Elizabeth Inchbald (née Simpson) (1753–1821) was an English novelist, actress, and dramatist.

3. **OBG (牛津商业集团)**: Oxford Business Group.

4. **SLO (学生学习成果)**: Student Learning Outcome.

New Words and Expressions:

1. proficiency [prəu'fiʃənsi]	n.	精通；熟练
2. taxonomy ['tæk'sɔnəmi]	n.	分类学；分类法
3. psychologist [psai'kɔlədʒist]	n.	心理学家，心理学者
4. transparency [træns'pærənsi]	n.	透明，透明度；幻灯片；有图案的玻璃
5. cognitive ['kɔgnitiv]	adj.	认知的；认识的
6. psychomotor [ˌpsaikə'məutə]	adj.	精神运动的
7. domain [dəu'mein]	n.	领域；域名；产业；地产
8. adequate ['ædikwit]	adj.	充足的；适当的；胜任的
9. hierarchy ['haiəˌrɑ:ki]	n.	层级；等级制度
10. milestone ['mailstəun]	n.	里程碑；划时代的事件
11. symptom ['simptəm]	n.	[临床] 症状；征兆
12. synonymous [si'nɔniməs]	adj.	同义的；同义词的
13. parameter [pə'ræmitə]	n.	参数；系数；参量
14. peripheral [pə'rifərəl]	adj.	外围的；次要的
15. segment ['segmənt, seg'ment, 'segment]	v.	分割
	n.	段；部分
16. competence ['kɑ:mpitəns]	n.	能力；胜任；权限；足以过舒适生活的收入
17. obsolete ['ɒbsəli:t, ˌɑ:bsə'li:t]	adj.	废弃的；老式的
18. anatomy [ə'nætəmi]	n.	解剖；解剖学；剖析；骨骼
19. physiotherapy [ˌfiziəu'θerəpi]	n.	物理疗法
20. overlap [ˌəuvə'læp, 'əuvəlæp]	n.	重叠；重复
	v.	与……重叠；与……同时发生
21. immunization [ˌimju:nai'zeiʃən, -ni'z-]	n.	免疫
22. homeopathic [ˌhəumiə'pæθik]	adj.	顺势疗法的；同种疗法的

23. vague [veig]		*adj.*	模糊的；含糊的；不明确的；暧昧的
24. empathy ['empəθi]		*n.*	同感；共情
25. tier [tiə]		*n.*	级；阶；等级
26. misinterpretation ['misin,tə:pri'teiʃən]		*n.*	误解；误释
27. unambiguous [,ʌnæm'bigjuəs]		*adj.*	不含糊的；清楚的；明白的
28. quantitative ['kwɔntitətiv, -tei-]		*adj.*	定量的；数量的
29. benchmark ['bentʃmɑ:k]		*n.*	基准；标准检查程序
30. manoeuvrability [mə,nu:vrə'biləti]		*n.*	机动性；可移动性；操纵的灵敏性

Exercises:

I. Vocabulary.

Match the word in Column A to the correct definition in Column B.

Column A	Column B
1. proficiency	A. connected with mental processes of understanding
2. cognitive	B. the quality of having great facility and competence
3. adequate	C. not clearly understood or expressed
4. synonymous	D. enough to meet a purpose
5. vague	E. (of words) meaning the same or nearly the same

II. Comprehension of the text.

Decide whether the following statements are true (T) or false (F) according to the passage.

1. Benjamin Bloom's group explored the hierarchy of educational objectives in psychomotor domain in the year 1972. ( )
2. Educational objectives determine learning contents. ( )
3. The "must know" segment comprises 60% of the total statements of educational objectives. ( )
4. Specific learning goals are different from instructional objectives. ( )
5. Any effort made towards realising national health needs adds relevance. It can therefore be said that relevance of educational objectives depends on the extent to which they conform to the national health needs. ( )

Unit 2　Educational Objective

III. Try to fill in the space with suitable words.

1. This group of psychologists identified that most of educational objectives can be grouped under three headings—cognitive, _____.

2. Educational objective can be defined as a statement of intent in an educational context, which is _____ on predetermined parameters.

3. _____ not only makes it easy to teach, but also provides a comprehensive structure to teaching.

4. Educational objectives can also be classified at three different levels. The broadest and most general form of goals are said to be _____.

5. SLOs, or _____ as they are more conventionally known, are explained in three different domains—cognitive, affective and psychomotor.

Supplementary Reading: Knowing Your Learning Target

The article discusses the importance of using learning targets in education. The author suggests that learning targets help students understand what they are meant to be learning during a lesson. The impact of learning targets on helping students achieve educational goals and meet instructional objectives is addressed. Several real-life classroom examples are presented in which learning targets for lessons in subjects such as mathematics and social studies are explained to students, who then become more engaged in lessons and take a more strategic approach to lessons and classwork.

The First Thing Students Need to Learn Is What They're Supposed to Be Learning

One of Toni Taladay's students walked into Lenape Elementary School wearing a colorful tie-dyed shirt with a tiny bull's-eye shape in the lower front corner. That small design caught the eye of his classmate, who exclaimed, "Look, Joey, you're wearing a learning target!" In the Armstrong School District in southwestern Pennsylvania, learning targets are everywhere: in lesson plans, on bulletin boards, in hallways—and as this story illustrates—firmly on students' minds.

What Is a Shared Learning Target?

If you own a global positioning system (GPS), you probably can't imagine taking a trip without it. Unlike a printed map, a GPS provides information about where you are, the distance to your destination, how long until you get there, and exactly what to do when you make a wrong

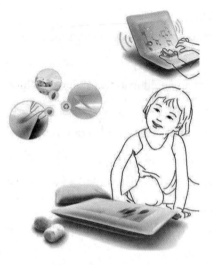

turn. But a GPS can't do any of that without a precise description of where you want to go.

Think of shared learning targets in the same way. They convey to students the destination for the lesson—what to learn, how deeply to learn it, and exactly how to demonstrate their new learning. In our estimation (Moss & Brookhart, 2009) and that of others (Seidle, Rimmele & Prenzel 2005; Stiggins, Arter, Chappuis et al., 2009), the intention for the lesson is one of the most important things students should learn. Without a precise description of where they are headed, too many students are "flying blind".

The Dangers of Flying Blind

No matter what we decide students need to learn, not much will happen until students understand what they are supposed to learn during a lesson and set their sights on learning it. Regardless of how important the content, how engaging the activity, how formative the assessment, or how differentiated the instruction, unless all students see, recognize, and understand the learning target from the very beginning of the lesson, one factor will remain constant: the teacher will always be the only one providing the direction, focusing on getting students to meet the instructional objectives. The students, on the other hand, will focus on doing what the teacher says, rather than on learning. This flies in the face of what we know about nurturing motivated, self-regulated, and intentional learners. (Zimmerman, 2001)

Students who don't know the intention of a lesson expend precious time and energy trying to figure out what their teachers expect them to learn. And many students, exhausted by the process, wonder why they should even care.

Consider the following high school lesson on *Jane Eyre*. The teacher begins by saying,

Today, as you read the next chapter, carefully complete your study guide. Pay close attention to the questions about Bertha—Mr. Rochester's first wife. Questions 16 through 35 deal with lunacy and the five categories of mental illness. The next 15 questions focus on facts about Charlotte Bronte's own isolated childhood. The last 10 items ask you to define terms in the novel that we seldom use today—your dictionaries will help you define those words. All questions on Friday's test will come directly from the study guide.

What is important for students to learn in this lesson? Is it how to carefully complete a study guide, the five types of mental illness, facts about Bronte's childhood, meanings of seldom-used words, or facts about Mr. Rochester's first wife? Your guess is as good as ours.

Constructing a Learning Target

A shared learning target unpacks a "lesson-sized" amount of learning—the precise "chunk" of the particular content students are to master. (Leahy, Lyon, Thompson & Wiliam, 2005) It describes exactly how well we expect them to learn it and how we will ask them to demonstrate that learning. And although teachers derive them from instructional objectives, learning targets differ from instructional objectives in both design and function.

Instructional objectives are about instruction, derived from content standards, written in teacher language, and used to guide teaching during a lesson or across a series of lessons. They are not designed for students but for the teacher. A shared learning target, on the other hand, frames the lesson from the student's point of view. A shared learning target helps students grasp the lesson's purpose—why it is crucial to learn this chunk of information, on this day, and in this way.

Students can't see, recognize, and understand what they need to learn until we translate the learning intention into developmentally appropriate, student-friendly, and culturally respectful language. One way to do that is to answer the following three questions from the student's point of view:

What will I be able to do when I've finished this lesson?

What idea, topic, or subject is important for me to learn and understand so that I can do this?

How will I show that I can do this, and how well will I have to do it?

Beginning to Share

When teachers in the Armstrong School District began sharing learning targets with their students, their early efforts were tentative and inconsistent. Not all teachers tried it, and some who tried did not share targets for every lesson. Some simply paraphrased instructional objectives, wrote the target statements on the board, or told students what they were going to learn at the beginning of a lesson. Yet, even their exploratory attempts became game-changers. When teachers consistently shared learning targets in meaningful ways, students quickly became more capable decision-makers who knew where they were headed and who shared responsibility for getting there.

At Lenape Elementary School, for example, teachers and administrators marveled at the immediate effect of shared targets and how quickly those effects multiplied. Principal Tom Dinga recalls a visit to a 1st-grade classroom during the first week of sharing learning targets. The teacher, Brian Kovalovsky, led the class in discussing the learning target for the math lesson that day—to describe basic shapes and compare them to one another. When he asked his students how they would know when they hit that target, one 6-year-old replied, "I'll be able to explain the difference between a square and a rectangle."

Invigorated by the changes they were witnessing, teachers and administrators used e-mail, peer coaching, peer observations, focused walk-throughs and professional conversations to share what was working in their classrooms and buildings and supported these claims with evidence that their students were learning more and learning smarter.

Students are now more actively engaged in their lessons as full-fledged learning partners. Because they understand exactly what they are supposed to learn, students take a more strategic approach to their work. Students have the information they need to keep track of how well a strategy is working, and they can decide when and if to use that strategy again. In other words, students not only know where they are on the way to mastery, but also are aware of what it will take to get there.

The Power of Meaningful Sharing

Learning targets have no inherent power. They enhance student learning and achievement only when educators commit to consistently and intentionally sharing them with students. Meaningful sharing requires that teachers use the learning targets with their students and students use them with one another. This level of sharing starts when teachers use student-friendly language—and sometimes model or demonstrate what they expect—to explain the learning target from the beginning of the lesson, and when they continue to share it throughout the lesson. Here are two powerful ways to do that.

- Designing a Strong Performance of Understanding

The single best way to share a learning target is to create a strong performance of understanding—a learning experience that embodies the learning target. When students complete the actions that are part of a strong performance of understanding, they and their teachers will know that they have reached the target.

When introducing the lesson, the teacher should explicitly share the learning target for the day and explain how each of the tasks that are part of the lesson will lead students toward that target. Remember the lesson on *Jane Eyre*? Consider this lesson introduction:

> Today we will learn more about how Bronte uses her characters to explore the theme of being unwanted. Remember, a theme is an underlying meaning of the story. Yesterday, we examined Jane Eyre's life experiences as they relate to the theme of being unwanted. Today we will do the same for Adele, Mr. Rochester's ward. As you read, find examples of Adele being unwanted, unloved, uncared for, or forgotten. Then, in your learning groups, discuss your examples and your reasons for choosing them. At the end of class, use your notes to draft a short paragraph that answers the question—How does the character of Adele deepen Bronte's theme of being unwanted in the novel *Jane Eyre*?

Note how the teacher explains what students will learn that day and how each task explicitly connects to that target. If students perform all of these actions, they will better understand how Bronte uses her characters to explore the theme of being unwanted. The tasks clearly lead students to the target, and the students can see how each task leads them to their goal. A strong performance of understanding helps students understand what is important to learn, provides experiences that will help them learn it, and gives them a chance to observe their growing competence along the way.

- Explaining the Criteria for Success

Success criteria are developmentally appropriate descriptions and concrete examples of what success in a lesson looks like. They are not the grades students should earn, the number of problems they must get right, or the number of times they should include something in a performance or product (for example, how many descriptive adjectives they should include in a paragraph).

"I can" statements are a great way to explain success. Another useful strategy is to ask students to examine work samples that represent various levels of quality and discuss what makes some samples better than others. Teachers can also use rubrics to define the elements of a successful performance or product and describe various performance levels for each element. An especially powerful way to do this is to have students apply a rubric's organized criteria to work samples with various levels of quality. Then ask students to explain their decisions using the language in the rubric. When students know the success criteria, they can be mindful of what success looks like as they use the rubric to guide their learning.

Empowering Every Student

Armstrong teachers began embedding learning targets into their lessons in October 2009. Now shared learning targets guide lesson planning, formative assessment, and classroom walk-throughs. But the most impressive transformation is that of students into full learning partners. Now that students know where they are going, they are more motivated to do the work to get there.

It's just this simple. Do we want classrooms full of empowered, self-regulated, highly motivated, and intentional learners? If we do, then it is time to own up to the obstacles that educators create by withholding the very information that would empower learners. Students cannot regulate learning, use thoughtful reasoning processes, set meaningful goals, or assess the quality of their own work unless they understand what success looks like in today's lesson.

Unit 3　Teacher & Student

Text A　The Teacher, the Student and the Classroom

> **导读**：教师是学生在知识的海洋中追随的灯塔，帮助学生明确目标，在学生遇到困难时及时地答疑解惑；而学生个人才是学习的主体，他们持有一把独一无二的钥匙，只有通过自身努力才能开启知识宝库和未来成就的大门。教师为学生铺路，学生沿着这条道路驶向目的地。在学生成长的过程中，他们会遇到许许多多不确定因素诱使他们偏离原先的道路。因此，教师应该不断鼓励学生抵制诱惑，认清方向，奋发向前。师生关系是教育教学过程中最基本的关系。新时代呼唤师生关系突破传统，实现重构，建立良好师生关系新模式——"师生共同体"。课堂本质上是一个空间概念，是个体空间同时又是群体空间，是教学关系的反映，是师生学习共同体的存在，是建构式的存在，也是生命性、复杂性的存在。

The road is not easy. We would acknowledge that what attract children are small colorful details hardly noticeable to the adult eye. Thus the onus is on the teachers to find a way to discover and then channel these attractions to the purpose of learning. The more we find how these minor details such as cartoons, games, jokes, songs, trivial chats etc., can be incorporated into our lessons with attached significance (teaching objective), the more we make the road more attractive to the student. Without this, there is nothing a student will look forward to in school.

Who then is a Good Teacher?

We can state that a good teacher is an educator or facilitator who leads the learner into the untrodden paths of knowledge. In doing so, the teacher (who in this case is a leader) needs to fulfill certain conditions in relation to whom he/she is leading. The best analogy for this situation is to compare a teacher to an army commander on the battlefield:

- Never leave anyone behind—a teacher must be ready to let all the students follow the lesson without anyone left behind. To concentrate on the fast learners at the expense of the slow coachers is unbecoming of a teacher. One must learn to strike a balance between the slow and the fast in a way that they are not boring to the fast or incomprehensible to the slow.

- Curry the weak/wounded—different lessons have different difficulties. Thus, the teacher must be cautious of those fast or otherwise who might have special problems with the topic. It is absurd to think that clever students would always follow the teacher without problems and also that slow students would always be a step behind. To curry the weak or wounded in this case is to create equilibrium in the flow of knowledge with a concentration on these with difficulty.

- Encourage the discouraged—for one reason or the other, students tend to have their favorite subjects. If yours is not the one a particular student likes, try to find the missing link. A student might be discouraged by the absence of challenges or the level and type of difficulty. (E.g. a science-oriented student might find arts to be very way out of their track and thus might do badly and consequently be discouraged.) The teacher must, therefore, encourage the student and direct them to perceive the subject in question with a different attitude.

- Motivate the lazy—some students might find a particular subject too easy for their ability. In the long run, they tend to be lazy (or spend little time on their work, do their tasks rapidly and carefree) and eventually fall behind or start performing badly. The teacher must use other means possible to motivate them to use the required amount of concentration in the subject.

- Give hope to the hopeless—some students seem not to absorb the knowledge in particular subjects. They can't get it right. After a couple of tries, they lose all hope and convince themselves that they can't learn that particular subject. Teachers should remember that psychology plays an equal amount of contribution towards anybody's performance and success. From this point of view, the teacher must find all viable means to give hope to the student. One way is to let the student work out simple tasks first (those his/her peers would scorn) and gradually increase the difficulty.

- Criticize less and praise often—some teachers seem to take criticizing and teasing as a hobby. Criticism, a more especially negative one, saps the criticized of all self-confidence. The student would eventually fear or shudder when responding to even a known question.

Unit 3 Teacher & Student

The contrary is also true, when you praise one for the effort they put in giving a wrong answer, they will confidently and zealously respond next time with greater chances of getting it right.

- Never shout but calmly chasten—a shout sends fear to the body but a calm whisper delivers wisdom to the heart. There are many ways of teaching a child but constant shouting is not one of them. The more one shouts, the more the recipient builds a wall of protection around oneself. This wall would be in form of a cold shoulder, a deaf ear, ignore, etc. At the end the teacher might call the student stubborn not knowing that teachers create stubborn students. (Stubborn children are not necessarily stubborn students.)

- Let everyone be your favorite—it is human nature to have favorites within a given group. However, in a classroom situation, favoritism should only be tolerated in extra-curricular activities. In most cases, good students tend to win favor in the teacher's eyes. In extreme cases, low achievers are sidelined and left in the darkness, even in other activities. The teacher must treat all students equitably, giving total concern to the deserving.

- Never label—some teachers are in a habit of openly classifying, sub-classifying and categorizing the students. Whilst this should be done in the teacher's report book, the task goes even in the classes such that the students know, and tend to live with it, how the teacher thinks of them. Like in a marathon race, some are slow starters but that does not mean they will remain at the tail. The difference is in the instance where their trainer constantly tells them that they are slow, and if they assimilate it they might take it that any effort to win the race might be a sheer waste of energy. From the teaching experience, we can concur that some slow starters sometimes finish first.

The school is the battlefield. The enemy is illiteracy. Everyone needs to have a good start for them to survive in the race for life. If students don't have a good foundation, they are unlikely going to survive by the time they reach middle school. Thus, we as teachers must be very careful with how and what we teach. We risk putting the future of the country in jeopardy. It is said, "Lack of education leads to elimination."

A good teacher is known for his/her ability to teach those who are slow or can't learn to learn and be able to apply the learned items in problem-solving situations be their exams or real life. If you teach the able to do what they are able to without difficulties, it is hard to draw a line whether you are a good teacher or not. "A good tradesman is known by the product not by the tool." In fact, one who has the worst tool but an up-to-date product is the master of them all.

Primary School Students

Building a foundation is the heaviest task for it will determine how long a building will last. In educational sense, primary school is the construction of the academic world foundation of the children. A carefree constructer (teacher) will cause the children to fall in times of rain and storm. All children (unless gifted) have the ability to benefit equally from the teacher. Thus, a strict yet captivating mode of instruction has to be used as teachers go about their teaching business. At this level, teachers must never consider students as grown-ups who know what they want from a school. They should bear in mind that some children are just forced to come to school and thus the last person they would like to meet is a bully or a teacher. Others don't have a slightest clue of what is going on at this stage of life. Yet still, others think school is a trick by parents to stop children from playing. Some take school as a drop-in centre, a community devised to take care of children while parents are at work. To the rich children, school could be an instrument poor people use to gain something, thus they see no reason to be there. The duty is for the teacher to construct a basic foundation on which all these contradicting thoughts are brought to book.

A primary school student is a child. Let's face it: the prime aim of children is "play". To be a teacher of this type of a person, one must be very understanding and tolerant. In teacher training programs, there is an emphasis on teachers lowering themselves to the level of their students. It is common knowledge that we learn best when the information comes from a familiar source or one we can easily identify with.

To the Primary School Student

- Play is the reason they exist—primary school age is a very delicate time for adventure and discovery. They want to explore and learn the latest activities and tricks seen on TV, read in books and talked about among peers. All these collectively make up child play. A classroom deprived of these would be to the child a nightmare. All the child would be looking forward to is break time. But if the teacher integrates these in his/her lessons, classroom would be a better place.

- Provoking/irritating others are a sport—students like making others for fun. If the teachers fall for this trap then the students would do everything to make the teacher angry. This requires a teacher to be at the same level as the students to be able to take charge and enhance learning.

- Disobedience is a standard—there are many reasons which may lead a child to be disobedient. A forceful teacher is one of them. A teacher who wants something to be done in a given way at a given time, without considering the students' creative ability is inviting

disobedience. Give room for personal creativity allows children to respect yours.
- Being directed is an offence—most children, just like adults, don't like to be told what to do. Everyone wants to be seen as being able to think independently. A teacher should lead by example. The tendency of directing is: one shows the way without having to tread.
- Mischief is fun—getting in trouble is one way of being noticed so many children enjoy that. However, a teacher must encourage being noticed through hard work and other worth activities.
- Jokes are entertainment—if a teacher should encourage entertainment then the class will be interesting. An ever-serious teacher is hard to follow because no one would like to be in that state for hours. Moreover, to say even none serious things seriously is bizarre.
- Being lazy is a "virtue"—in management psychology we learn that humans have an innate tendency of not wanting to do work. Therefore, instead of punishing them for their attitude, we must find ways to motivate them. The best ways to curb laziness are therefore through reward and motivation.
- Nothing is good enough—for most children at this age (school-going age) they don't know what they want in life. They are at the breaking age of discovery and are still discovering themselves. What interests them today might not be tomorrow. What they need most is moderation. Accept them as they are while carefully giving viable advice.
- Being underestimated is fatal—it is hard without proper assessment to determine what the children are capable of. However, to take things for granted and make it general that they don't know ABC will be making a grave mistake. This might affect the chills perception of self. If the perception is duly negative, then the child might lose self-confidence and esteem.

We mentioned earlier that the student is the sole holder of the key to success. The question arises: how can someone who doesn't know what life is all about hold the key? The answer to the question lies in the understanding that one can never force a donkey to drink water. In the classroom situation, the teacher should win, through tricks if necessary, the confidence and interest of the students. Children, due to a lack of understanding of consequences, are very good at giving deaf ears. They can even decide to "turn off" their minds from the teacher. This could be evident when they are tired or the teacher is "killing" them with boredom; and the bell goes, one can see them jump and cheer while, as though planned, dashing to the door.

We should understand that while the teacher holds the key to imparting knowledge, the learner holds the key to receiving the knowledge. The teacher cannot learn on behalf of the student, thus he can never claim the key. Some teachers think they can beat, force or shout lessons into the students. The more they do it, the harder it is for the students to understand. They build numerous rules and rigorous regulations, standards and values for their classes which have little to do with teaching and learning. They use corporal punishments for academic flouting. In doing so, the relationship between the teacher and the students change to "cat and mouse". When the teacher goes away, all the students sigh.

The Classroom

If teachers are commanders and the students are soldiers, then the classroom is the battlefront. (Remember we are shooting down illiteracy not personality) Unlike where the enemy is external, the teacher like a doctor must see the symptoms and use them to cure the infected person. The teacher must carefully scrutinize each case and find ways to help the victim. He should, however, also bear in mind that each case is unique and must be treated unequally.

Thus the classroom is a treatment area and every teacher must:

- Avoid taking in personal complaints—there is nothing sickening than a teacher who always has a personal problem and seeks sympathy from the students. In the long run, the students may consider their teacher as their big baby they need to protect rather than someone they look up to for help.
- Avoid releasing frustrations on the students—we all have our sets of frustrations, but to release these to our innocent children will cause not only a bad relationship but also uncalled-for tension between the teacher and the students. This causes a blockage in learning.
- Avoid bringing in home issues—social problems, especially adult related, are not to be taken into the classroom (this we know). Most teachers however forget that the teacher's uniform shields them from portraying any social related problems (just as it is unbecoming of the doctor to show that he can too get sick). Though not perfect, a teacher can be well-received and respected if they are blemish free.
- Avoid ignoring "simple" behavioral outbursts—the key to controlling a class lies in the way the teacher checks nonsensical behavioral attitudes. In language teaching, these attitudes include those that deal with student's verbal behavior, participation, response etc.
- Never release their anger to the students—there is no room for anger in the classroom.

Consider a classroom as a dispensary; it would be absurd for a doctor to be angry at the patients. The students come to school to seek help in their world of knowledge. If they do any unbecoming thing, it is digging a pit to bury another pit if the teacher rages with anger to correct a child.

- Never tease lazy students—negative teasing which sends the child into self-pity and sups confidence should be discouraged at all times. Some children don't know things not because they are dull but due to many other factors. A teacher should aim at correcting the child rather than playing him or her for a fool. There are honest mistakes which must be taken seriously.
- Tell students that they will definitely fail—even to a nonstarter child; straightforward negative talk will send them back into their hole. However, they will be satisfied that at least people understand their situation and that even though they don't do anything about it is still okay.

However, as teachers, we should expect students to come to class with all of the above. The onus again is on the teachers not to castigate the children but to help them get over their many problems including age.

A good teacher always has good results and contributes positively to the general growth of the children and the nation as a whole. A classroom is a place for the dissemination of information and a treatment area for problems. Whether in or outside the four walls a teacher is still a teacher and must as though impelled, curry the classroom tendencies wherever they go. A student is a learner whether within or without the classroom and they address teachers as teachers even in the supermarket. This serves to mean that our classroom is not limited to the four walls but in the abstract sense to the world of teaching and learning. The students are the people that make the profession worthwhile. Without them, all that is called teaching would be rendered useless. Thus, to help them learn is the teacher's main objective, and the teacher should do so with courtesy and dedication.

Note:

Verbal behavior (言语行为): Verbal Behavior is a methodology that is based upon behavioral principles, but combines the functionality and generalization of Floortime.

New Words and Expressions:

1. perpetually [pə'petʃuəli]	adv.	永恒地；持久地	
2. onus ['əunəs]	n.	责任；义务；负担	
3. channel ['tʃænəl]	v.	引导，开导；形成河道	
	n.	通道；频道；海峡	
4. trivial ['triviəl]	adj.	不重要的；琐碎的	
5. analogy [ə'nælədʒi]	n.	类比；比喻	
6. equilibrium [ˌi:kwi'libriəm]	n.	均衡；平静；保持平衡的能力	
7. viable ['vaiəbl]	adj.	可行的；能养活的；能生育的	
8. sap [sæp]	n.	[植] 树液；精力；活力；坑道	
	v.	使衰竭；使伤元气；挖掘以破坏基础	
9. shudder ['ʃʌdə]	n.	发抖；战栗；震动	
	v.	发抖；战栗	
10. zealously ['zeləsli]	adv.	热心地，积极地	
11. chasten ['tʃeisən]	v.	惩罚；磨炼；抑制	
12. whilst [hwailst]	conj.	同时；有时；当……的时候	
13. illiteracy [i'litərəsi]	n.	文盲；无知	
14. jeopardy ['dʒepədi]	n.	危险；（被告处于被判罪或受处罚的）危险境地	
15. captivating ['kæptiveitiŋ]	adj.	迷人的；有魅力的	
16. provoke [prəu'vəuk]	v.	驱使；激怒；煽动；惹起	
17. bizarre [bi'zɑ:]	adj.	奇异的（指态度、容貌、款式等）	
18. curb [kə:b]	n.	抑制；路边；勒马绳	
	v.	控制；勒住	
19. moderation [ˌmɔdə'reiʃən]	n.	适度；节制；温和；缓和	
20. rigorous ['rigərəs]	adj.	严格的；严密的；严酷的	
21. corporal ['kɔ:pərəl]	adj.	肉体的，身体的	
	n.	下士	
22. scrutinize ['skru:tinaiz]	v.	细阅；作详细检查	
	n.	仔细或彻底的检查	
23. unbecoming [ˌʌnbi'kʌmiŋ]	adj.	不适当的；不合身的；不得体的	
24. blemish ['blemiʃ]	n.	瑕疵；污点；缺点	
	v.	玷污；损害；弄脏	

25. nonsensical [nɔn'sensikəl]   *adj.*   无意义的；荒谬的
26. dispensary [dis'pensəri]   *n.*   药房；（学校、兵营或工厂的）诊疗所；防治站
27. castigate ['kæstigeit]   *v.*   严惩；苛评；矫正；修订
28. courtesy ['kə:tisi]   *n.*   礼貌；好意；恩惠
   adj.   殷勤的；被承认的；出于礼节的

Exercises:

I. Vocabulary.

Fill in the blanks with the most suitable words. Change the form when necessary.

| onus | trivial | shudder | zealously | illiteracy |
| captivating | provoke | blemish | nonsensical | courtesy |

1. The main task of our government is eliminating poverty, disease and _____.
2. It's very annoying and the most _____ business situation I have ever been involved in.
3. I still _____ when I think of that moment.
4. Who could look away from Suzanne Somers's sad but _____ efforts to turn back time?
5. The _____ is on the government to create the necessary conditions for credible and inclusive elections.
6. Those measures sought to _____ a court challenge of the U.S. Supreme Court's 1973 Roe v. Wade.
7. Nevertheless, women of all ages still appreciate this _____.
8. A lawyer should represent a client _____ within the bounds of the law.
9. The extra security precautions are not _____ and affect most communication technology on the market.
10. That is no doubt my fault, and a great _____ in me.

II. Comprehension of the text.

Decide whether the following statements are true (T) or false (F) according to the passage.

1. What attract children are small colorful details which are also noticeable to the adult eye. ( )
2. A teacher must be ready to let most of the students follow the lesson and can leave some

students behind. ( )

3. The school is the battlefield. The enemy is illiteracy. If students don't have a good foundation, they are still likely going to survive by the time they reach middle school. ( )

4. Instead of punishing students for their attitude, we must find ways to motivate them. The best ways to curb laziness are therefore through reward and motivation. ( )

5. We should understand that while the teacher holds the key to imparting knowledge, the learner holds the key to receiving the knowledge. ( )

III. Try to fill in the space with suitable words.

1. _____ is the sole holder of the key to personal glory and success in school.

2. The teacher should be close enough to perpetually _____ the student to ignore the attractions and continue on his/her journey.

3. We can state that a good teacher is an educator or _____ who leads the learner into the untrodden paths of knowledge.

4. A student might be discouraged by _____ of challenges or the level and type of difficulty.

5. _____ is the heaviest task for it will determine how long a building will last.

Text B Teacher-Student Attachment and Teachers' Attitudes Towards Work

> 导读：无论是在课内还是在课外，教师都被认为是学生学习的榜样。榜样教育作为传统德育的一种形式，广泛运用于古今中外的教育实践当中。罗丝曾经对教育者在正式或非正式场合所起到的榜样作用进行调查研究，并强调了榜样对群体的某些态度、观点和生活方式的影响；罗丝发现学生通常把教师视为与其父母同等重要的榜样。凯尔认为："不论一个教师教的是哪门学科，他都在孩子的教育过程中起到榜样的作用。教师应该为人正直，不赌博，不酗酒，不做荒淫的勾当，不与不道德的人为伍。"

Introduction

Teachers are expected to be positive role models for their students, both inside and outside the classroom. Teachers who are able to accurately interpret the underlying teacher-student relationship processes can learn to proactively, rather than reactively, influence the dynamics of any class. Having examined the role of educators as role models in both formal and informal education, Rose (2005) stressed that role models can expose groups to specific attitudes, lifestyles and outlooks. Children often regard their teachers as important role models as their parents. Carr (2000) pointed  out that regardless of subject area, teachers play a moral role in education. It is the teachers' duty to be socially acceptable by keeping themselves morally upright, refraining from excesses like abhorring drunkenness, gambling, and avoiding immoral relations.

The powerful attachment bond some students feel toward the teacher, as a significant "other" in their life, is also felt by the teacher. However, referring to Kearney, Plax, Hays et al. (1991), researchers often tend to overlook teachers as a potential source of problems in the classroom. Unfortunately, Sava (2001) reported that teachers' actions could actually have some lasting negative effects on students.

Compared to the majority of literature that focuses on positive teacher communication behaviors, fewer studies have been done on negative teacher communication behaviors. Concurrently, educational reform tends to focus only on curricula, neglecting the importance of effective teacher-student interaction. Teacher support can be conceptualized similarly to social support in schools, which is strongly related to a student's psychological well-being (acceptance, care, encouragement and approval from others) and may improve students' self-esteem and self-evaluation. On the other hand, Bru, Boyesen, Munthe et al. (1998) asserted that lack of teacher support would hinder students from developing a positive self-concept. In spite of all these compelling reasons to study teachers' behavior, researching negative teacher-student interactions is often considered a taboo, making study in this area difficult.

Teacher-Student Attachment

The relationship between the teacher and the student provides the underpinning of a professional identity for the teacher, a learning identity for the students and a professional working relationship for both. Ainsworth and her colleagues were the first to provide empirical evidence for Bowlby's (1988) attachment theory. Using the strange situation procedure, Ainsworth and Bell classified infants into one of three categories: (1) secure, in which infants use the mother as a secure base for exploration and seek contact with her after separation; (2) anxious-ambivalent (later called "resistant"), in which infants are unable to use the mother as a secure base and are often angry and push her away upon reunion; (3) anxious-avoidant, in which infants fail to use the mother as a secure base for exploration and avoid the mother upon reunion or approach her only indirectly. More recent work presented a fourth category (disorganized-disoriented), in which infants have no predictable or effective pattern of eliciting care-giving behaviors when stressed. Across the lifespan, each attachment classification falls on a continuum of emotional regulation for managing affect, events, and relationships. This conceptualization places the anxious–avoidant style, with its overly organized strategies for controlling and minimizing affect, at one end of the continuum, and the relatively uncontrolled, poorly managed effect of anxious–resistant styles at the opposite end. Secure attachment, falling along the midpoint of the emotional continuum, reflects a balance of the two extremes of emotional regulation. Those with disorganized-disoriented attachment classifications may present a range of behaviors involving under-controlled emotional reactions such as impulsive verbal or physical aggression or over-controlled responses in which emotions are difficult to express and behavior may reflect withdrawal and difficulty handling conflict. Thus, their emotional reactions are unpredictable and typically maladaptive.

Referring to Bowlby (1988), attachment is a special emotional relationship that involves an exchange of comfort, care, and pleasure. Previous research has found that adults differ according to their own attachment style in their ability to act as a secure base for children in their care. Secure adults are typically better at realistically evaluating their own relationship histories and responding sensitively and appropriately to a child's attachment needs (Crowell & Feldman, 1988) than adults with an insecure attachment history. Pianta, Steinberg and Rollins (1995) define positive teacher-student relationships as "warm, close, communicative", and such relationships are linked to behavioral competence and better school adjustment. Teacher and student attachment has been identified as a significant influence on students' overall school and behavioral adjustment. Fisher and Cresswell (1999) asserted that interaction with other people (students, other teachers, and staff) is actually a major part of most teachers' school days. Therefore, it is important to study the naturalness and quality of teacher-student relationships, as it influences the quality of their relationships. According to researchers, the qualities that lead to effective teacher-student relationships are positive affection, warm attitude, tact in teaching, teacher immediacy and teacher power, teacher assertiveness and responsiveness, and low differential treatment. Lack of any of these traits may negatively influence teacher-student interaction.

It is logical to infer that the internal working model plays a role in the choice of career. An insecurely attached person may be attracted to the teaching profession as a result of a positive experience of teachers as a student, or the promise of having students to attach to. Both offer the chance of a corrective relational experience for the teacher.

A secure teacher's interest is mainly focused on understanding her students. She is glad to depend on them and have them depend on her. If this trust is broken and the teacher is let down by a student, she is more likely to view it as an aberration rather than the norm. It disconfirms her inner working model of others and perhaps drives an investigation into how she can improve the delivery of the information, or the quality of the interaction, so that the student gains understanding and therefore pleasure from the learning experience along with an increased curiosity about the world. This teacher uses the experience to shape and improve her own practice. She seeks to have her internal working model confirmed and does so in ways that benefit the students, the teacher and the relationship between them.

A preoccupied teacher may appear to be inconsistent in her treatment of students, over valuing some and devaluing others. The students held in high regard may be able to do no wrong in the eyes of the preoccupied teacher, while others appear to do nothing right. The teacher could not afford, in attachment terms, to lose favour with students she deemed special, for instance those who appeared to influence other students either positively or negatively toward the teacher. This might lead to over involvement with preferred students. The preoccupied teacher can choose who she would like to be close to and may engineer many opportunities for closeness to preferred students. However, if students reject the closeness, raising separation anxiety in the teacher, as many students with a dismissing or fearful type would, the teacher may find herself displaying separation protest behaviours to those students. The preoccupied type maybe more attracted to teaching than the other types. Possibly it could be because they perceive that they will get the rewards of students liking them while remaining largely in control of the relationship, thus reducing the anxiety associated with being liked.

A dismissing teacher is not likely to be attracted to teaching in large numbers due to the forced proximity and interaction with a large number of people. The dismissing teacher may tend to "stay on the case" of certain students, always catching them behaving badly and always failing to catch them doing well or being socially proactive. If the teacher were to catch the bad student doing good things this would increase her emotional dissonance and therefore challenge the inner working model. To maintain the avoidant attachment she must remain emotionally and symbolically, if not physically, distant from the students. However, this is likely to increase the chances of separation anxiety, or even protest, in the students. They may attempt to regain emotional proximity to the teacher to satisfy their attachment needs. This in turn increases the teacher's level of anxiety about the level of intimacy and might lead to increased chances of the teacher misbehaving to remain distant from students who wish to be close. It might be expected that the dismissing teacher may suffer from more classroom discipline issues as the students try to attach to her.

A fearful teacher may find herself in a heightened state of attachment arousal most of the time. For her, proximity is both sought and avoided at the same time. This creates a number of unique difficulties in a classroom situation where physical proximity is forced upon all. The fearful teacher experiences an increased sense of unworthiness when compared to the other attachment styles. She may feel less able than her peers in her professional capability and is also likely to fear that significant others, such as colleagues, students and parents, will find this out and become negatively disposed toward her as a result. This makes the fearful teacher more vulnerable to the expectations of others and she would have greater difficulty in managing the competing demands of the people that she deals with daily, including in particular her immediate superiors. Yet, this would also suggest that the immediate superiors have a significant role in the fearful teacher's professional identity. Support by the principal and other superordinates may significantly lessen feelings of inadequacy for the fearful teacher, unlike the dismissing teacher who would not place much value on the opinions of others.

The organizational climate in schools, teachers' ideologies, and their level of burnout (outcome of stress) could harm teacher-student relationships. Affected teacher-student relationships can in turn cause teacher-conflict-inducing attitudes (lack of teacher emotional support, teacher misbehavior or hostility). According to Sava (2001), the quality of teacher-student relationships can influence students' educational and psychosomatic outcomes. Concurrently, high incidences of educational, psychological and somatic complaints are seen in students whose teachers they characterize as more hostile in their attitude towards them. Teachers with lower morale due to school climate conditions and who are more likely to burn out tend to adopt conflict-inducing attitudes towards students, which will in turn lead to educational and psychosomatic complaints in students.

Abidin and Kmetz (1997) reported that teacher-student relationships are one of the factors that influence teachers' stress, and the stresses developed by teachers are reflected in their behavior towards students. Teachers, as reported by Abidin and Kmetz (1997), have different perceptions and experienced different stress levels with regard to specific students in classroom (behaviorally challenging students and typical students). These perceptions and stress levels are linked to their classroom behaviors and may bias a teacher's behavior towards those students. Furthermore, teachers' behavior towards challenging students involved greater amounts of negative and neutral behaviors compared to the control students. Briefly, if teachers' stress levels increase, this will decrease their positive behavior towards the students, and the teacher will avoid contact or ignore the students. The more stress induced by the students, the less engaged the teacher will be with the students, which affects the teacher-student relationship.

Teachers' Attitudes Towards Work

Teaching is said to be a demanding profession. Aside from the tedious classroom preparations and the task of dealing individually with many kinds of learners, teachers are also expected to be involved in different kinds of community activities and other out-of-school assignments. Hence, these various roles which teachers face seem to be exhausting and stressful. Meador (2013) described teaching as a difficult profession. However, Guneyli and Aslan (2009) stated that prospective teachers posited to be happy to teach even under difficult conditions. To other teachers, such additional work assignments could also be a source of joy and self-fulfillment. While other teachers grumble, complain and avoid the job, others regard teaching as a rewarding profession and would even commit their lifetime in the teaching profession. To them, their love and passion for teaching prevails than their personal concerns. How a teacher faces the tough job of being a teacher depends on attitudes and work values. Thus, variation in the attitude and work values of teachers may be expected.

According to Kreitner and Kinicki (2007), there are three components of attitudes: affective, cognitive and behavioral. The affective component is a feeling or an emotion one has about an object or situation. The cognitive component is the beliefs or ideas one has about an object or situation, whereas the behavioral component of attitude reflects how one intends to act or behave towards someone or something. In most situations, the three components appear concomitantly to shape teachers' classroom postures, through direct and indirect interaction between society, school and teachers. Moreover, teachers' styles and attitudes are strong context outcomes rooted in experience. They do not become automatic routine behaviors, in the sense that they are developed through very slow interactions (action and reaction), and become well-established constructs for each individual only after some time. In that sense, as noted by Carr (1990), attitudes can be modified only by each individual, when they become aware, through elements and evidence, that new postures would be better to deal with the surrounding world.

Attitudes towards work mean perceptions that affect employees' performance in their positions. Referring to Brophy and Good (1974), many educational researchers have supported the idea that teachers' attitudes and expectations can be self-fulfilling prophecies. Brophy and Good (1974) also pointed out that once teachers develop a particular attitude or belief, they may begin to treat students differently in ways that help bring about the outcomes that they expect. On the other hand, Petty and Cacioppo (1986) asserted that attitude and behavior are defined comprehensively as individuals' general evaluations about themselves, others, other objects, events and problems. Briefly, attitudes do predict people's behavior. In order to understand teachers' attitudes and understand how attitude reflects teachers' behavior, we could examine many components of attitude in context of organizational behavior. The following are four components of attitude used to assess teachers' attitude towards work: job satisfaction, commitment, communication, and alienation.

Job satisfaction is the most important and frequently studied attitude. It reflects the extent to which people like their jobs. As expected, teachers' working conditions, assessed by their level of job satisfaction, affect teacher-student interaction. Hence, higher levels of job satisfaction improve teachers' morale, which students perceive positively.

Commitment is an important work attitude, because it can distinguish those who are "caring", "dedicated", and who "take the job seriously" from those who "put their own interests first". Committed individuals are expected to be willing to work harder to achieve their goal and remain employed. However, teachers do not all have the same level of commitment to their job. For some teachers, commitment is a major part of their lives, and they afford it extensive consideration and high priority. Others may view it differently, perceiving teaching as just a job. Referring to Jackson, Boostrom and Hansen (1993), Goodlad (1990) and Sockett (1993), the moral purposes of teachers are described by words such as "courage", "integrity", "care", "fairness" and "honesty". It is easy to see how these words may be linked to commitment. The more obvious signs of commitment are enthusiasm for the job and for the people with whom one works.

Communication manifests itself in attitudes as accuracy and openness of information exchange. Effective communication is the heart of creating and maintaining an effective school. Communication that occurs within schools is crucial in shaping teachers' social reality. School excellence is directly related to what teachers think and do. Teachers' attitudes and behavior strongly rely on their perceptions about their schools.

Attitude is alienation, according to Rafferty (2003), meaning the extent to which staff members feel disappointed with their careers and professional development. On the whole, the concept of positive student-teacher interaction is multi-dimensional, as it involves organization, workload (difficulty), expected fairness of grading, instructor knowledge, and perceiving learning.

Teaching has been identified as a stressful profession. Teachers' relationships with their students significantly affect their stress levels. Several studies show that teacher stress predicted negative teacher and student relationships. Significant correlations were found among teacher stress and negative teacher-student relationships. Teacher stress arises from being unable to discipline pupils in the way they would prefer. Mancini, Wuest, Vantine et al. (1984) pointed out that teachers with depersonalization (an "alteration" in the perception or experience of the self so that one feels "detached" from one's mental processes or body) will behave immorally and fail to give information to their students.

Teacher commitment has been a critical predictor of teachers' work performance, absenteeism, retention, burnout and turnover. Day, Elliot, and Kington (2005) suggested that teachers remained committed to their beliefs throughout their professional life. Although their levels of engagement with particular practices were modified through various life events and activities, their commitment to their ideological positions did not diminish. However, some teachers' commitment might vary over time, because different people have different levels, and some can plateau earlier or later than others. Commitment was moderated through a range of factors; some of which were sustaining and some diminishing. Teachers were less likely to engage in particular activities or behave in particular ways at one point in time, depending on various work and life contextual factors such as school contexts, and relationships with students and colleagues. These seemed to be the major work and life factors that diminished commitment.

Bindhu and Kumar (2007) discovered a significant and positive correlation between job satisfaction and stress coping skills, which are self-reliance, pro-active attitude, adaptability and flexibility, and total stress coping skills. Briefly, the ability to deal with stress can increase teachers' job satisfaction.

Note:

Role model (行为榜样): The term role model generally means any "person who serves as an example, whose behavior is emulated by others". The term first appeared in Robert K. Merton's socialization research of medical students. Merton hypothesized that individuals compare themselves with reference groups of people who occupy the social role to which the individual aspires.

New Words and Expressions:

1. abhor [əb'hɔː]	v.	痛恨；憎恶
2. excess [ik'ses]	n.	放肆行为；过度；超过的量
3. assert [ə'səːt]	v.	断言；主张；声称；维护
4. hinder ['hində]	v.	阻碍；打扰
	adj.	后面的
5. compelling [kəm'peliŋ]	adj.	引人注目的；强制的；激发兴趣的
6. ambivalent [ˌæmbi'veilənt, æm'bivə-]	adj.	矛盾的；好恶相克的
7. elicit [i'lisit]	v.	抽出；引出；引起
8. overly ['əuvəli]	adv.	过度地；极度地
9. resistant [ri'zistənt]	adj.	抵抗的；反抗的；顽固的
	n.	抵抗者
10. withdrawal [wið'drɔːəl, wiθ-]	n.	撤退；收回；提款；取消；退股
11. maladaptive [ˌmælə'dæptiv]	adj.	适应不良的；不适应的；不利于适应的
12. assertiveness [ə'səːtivnis]	n.	魄力；自信
13. responsiveness [ri'spɔnsivnis]	n.	响应能力；有同情心
14. abberration [ˌæbə'reiʃn]	n.	脱离常规，反常现象
15. proximity [prɒk'siməti]	n.	接近；靠近
16. ideology [ˌaidi'ɔlədʒi, ˌidi-]	n.	意识形态；思想意识；观念学
17. concurrently [kən'kʌrəntli]	adv.	同时发生地
18. hence [hens]	adv.	因此；今后
19. morale [mɔ'rɑːl, -'ræl]	n.	士气，斗志
20. dedicated ['dedikeitid]	adj.	专用的；专注的；献身的
21. reflexive [ri'fleksiv]	adj.	反身的；[物] 反射的
22. inconsistent [ˌinkən'sistənt]	adj.	不一致的；前后矛盾的
23. manifest ['mænifest]	v.	证明；表明；显示
24. alienation [ˌeiljə'neiʃən]	n.	疏远；转让；精神错乱；[哲]异化；[戏]间离效果
25. depersonalization [diːˌpəːsənəlai'zeiʃən, -li'z-]	n.	[心理] 人格解体；人性之丧失
26. absenteeism [ˌæbsən'tiːizəm]	n.	旷工；旷课；有计划的怠工；经常无故缺席

Unit 3   Teacher & Student

Exercises:

I. Vocabulary.

Fill in the blanks with the most suitable words. Change the form when necessary.

| abhor | assert | hinder | compelling | maladaptive |
| assertiveness | proximity | concurrently | morale | manifest |

1. Even now, I still believe the logic is _____.
2. He _____ a pleasing personality on stage.
3. They _____ all forms of racial discrimination.
4. The National Trust opposes the development because of its _____ to the UNESCO world heritage site.
5. _____, a serious diplomatic effort is needed to address the major anomaly of the Afghan war.
6. Before panic spreads, it is worth noting that Japan's new _____ reflects weakness as well as strength.
7. Schizophrenia—A group of disorders manifested in delusions, disturbances in language and thought, mood shifts, and _____ behaviors.
8. Its statesmen used to _____ that Germany had no independent foreign policy, only a European policy.
9. Low pay in recent years has led to low _____.
10. Officials say Williams' death could _____ the work of non-government groups in the country.

II. Comprehension of the text.

Decide whether the following statements are true (T) or false (F) according to the passage.

1. Teachers are expected to be positive role models for their students only inside the classroom. ( )
2. According to Ainsworth and Bell's classification, anxious-avoidant infants use the mother as a secure base but are often angry and push her away upon reunion. ( )
3. Bru, Boyesen, Munthe and Roland asserted that lack of teacher support would prevent students from developing a positive self-concept. ( )
4. The quality of teacher-student relationships rarely influences students' educational and

psychosomatic outcomes. (　)

5. Communication which occurs within schools plays a crucial role in shaping a teacher's social reality. (　)

III. Try to fill in the space with suitable words.

1. In spite of all these compelling reasons to study teachers' behavior, researching _____ is often considered a taboo, which can make study in this area difficult.

2. Referring to Bowlby, _____ is a special emotional relationship that involves an exchange of comfort, care, and pleasure.

3. According to Kreitner and Kinicki, there are three components of attitudes: affective, _____ and behavioral.

4. A dismissing teacher is not likely to be attracted to teaching in large numbers due to the forced proximity and _____ with a large number of people.

5. There is a significant and positive correlation between job satisfaction and _____.

Supplementary Reading: Teacher Effectiveness: What Do Students and Instructors Say?

Teaching effectiveness is a topic of significant conversation and attention in the media, the legislative area, and education, but there is little agreement about what "teacher effectiveness" actually means. Teaching effectiveness is a complex phenomenon, and educators are no closer to reaching a consensus about the characteristics that determine teacher effectiveness.

However, increasingly, policy conversations frame teacher effectiveness as a teacher's ability to produce higher than expected gains in students' standardized test scores. This focus on attributing gains on standardized tests to teachers and measuring the result of teaching by averaging test score gains has a number of strengths. It has a certain amount of credibility—most would agree that an effective teacher should help students learn more than expected. This definition does, however, have serious limitations.

One critique concerns the problem of the assumptions of causality that underlie this approach. The approach requires the establishment of what part of an effectiveness score is attributable solely to the teacher. Making this determination is problematic not just for practical reasons but for logical reasons—assumptions are required that may be unreasonable. If we presuppose a blank, receptive mind, encased within a compliant and passive learner, then we need travel only a very short logical distance to infer that teaching produces  learning, and hence that what teachers do determines whether students learn. In the passive recipient view, it makes some sense to think of successful teaching arising solely from the actions of a teacher. That is, assuming that the formulation offered above has merit, then it follows that success at learning requires a combination of circumstances well beyond the actions of a teacher.

It can be argued that narrowing the definition of teacher effectiveness to reflect only student growth on standardized achievement takes this assumption too far. It is important to note that measures of teacher effectiveness can be calculated without regard to what takes place in classrooms and schools, if teacher effectiveness is narrowly defined as a given teacher's impact on the learning of his or her students as measured by standardized tests. With this narrow definition, other important ways that teachers contribute to successful students, communities, and schools are overlooked. Similarly, other influences on student outcomes, including other teachers, peers, school resources, community support, leadership, and school climate or culture, cannot be "parceled out" of the resulting score.

In the narrowest definition of teacher effectiveness, in which effectiveness is determined solely by student achievement gains, a teacher can be deemed effective compared to other teachers because his or her students performed better on the state test than the students' prior achievement would have predicted, without consideration of any other factors. In that case, it would be impossible to say whether the growth in achievement as reflected by test scores was the result of class time spent narrowly on test-taking skills and test preparation activities or whether achievement growth was the result of inspired, competent teaching of a broad, rich curriculum that engaged students, motivated their learning, and prepared them for continued success.

Another critique of a teacher effectiveness model based on test scores concerns the degree to which innovations in measurement drive how teacher effectiveness is defined. Campbell, Kyriakides, Muijs et al. (2003) contend that trends in measurement of teacher effectiveness seem to follow the development of new instruments and technologies, focusing on the ability to measure something, rather than first defining effectiveness and then determining a technology for measuring it.

The increased availability of data in which student achievement is linked to teachers along with statistical innovations in analyzing these data may be partly responsible for what appears to be a growing emphasis on measuring teachers' contributions to student achievement and a concomitant narrowing of the definition of teacher effectiveness. Students' knowledge is summarized in a test score, whereas teachers' effectiveness is reflected in their contribution to that test score. Value-added models provide a classic example of a measure of teacher effectiveness driven by technological development.

In addition to students' test scores, teacher effectiveness has been assessed in other different ways, including: instructors' qualifications, their behavior/characteristics, the instructional practices used, or a combination of these factors. Especially in higher education, students' perceptions are often regarded as a central element in determining teacher effectiveness. Universities have used student course evaluations extensively as a means for measuring teacher effectiveness. Faculty evaluations have been used in at least three different ways: as formative measures to help faculty improve teaching and course content, summative evaluations of teaching effectiveness, and as information to aid students in selecting courses and instructors. In addition, much research has been conducted in an attempt to identify the characteristics of effective teachers. The results indicated that students felt effective instructors' possessed important cognitive and affective components. The cognitive skills included content, organization of ideas, clarity of concepts, and effective presentation skills. Four affective components of increasing student interest, encouraging participation, developing interpersonal relations, and enhancing communication were identified.

By contrast, in the qualitative study of teacher effectiveness, Madsen and Cassidy (2005) examined educators' perception of effective teaching behaviors rather than students' perceptions of effective teaching. In analyzing their data, Madsen and Cassidy focused on categories of behaviors rather than listing individual teaching characteristics. Experienced instructors, student teachers, and beginning education students with no teaching experience observed videos of instructors and analyzed the instruction across 5 pre-identified dimensions of teacher behavior: instructional practices, content delivery, classroom environment, student learning, and student social interaction. The study participants identified teachers' instructional practices as the most important component that differentiated effective instructors from those who were perceived as less effective, while teacher delivery was the least important characteristic and according to their results had little impact on teacher effectiveness. Stronge, Ward, and Grant (2011) in their research placed the emphasis of teacher effectiveness on student achievement rather than teacher instructional practices. Stronge, Ward, and Grant determined teacher effectiveness by comparing the characteristics of teachers whose students had high academic growth to those whose students experienced low academic growth. The two groups of instructors were compared across 15 characteristics which Stronge, Ward, and Grant then organized into 4 dimensions: instructional delivery, student assessment, classroom learning environments, and personal qualities. Differences were found between the instructors of high and low achieving students in two of the dimensions: classroom environment and personal qualities. However, in contrast to Madsen and Cassidy's findings, no difference was found between the groups in the dimensions of teacher instructional delivery and student assessment. The dimensions of students' social interactions and teachers' personal characteristics were not examined in this study.

Instructors of high achieving students scored significantly higher in the dimension of the classroom learning environment and its two components: managing and organizing the environment. Managing the classroom environment included establishing classroom routines, monitoring student behavior, and managing time efficiently and effectively. The other dimension of the classroom environment encompassed classroom organization, which included the availability of student materials, the classroom layout, and effective use of space.

Significant differences were found in two dimensions of personal qualities between academically effective and less academically effective teachers. Instructors of high achieving students scored higher in the areas of respect and fairness. In addition, they also evidenced stronger positive relationships with their students when compared with the instructors of lower achieving students.

These results were similar to those found in an earlier exploratory study analyzing the educational practices of more and less academically effective instructors. Depending on whose perspective is considered, effective teaching practices may be identified differently. Kern determined that students and teachers have different classroom expectations. Williams and Burden (1997) found that this difference can negatively affect learners' satisfaction, motivation and interest in learning, and their academic achievement. In contrast, a close match between students' and teachers' perceptions as to what constitutes effective instruction may result in greater student gains and motivation. Despite the importance of achieving consensus between

instructors and students, few studies have compared teachers' and students' perceptions of effective teaching.

For both online and on-ground instructors, "Knowledgeable" was the most important characteristic. This characteristic/behavior has remained consistent even though we are currently educating a new generation of learners using both on-ground and online formats. The three most important characteristics for effective online instructors were: "Respectful", "Knowledgeable", and "Approachable". Instructors should take note that students seemed to value approachable instructors, more than those that demonstrate responsiveness or professionalism.

The quality of the educators' instructional practices to be more important than delivery method used. This added more to our understanding of the qualities that exemplify effective instructors by identifying that the top three and lowest three characteristics/behaviors of effective instructors were the same whether the course was delivered online or on-ground. The data also indicated that the top three qualities of instructors were closely aligned. This is very interesting in that it suggests that the delivery method does not necessarily mean the characteristics/behaviors of instructors should change.

In other words, good teaching is whether it occurs online or on-ground. This also furthered our understanding of types of students and their perceptions of good instructors. No matter their gender, age, major, level of education, or location, all students tended to rate good instructor characteristics/behaviors and qualities similarly. The only significant difference was found for younger students and undergraduate students, who rated use of humor as more important than older, graduate level students did. For educators to be perceived as effective they can use the same characteristics/behaviors and exhibit the same qualities for all students no matter their age, gender, or program of study. Use of humor, however, is recommended when teaching younger, undergraduate students.

Unit 4　Teaching Methods

Text A　Refuting Misconceptions about Classroom Discussion

导读：长期以来，小组讨论法被普遍认为是一种能培养学生批判性思维、小组合作精神，提高学生理解能力的有效教学手段。但是，在现实教学情景下，受到一些条件的限制，小组讨论法经常被误用，以至于达不到理想效果。本文探讨了四个对课堂讨论法的错误性认知，并对这些错误观点进行反驳，减少教学者对采用这种教学法的顾虑。

Social studies educators advocate discussion as an influential instructional method to encourage students to apply knowledge and develop higher-order thinking and understanding. Firstly, telling students about something does not necessarily ensure their comprehension, but discussing a topic helps students strengthen and extend their existing knowledge of the topic and increase their ability to think about it. Secondly, discussion promotes students' involvement and engagement. Researches, as well as the wisdom of experienced teachers, demonstrate that for true learning to take place students must take responsibility for their own learning and not depend solely on a teacher. Using discussion is one means of doing this. It gives students public opportunities to talk about and play with their own ideas and provides motivation to engage in discussion beyond the classroom. Thirdly, discussion is used by teachers to help students learn important communication skills and thinking process. Because discussions are public, they provide a means for a teacher to find out what students are thinking and how they are processing the ideas and information being taught. Discussions thus provide social settings in which teachers can help students analyze their thinking process and learn important communication skills such as stating ideas clearly, listening to others, responding to others in appropriate ways, and learning how to ask good questions.

In classroom reality, however, teachers only use the discussion method sparingly. Instead, teachers predominantly use a quasi-discussion form called recitation to involve students in demonstrating their knowledge of the subject matter. The problem is compounded by the fact that teachers generally refer to all major interaction sessions with students in the classroom as "discussions" when, in reality, they are recitations. Although both forms of interaction are effective in achieving their intended purposes, discussion is vastly more appropriate and effective in developing in students the widely endorsed citizenship competencies associated with rational and humane decision-making and problem-solving necessary for the common good.

Social studies teachers do not use discussion in their classrooms for many reasons, including a lecture-recitation instructional tradition, a long tradition of discipline-based curriculum design, emphasis on speedy and superficial coverage of content, fact-based textbooks and the limited availability of issue-based materials. It is hypothesized that one reason teachers avoid discussion is that they are relying on common misconceptions about the discussion method to make judgments about its use. Those misconceptions diminish the role that discussion can play in the classroom to help achieve the purpose of social studies. Logically, we can further assume that reflective and conscientious teachers might consider using discussion more often if their misconceptions were refuted with accurate and practical information. Possessing reliable and up-to-date information is the first step teachers need to consider when evaluating discussion as a viable instructional method.

Discussion Misconception 1: A discussion consists of a teacher asking questions and students answering them.

If we substitute the word recitation in place of discussion, that statement would not be a misconception. A recitation does consist of a teacher asking questions and students answering them, but a discussion is much more. Therefore, a recitation is not a discussion; it is, at the most, a quasi-discussion.

The traditional recitation method emphasizes finding out whether students know certain facts, often to prepare them for objective tests. As an instructional method, the use of the recitation method is very effective in achieving goals related to knowing content. It has been the dominant interaction form in classrooms throughout the past century, and it is characterized by the interaction pattern of a teacher question, usually at the lower cognitive levels, followed by a student response, and then a teacher evaluation. This procedure is referred to as the IRE (teacher initiation, student response, teacher evaluation) pattern. One reason the pattern has persisted in the classroom is that it helps teachers manage and direct the flow of interaction. Teachers continuously need to reaffirm their authority when dealing with groups of twenty to thirty students, many of whom are reluctant learners.

Discussions physically look and sound different from recitations. Discussion has a different purpose, interaction structure, and cognitive focus. It has as it emphasizes that students should apply what they have read or learned through the oral exploration of ideas, issues, and problems. A teacher's interaction with students aims at encouraging students to make connections between the new content and their past knowledge and perspectives. The general goal is for students to understand the material more fully. Key to achieving that is the use of authentic questions that request new information rather than memorized facts from the text. The interaction pattern is much more variable than the pattern of a recitation with teacher and students asking and answering questions and making comments. A discussion more closely approximates natural conversation than recitation because it is slower paced and not driven by the questions or evaluations of one person. It is an educative conversation with and among students. For example, a teacher might initiate a discussion with a higher cognitive-level question and may redirect that question to several students who have different perspectives on the issue being discussed. The teacher may probe one or more of the students for clarification of their responses and for elaboration or extension of their thinking. Students may converse with one another, sharing or questioning perspectives, and asking for evidentiary support for perspectives. It is not uncommon during genuine discussions for students to assume discussion leadership at various points.

Discussion Misconception 2: Teachers cannot get students involved in discussions if the students do not want to participate.

This misconception applies to reluctant students, not to those students who adamantly refuse to participate in class for whatever reason. That is extreme behavior. Teachers can get students involved who appear apprehensive, who do not raise their hands, who say "I don't know", who sit in the back of the room, who appear disinterested, and who are silent most of the time.

The classroom climate a teacher creates is very important in encouraging student participation. In an international study, Klinzing and Klinzing-Eurich find that teachers tend to control discussions excessively by moving discussions back to themselves. They inadvertently do this by reacting in one way or another to almost every student response, question, or comment. Instead, they should only intervene with a comment or question at key points during the discussion and encourage more student-student interaction. Teachers who use those discussion techniques will give students more freedom to converse.

Teachers can employ many questioning techniques to encourage students to participate, including probing students' initial responses, redirecting questions to several students, and calling on non-volunteering students. During discussions, students sometimes lack the skill and confidence to express themselves at the higher cognitive levels. Resulting responses to questions can be ambiguous and incomplete. Teachers find that probes are useful follow-up questions to encourage students to complete, clarify, expand, or support their answers, especially with younger students as they begin to articulate the basics of reflective thinking during discussions. Questions such as "Why?" "What evidence do you have?" and "How can you support your view?" are common in discussions about societal issues and problems. A teacher leading students in discussion will need to be particularly diligent in listening to students' initial responses to follow-up with appropriate probes. Another useful approach to stimulate student participation in discussion is to direct one question to several students. The redirection could be prompted by an unanswered question or a desire to get additional responses to the same question and can involve volunteering and non-volunteering students.

Another questioning approach to stimulate participation during discussions is to have students formulate questions. Students ask few information-seeking questions so they need to be prompted to formulate questions related to the issue or problem being discussed. For example, a teacher might ask that all students write one question in response to the request, "If you had an opportunity to participate in a presidential press conference, what question would you ask him related to his policy on terrorism?" A question of this type will encourage all students to think and get involved. Having students ask questions of each other is another approach to consider because students tend to respond in more complex ways to each other than to teachers' questions.

The key to encouraging students to get involved in discussions is to create the conditions under which they want to contribute to discussions. The most obvious one is to rearrange students from seating in rows facing the teacher to seating them in a circle or semicircle to face each other, thereby facilitating communication. Another seating arrangement is referred to as the parliamentary style with two sets of rows facing each other. Establishing a positive social-emotional climate where students' responses, comments, and questions are respected, encouraged, and supported by both teacher and students is essential. Rules might be established by the teacher or the students to create discussion-behavioral expectations and guide the development of students' civic behaviors.

Other approaches to encourage participation include "pump priming" techniques such as having students write a response to a question first before answering, using a "think-pair-share" approach to get them to test a response with a peer first rather than with the whole class, or using small groups of two to three students to have them reflect on questions related to issues and problems. The key is getting students to discuss with each other, which they find is much less threatening than having to "be on stage" in front of the whole class. A student's "stage performance" will improve after having presented "off-Broadway" first.

There are many other instructional activities to get students to think and contribute responses to higher-order questions that can then be used as a base for a discussion:

1. Response cards. Pass out index cards and ask for anonymous answers to your discussion questions. Then group the responses to structure a class discussion or identify an issue for the class to explore through discussion;

2. Polling. Use a verbal survey by asking for a show of hands-on positions related to an issue. Then follow up the diagnosis of group sentiment with a discussion based on support for positions;

3. Whips. Go around the group and obtain each student's point of view or a random sample of views. Use whips when you want to obtain something quickly from each student. The information might be used to form small groups representing different perspectives on an issue or solutions to a problem;

4. Informal panel. Invite a small number of students to present their views in front of the entire class;

5. Discussion chip. Distribute the same number of chips or pennies (three to five) to each member in a small group of students. Tell them that they are to use one chip for every answer, comment, or question as part of a discussion. Students need to use up all their chips before the discussion is completed or redistribute another equal number of chips for the discussion to continue;

6. Talking ball. Toss a small foam ball to a student with the understanding he or she must provide an answer to the discussion question, make a comment, or ask a question. That student then tosses the ball to another student, and so on.

Discussion Misconception 3: Teachers are unbiased when encouraging students to make discussion contributions.

Although social studies teachers claim they take student diversity into account when involving students in discussion, observation of their discussion practices suggests a differentiated approach. In an in-depth study of five social studies teachers, Larson found that student diversity is a factor teachers said they consider when deciding whether to engage their students in discussion. Components of this factor are cultural background, ethnicity, gender, race, learning styles, and ability. Students representing different backgrounds were perceived as potentially valuable for discussion because an opportunity was provided to have a variety of viewpoints represented on an issue.

Evidence had shown that teachers, generally, expose low-ability students to an "impoverished curriculum", which translates to limited and repetitive content, emphasis on factual recitation rather than on lesson-extended discussion, stress on drill and practice tasks rather than application and higher-level thinking tasks. In other research, it was also found that male students were given more time to talk in classrooms and received more remediation, praise, and criticism than female students.

Discussion Misconception 4: Teachers cannot objectively evaluate students' contributions during classroom discussions.

Through the use of rubrics, teachers can assess more objectively the quantity and quality of students' verbal contributions during classroom discussions. During the past decade, there has been a movement toward integrating assessment of students' learning with instruction. One of the trends is the emphasis on moving away from what have been, until recently, the "tried and true" means of assessing student achievement and skills—traditional objective tests. In the old paradigm, the primary and major evaluation, usually a test was something that followed instruction to determine if students had learned the lesson material. Today, alternative and authentic assessment is more closely linked to instruction so that assessment becomes the means and ends of instruction.

Instruction involves formative and summative assessment of students by using authentic approaches or approaches that reflect the real world. Discussion is considered to be one such alternative and authentic instructional approach because it is how we communicate in many different venues—schools, works, communities, and families, for example. And, we can measure and assess discussion in terms of the content of the discussion and the process of discussing.

Over the past ten years, new techniques can help teachers to assess students' contributions during discussions more objectively. One such technique is a discussion rubric, which is a description of the teacher's requirements for varying degrees of student performance as the students attempt to meet the established criteria for an effective discussion. Harris created a rubric for assessing classroom discourse about civics that is based on standards and criteria. The teacher's goal in assessing each student engaged in a small group discussion of an issue is to judge the extent that a student's contribution to clarifying the issue under consideration and assisting the group toward an understanding and resolution of the issue. Students are assessed on substantive criteria aiming at evaluating students' understanding of the issue and procedural criteria that focus on students' ability to engage one another in discussion about the issue. The procedural criteria include positive (e.g. "inviting contributions of others" and "summarizing points of agreement and disagreement") and negative (e.g. "irrelevant distracting statements" and "personal attack") components. Three elements of performance focus the assessment: whether or not the student has presented accurate knowledge related to the policy issue, employed skills for stating and pursuing related issues, and engaged others in constructive dialogue.

Note:

Off-Broadway (在纽约市戏院区以外的戏院上演的戏剧，多半是非主流的，制作费较少，或是实验剧): It is a term for a professional venue in New York City with a seating capacity between 99 and 499, and for a specific production of a play, musical or revue that appears in such a venue, and which adheres to related trade union and other contracts. These theatres are smaller than Broadway theatres.

New Words and Expressions:

1. compound ['kɔmpaund, kəm'paund]   v.   混合；调和；使严重
2. diminish [di'miniʃ]   v.   减少；减损；贬低
3. viable ['vaiəbl]   adj.   能生存的；可行的
4. reluctant [ri'lʌktənt]   adj.   不情愿的；勉强的
5. adamantly ['ædəməntli]   adv.   坚决地；顽固地
6. inadvertently [ˌinəd'və:təntli]   adv.   不注意；疏忽地；非故意地
7. ambiguous [æm'bigjuəs]   adj.   模棱两可的；含糊不清的
8. remediation [riˌmi:di'eiʃən]   n.   纠正；补习
9. rubric ['ru:brik]   n.   种；类；题目；标题；注释
    adj.   红色的；用红色写的
10. paradigm ['pærədai:m]   n.   范例；示范；典范

Exercises:

I. Vocabulary.

Fill in the blanks with the most suitable words. Change the form when necessary.

| compound | diminish | reluctant | ambiguous | paradigm |

1. He's _____ to begin, but when he does you should see him go into action.
2. We were lost in bewilderment due to his intentionally noncommittal or _____ statement.

3. Several unpopular decisions _____ the governor's popularity.
4. The painting provides us with one of the earliest _____ of the use of perspective.
5. He _____ various ingredients into an effective drug.

II. Comprehension of the text.

Decide whether the following statements are true (T) or false (F) according to the passage.

1. Instead, teachers predominantly use a quasi-discussion form called recitation to involve students in demonstrating their knowledge of the subject matter. ( )
2. A discussion more closely approximates natural conversation than recitation because it is quicker-paced and driven by the questions or evaluations of one person. ( )
3. To encourage students to get involved in discussions, it is essential to create the conditions under which they want to contribute to discussions. ( )
4. It was found that male students were given more time to talk in classrooms and received more remediation, praise, and criticism than female students. ( )
5. Response cards, polling, and informal panel are used to help teachers to objectively evaluate students' contributions during classroom discussions. ( )

III. Translate the following phrases into Chinese.

communication skills _____
up-to-date information _____
substitute A in place of B _____
integrate...with... _____
meet criteria _____

Text B   Brainstorming: A Creative Way to Learn

导读：头脑风暴这一问题解决方法不仅在商业机构、政府机构等领域大受推崇，在教育界，头脑风暴也成为一种教学手段。采用"头脑风暴法"进行教学，需要教师转换教学观念，给学生提供互相学习和交流的机会，让学生不断修正自己的观点。本文从使用这一教学手段该遵守的原则，以及在课堂实践中实施的具体步骤两方面入手，给教育工作者提出了如何最有效率地使用该方法的意见。

Unit 4   Teaching Methods

Man is a highly creative creature who prefers to learn by doing, exploring, testing, questioning, and modifying ideas. However, the traditional school has not usually found it "economical" to foster learning by a process that is so natural to students. Education for today and the future must be relevant and meaningful. It must equip each student with a process by which he may solve many complex problems that will eventually evolve. Brainstorming is a creative problem-solving technique that has been used successfully in business, government, industry, and to a limited degree in the field of education. In the classroom, brainstorming can provide a student with the means by which early contact with peers becomes a stimulating and challenging experience. Children might be asked to solve practical problems that arise during the day or to solve problems that might be proposed by the teacher or students during a social studies lesson. Researchers have found that even first-grade children can profitably use the brainstorming technique.

Small group interaction has long been cited as an effective teaching technique. This interaction is of importance because the pupil has the opportunity to become actively involved in the process of learning. Developing a positive self-concept by active participation would be one of the major benefits derived from group brainstorming. Educators often promote brainstorming as a useful technique in gifted education. There are many who claim that in a search for ideas there can be no implicit techniques, and rightly so, if the technique means a rigid set of rules. Any attempt to lay down hard-and-fast methods would be nothing but terminology masquerading as technology, but, there can be and are certain principles in the form of guides to procedure.

Brainstorming Principles

Alex F. Osborn, the father of modern-day brainstorming outlined four basic principles for effective brainstorming:

1. Critical judgment is ruled out; criticism of ideas must be withheld until later. Many creative thoughts have been lost simply because a person doubted that others would think his ideas insignificant and of no value. Many students start their question with "This may be a stupid question, but..." Education and experience have trained most children and adults to think critically rather that creatively, and this preface to a question is an example.

As a result, they tend to impede their fluency of ideas by applying their critical power too soon. By deferring judgment during a brainstorming session, children will be able to conceive a large number of creative ideas.

2. "Freewheeling" is welcomed. The wilder the idea, the better; it is easier to tame down than to think up.

3. Quantity is wanted. The greater number of ideas, the more likelihood of potential solutions. Practically all the experiences with group brainstorming confirm the principle that quantity helps breed quality.

4. Combination and improvement are sought. In addition to contributing ideas of their own, participants should suggest how ideas of others can be turned into better ideas, or how two or more ideas can be combined to make one.

Steps to Successful Brainstorming in the Classroom

1. Description of brainstorming and statement of instructions. Explain to the children that brainstorming is a way of stating a greater number of ideas in a limited amount of time. Emphasize the idea of spilling out ideas as quickly as possible while applying the deferred judgment principle. A short practice session can be attempted by asking the children to write a list of as many items as possible under the heading, "things we do at school". After several minutes, stop the listing and compile the number of different ideas on the chalkboard. You may wish to discuss with the children the following questions: Did each of you contribute some ideas? Were you able to avoid being critical of each other's contributions? This deferred judgment principle must be accomplished before effective brainstorming can take place.

2. Divide the class into brainstorming groups. Beginning groups seem to function well with 3 to 11 members. The groups can be all boys, all girls, or mixed. An odd number in the group might assure the availability of a majority, and thus avoid the danger of a split between two children of equal number. It will help if the teacher selects a few individuals who serve as self-starters for each group. With proper planning and guidance, the whole room can brainstorm a problem or just one individual can use this technique. Several groups can be brainstorming at one time within the classroom.

3. Selection of a group leader and secretary. Each group should have a leader who would present the problem and keep the group actively engaged in the brainstorming process. The function of the secretary would be to write in brief form all ideas as they are presented. At times the ideas may tumble out so fast that even a shorthand expert would have difficulty recording them. It may be necessary to have two secretaries, each one jotting down every other idea.

4. Selection of the problem. The problem to be brainstormed should be one that will arouse student interest. This may not be easy to do, but a way usually can be found to make the problem relevant to many interests. Many times a functional problem, like what to do during the upcoming party could be used as a starting point. After the technique is refined, problems dealing with academic topics could be brainstormed. Students should assist in the selection process.

5. Statement of the problem. Problems can be presented that will encompass several areas of study. Social studies is a particularly good area in which children can brainstorm. The major objective in selecting a problem and stating the problem properly is to make sure that it is specific, not general.

The guiding principle is that a problem should be simple rather than complex. Failure to narrow the problem to a single target can seriously mar the success of any brainstorming session. Sometimes a session can be conducted to break down broad problems into their specific components. But in the normal course of events, make sure the problem is simple and specific.

Another principle to be considered is that the problem must be one that lends itself to many possible answers. If there are just a few possible solutions to the present one, then it would be wise to select another problem.

6. The brainstorming session begins. The problem should be explained, and the group leader should then discuss the four basic principles. Placards stating these principles could be displayed to act as a constant reminder to the children.

After these preliminaries are completed, the leader then calls for suggestions on how the problem could be solved. What happens if all of the children's hands go up? If this occurs the group leader could simply go around the table and let each person present one idea in turn. One student should present only one idea at a time. The fun is just beginning! If a child has some idea that is directly related to the previous statement, he can snap his fingers to be recognized by the leader. The leader should give priority to the finger snappers and thus make the most of the power of association. The students will find this exciting and challenging! Throughout this entire procedure, the secretary should be taking brief notes.

Past experiences indicated the optimum time for beginners using brainstorming is about ten minutes. As their experience in this activity increases so can the time period.

As the children's brainstorming skills become more sophisticated with time, new variations can be tried. After a brief amount of time on a problem, the leader can stop the session and ask the group members to keep the problem on their minds until the next day when they will be asked for their afterthoughts. Maybe you can come up with some new variations.

7. Evaluations of the presented ideas. After the brainstorming session has been completed, the secretary of the group should prepare a list of all ideas suggested during the session. At this point, the teacher has to make a decision. Should the ideas be evaluated by the group of students who think up the ideas or by an entirely different group? It is usually wise to have the final evaluation done by those directly responsible for the problem. This may or may not be the group

that does the brainstorming. The teacher has a great deal of latitude when choosing the method of evaluation. To facilitate this evaluation, it is often advisable to prepare a checklist of criteria by which students and teachers can evaluate the ideas. The following criteria could be used to evaluate each idea: Is it feasible? Is the idea simple enough? Is it timely? Is it appropriate? Is it efficient? Is it an improvement?

It is important that the criteria are appropriate for the problem being brainstormed. With each new problem, you may need to create a new checklist. The entire class can work together to determine the relative worth of the presented ideas. This evaluation process usually develops into a most effective and meaningful type of group interaction. During the final evaluation, the students should attempt to apply the final ideas to the problem to determine whether or not the ideas are applicable.

If application is not feasible, the children can conduct a debate or continue with class discussion on the relative worth of the ideas.

At this point, a very important concept must be noted. In many areas of instruction, particularly in social studies, there is no "right" or "wrong" answer. From this type of learning experience students will have the opportunity to discover the dichotomies in our society. It is important that students find out how the real world operates and how to evaluate real problems. The teacher should integrate the final evaluated ideas into his teaching lesson.

Most practitioners of group brainstorming recommend that brainstorming groups be assisted by trained facilitators. These facilitators can ensure that group members follow the rules for effective brainstorming. For example, they might remind group members not to criticize or evaluate each other's ideas. Facilitators can also keep groups from drifting into issues or topics not directly related to the central problem being discussed. Group members who do not actively participate because of fear or lack of motivation can be encouraged to contribute to the group effort. When groups hit dry spells, the facilitator can suggest some areas or angles they have not considered and encourage them to keep trying by mentioning high-performance levels attained by other groups. Several studies have shown that facilitators that use these strategies can in fact help brainstorming groups attain relatively high levels of performance.

It is often not feasible to have a facilitator work with each brainstorming group. Teachers who divide their classes into groups for brainstorming sessions cannot effectively monitor and facilitate each one of these groups. It is also difficult and expensive to provide facilitators for group brainstorming sessions in organizations. A more useful strategy is to train students to be effective group brainstormers. Experience in group brainstorming with an effective facilitator greatly enhances group brainstorming in subsequent sessions without facilitators.

  Computers also appear to be useful in facilitating group brainstorming. Many corporations and university laboratories employ a group decision support system that allows participants to exchange ideas by means of a computer network. Ideas can be entered in the lower section of the computer screen while ideas generated by others in the group network are shown at the top of the screen. Studies have shown that this type of group brainstorming is as effective as individual brainstorming. It appears to be especially useful when dealing with large groups of 12 or more, in part because participants do not experience the interference of conventional group brainstorming. They can type their ideas at any time and do not have to wait until others have expressed their ideas. Unfortunately, this type of computer-based brainstorming requires equipment and software not easily available in most educational contexts. However, simply having students in a group type their ideas on computers as they share them aloud appear to be an effective alternative. Even though there is still some potential distraction from hearing others generate ideas, one does not have to wait for one's turn to generate ideas. Moreover, there is a record of each person's ideas which should minimize the tendency to loaf in groups.

Notes:

1. **Brainstorming (头脑风暴):** A group creativity technique by which a group tries to find a solution for a specific problem by gathering a list of ideas spontaneously contributed by its members.
2. **Alex F. Osborn** (May 24, 1888—May 13, 1966): Osborn was an advertising executive and the author of the creativity technique named brainstorming.

New Words and Expressions:

1. foster ['fɔstə]	v.		领养；培养；促进；鼓励；抱有（希望等）
2. derive [di'raiv]	v.		获取；得自；起源于
3. rigid ['ridʒid]	adj.		严格的；固执的；刻板的
4. impede [im'pi:d]	v.		妨碍；阻止
5. freewheeling [ˌfri:'wi:liŋ]	adj.		随心所欲的；无拘无束的
6. spill out			倾诉；涌出
7. tumble ['tʌmbl]	v.		（使）跌倒；翻滚；暴跌
8. encompass [in'kʌmpəs]	v.		围绕；包围；包括；完成

9.	preliminary [pri'limin əri]	*adj.*	初步的；预备的；开始的
		n.	初步行动；准备；初步措施
10.	optimum ['ɔptiməm]	*adj.*	最佳的；最适宜的
11.	sophisticated [sə'fistikeitid]	*adj.*	老练的；精密的；复杂的；久经世故的
12.	dichotomy [dai'kɔtəmi]	*n.*	两分；分裂；二分法
13.	distraction [dis'trækʃən]	*n.*	分心；分心的事物；注意力分散

Exercises:

I. Vocabulary.

Fill in the blanks with the most suitable words. Change the form when necessary.

derive	encompass	rigid	optimum	sophisticated

1. She enjoys doing yoga because she can not only keep fit but also _____ happiness from it.
2. In the _____ college entrance exam, he stood out and was admitted into Peking University.
3. Nowadays, iPhone enjoys immense popularity because it is very _____.
4. Both the weather and also the market offered _____ conditions for the sale of this product.
5. The general arts course at the university _____ a wide range of subjects.

II. Comprehension of the Text.

Decide whether the following statements are true (T) or false (F) according to the passage.

1. Brainstorming is a creative problem-solving technique that has been used successfully in business, government, and industry, but not in the field of education. (　)
2. Researchers have found that even first-grade children can profitably use the brainstorming technique. (　)
3. The greater number of ideas, the more likelihood of potential solutions. (　)
4. Beginning brainstorming groups function well with more than 11 members. (　)
5. Assisted by trained facilitators, it is more likely that group members will follow the rules for effective brainstorming. (　)

III. Translate the following sentences into Chinese.

1. Man is a highly creative creature who prefers to learn by doing, exploring, testing, questioning, and modifying ideas.
2. Critical judgment is ruled out; criticism of ideas must be withheld until later. Many creative thoughts have been lost simply because a person doubted that others would think his ideas insignificant and of no value.
3. In addition to contributing ideas of their own, participants should suggest how ideas of others can be turned into better ideas, or how two or more ideas can be combined to make one.
4. The function of the secretary would be to write in brief form all ideas as they are presented. At times the ideas may tumble out so fast that even a shorthand expert would have difficulty recording them.
5. Ideas can be entered in the lower section of the computer screen while ideas generated by others in the group network are shown at the top of the screen.

Supplementary Reading: Learning Styles and Teaching Styles

Students learn in many ways—by seeing and hearing; reflecting and acting; reasoning logically and intuitively; memorizing and visualizing and drawing analogies and building mathematical models; steadily and in fits and starts. Learning styles have profound effects on material processing, exercises designing, teachers' instruction options, and performance assessments. Teaching methods also vary. Some instructors lecture, others demonstrate or discuss; some focus on principles and others on applications; some emphasize memory and others understanding. How much a given student learns in a class is governed in part by that student's native ability and prior preparation but also by the compatibility of his or her learning style and the instructor's teaching style. Therefore, it is important for teachers to know their learners' preferred learning styles because this knowledge will help teachers to plan their lessons to match or adapt their teaching and to provide the most appropriate and meaningful activities or tasks to suit a particular learner group at different stages.

In addition to the traditional skills of analysis, reason, and sequential problem solving, educators should place emphasis on intuition, feeling, sensing, and imagination. Teachers should design their instruction methods to connect with all learning styles, using various combinations of experience, reflection, conceptualization, and experimentation. Instructors can introduce a wide variety of experiential elements into the classroom, such as sound, music, movement, experience, and even talking. Teachers should employ a variety of assessment techniques, focusing on acquiring the essential language skills.

Models of Learning & Teaching Styles

A student's learning style may be defined in large part by the answers to five questions (see Figure 4-1):

(1) What type of information does the student preferentially perceive: sensory (external)—sights, sounds, physical sensations, or intuitive (internal)—possibilities, insights, hunches?

(2) Through which sensory channel is external information most effectively perceived: visual—pictures, diagrams, graphs, demonstrations, or auditory—words, sounds? (Other sensory channels—touch, taste, and smell—are relatively unimportant in most educational environments and will not be considered here.)

(3) With which organization of information is the student most comfortable: inductive—facts and observations are given, underlying principles are inferred, or deductive—principles are given, consequences and applications are deduced?

(4) How does the student prefer to process information: actively—through engagement in physical activity or discussion, or reflectively— through introspection?

(5) How does the student progress toward understanding: sequentially—in continual steps, or globally—in large jumps, holistically?

Teaching style may also be defined in terms of the answers to five questions (see Figure 4-1):

(1) What type of information is emphasized by the instructor: concrete—factual, or abstract—conceptual, theoretical?

(2) What mode of presentation is stressed: visual—pictures, diagrams, films, demonstrations, or verbal—lectures, readings, discussions?

(3) How is the presentation organized: inductively—phenomena leading to principles, or deductively— principles leading to phenomena?

(4) What mode of student participation is facilitated by the presentation: active—students talk, move, reflect, or passive—students watch and listen?

(5) What type of perspective is provided on the information presented: sequential—step-by-step progression (the trees), or global—context and relevance (the forest)?

Preferred Learning Style		Corresponding Teaching Style	
sensory intuitive } perception		concrete abstract } content	
visual auditory } input		visual verbal } presentation	
inductive deductive } organization		inductive deductive } organization	
active reflective } processing		active passive } student participation	
sequential global } understanding		sequential global } perspective	

Figure 4-1 Dimensions of Learning and Teaching Styles

Sensing and Intuitive Learners

Sensing and intuition are the two ways in which people tend to perceive the world. Sensing involves observing, gathering data through the senses; intuition involves indirect perception by way of the unconscious—speculation, imagination, hunches. Everyone uses both faculties, but most people tend to favor one over the other.

Sensors like facts, data, and experimentation; intuitors prefer principles and theories. Sensors like solving problems by standard methods and dislike "surprises"; intuitors like innovation and dislike repetition. Sensors are patient with detail but do not like complications; intuitors are bored by detail and welcome complications. Sensors are good at memorizing facts; intuitors are good at grasping new concepts. Sensors are careful but may be slow; intuitors are quick but may be careless. These characteristics are tendencies of the two types, not invariable behavior patterns: any individual—even a strong sensor or intuitor—may manifest signs of either type on any given occasion. An important distinction is that intuitors are more comfortable with symbols than are sensors. Since words are symbols, translating them into what they represent comes naturally to intuitors and is a struggle for sensors. Sensors' slowness in translating words puts them at a disadvantage in timed tests: since they may have to read questions several times before beginning to answer them, they frequently run out of time. Intuitors may also do poorly on timed tests but for a different reason—their impatience with details may induce them to start answering questions before they have read them thoroughly and to make careless mistakes.

Visual and Auditory Learners

The ways people receive information may be divided into three categories, sometimes referred to as modalities: visual—sights, pictures, diagrams, symbols; auditory—sounds, words; kinesthetic—taste, touch, and smell. An extensive body of research has established that most people learn most effectively with one of the three modalities and tend to miss or ignore information presented in either of the other two. There are thus visual, auditory, and kinesthetic learners. Visual learners remember best what they see: pictures, diagrams, flow charts, time lines, films, demonstrations. If something is simply said to them they will probably forget it. Auditory learners remember much of what they hear and more of what they hear and then say. They get a lot out of discussion, prefer verbal explanation to visual demonstration, and learn effectively by explaining things to others. Most people of college age and older are visual while most college teaching is verbal—the information presented is predominantly auditory (lecturing) or a visual representation of auditory information (words and mathematical symbols written in texts and handouts, on transparencies, or on a chalkboard).

Inductive and Deductive Learners

Induction is a reasoning progression that proceeds from particulars (observations, measurements, data) to generalities (governing rules, laws, theories). Deduction proceeds in the opposite direction. In induction one infers principles; in deduction one deduces consequences. Induction is the natural human learning style. Babies do not come into life with a set of general principles but rather observe the world around them and draw inferences: "If I throw my bottle and scream loudly, someone eventually shows up." Most of what we learn on our own (as opposed to in class) originates in a real situation or problem that needs to be addressed and solved, not in a general principle; deduction may be part of the solution process but it is never the entire process. On the other hand, deduction is the natural human teaching style, at least for technical subjects at the college level. Stating the governing principles and working down to the applications is an efficient and elegant way to organize and present material that is already understood.

Active and Reflective Learners

The complex mental processes by which perceived information is converted into knowledge can be conveniently grouped into two categories: active experimentation and reflective observation. Active experimentation involves doing something in the external world with the information— discussing it or explaining it or testing it in some way—and reflective observation involves examining and manipulating the information introspectively. An "active learner" is someone who feels more comfortable with, or is better at, active experimentation than reflective observation, and conversely for a reflective learner. Active learners do not learn much in situations that require them to be passive (such as most lectures), and reflective learners do not learn much in situations that provide no opportunity to think about the information being presented (such as most lectures). Active learners work well in groups; reflective learners work better by themselves or with at most one other person. Active learners tend to be experimentalists; reflective learners tend to be theoreticians. At first glance there appears to be a considerable overlap between active learners and sensors, both of whom are involved in the external world of phenomena, and between reflective learners and intuitors, both of whom favor the internal world of abstraction. The categories are independent, however. The sensor preferentially selects information available in the external world but may process it either actively or reflectively, in the latter case by postulating explanations or interpretations, drawing analogies, or formulating models. Similarly, the intuitor selects information generated internally but may process it reflectively or actively, in the latter case by setting up an experiment to test out the idea or trying it out on a colleague.

Sequential and Global Learners

Most formal education involves the presentation of material in a logically ordered progression, with the pace of learning dictated by the clock and the calendar. When a body of material has been covered the students are tested on their mastery and then move to the next stage. Some students are comfortable with this system; they learn sequentially, mastering the material more or less as it is presented. Others, however, cannot learn in this manner. They learn in fits and starts: they may be lost for days or weeks, unable to solve even the simplest problems or show the most rudimentary understanding, until suddenly they "get it"—the light bulb flashes, the jigsaw puzzle comes together. They may then understand the material well enough to apply it to problems that leave most of the sequential learners baffled. These are the global learners. Sequential learners follow linear reasoning processes when solving problems; global learners make intuitive leaps and may be unable to explain how they came up with solutions. Sequential learners can work with material when they understand it partially or superficially, while global learners may have great difficulty doing so. Sequential learners may be strong in convergent thinking and analysis; global learners may be better at divergent thinking and synthesis. Sequential learners learn best when material is presented in a steady progression of complexity and difficulty; global learners sometimes do better by jumping directly to more complex and difficult material. School is often a difficult experience for global learners. Since they do not learn in a steady or predictable manner they tend to feel out-of-step with their fellow students and incapable of meeting the expectations of their teachers. They may feel stupid when they are struggling to master material with which most of their contemporaries seem to have little trouble. Some eventually become discouraged with education and drop out. However, global learners are the last students who should be lost to higher education and society. They are the synthesizers, the multidisciplinary researchers, the systems thinkers, the ones who see the connections no one else sees. They can be truly outstanding engineers—if they survive the educational process.

Teaching Techniques to Address All Learning Styles

Traditionally, teaching is dominated by a teacher-centered, book-centered, grammar-translation method and an emphasis on mechanical memory. These traditional language teaching approaches have resulted in a number of typical learning styles, with visual learning being one of them. A teacher must design her lesson plan around her students. After you know the students' learning styles, you should set goals for your teaching strategies. This requires you to differentiate instruction through use of the learning styles. Ideally you want to incorporate all of the learning styles so that each student may learn in a way that suits them best for the day.

Studies show that matching teaching styles to learning styles can significantly enhance student attitude and student behavior. This is not to say that the best thing one can do for one's students is to use their preferred modes of instructions exclusively. A point no educational psychologist would dispute is that students learn more when information is presented in a variety of modes than when only a single mode is used. The following are some techniques employed in teaching practice:

(1) Provide a balance of concrete information (data, facts, experiments and results) and abstract concepts (principles, theories).

(2) Balance material that emphasizes practical problem-solving methods with material that emphasizes fundamental understanding.

(3) Use pictures, graphs and simple sketches liberally, during and after the presentation of verbal material. Show films or provide demonstrations, if possible.

(4) Don't fill every minute of class time lecturing and writing on the blackboard. Set aside intervals, however brief, for students to learn what have been told on their own. Raise questions and problems to be worked on.

(5) Talk to students about learning styles, both in advising and in class. Students are reassured to find their academic difficulties may not all be due to personal inadequacies. Explaining to students how they learn most efficiently may be an important step in helping them

reshape their learning experiences so that they can be successful.

(6) Try to design some activities which involve students' senses as many as possible, using all the senses to help improve English learning. For example, relatively long passage dictations, and games, which require students to write down what they are told by their classmates, who already have learnt that by heart.

(7) Encourage students to learn something online. In terms of English learning, students can write assignments through e-mail or read materials given online (the students in the experimental class use the new horizon college English book, a web-assisted textbook).

(8) Motivate learning. As much as possible, teach new material in the context of situation to which students can relate in terms of their personal experiences, rather than simply as more material to memorize.

Teachers confronted with this list of techniques might feel that is impossible to do all that in the class and cover the syllabus and requirements. The idea, however, is not to adopt all the techniques at once but rather to pick several that look feasible and try them on an occasional basis, and try one or two more later in class. In this way a teaching style that is both effective for students and comfortable for teachers will evolve naturally, with a potentially dramatic effect on the quality of learning.

Nowadays, technology is being used in a variety of ways to improve classroom instruction. Technology is enhancing instruction in variety of school types. Additionally, teacher and student roles are being altered in ways that are reflective not only of the presence of technology, but also the efforts at systemic school reform. These findings highlight different roles that students and teacher adopt in the course of their interaction with technology-supported pedagogical practices that inquiry-based learning. These practices:

- promote active and autonomous learning in students;
- provide students with competencies and technological skills that allow them to search for, organize, and analyze information, and communicate and express their ideas in a variety of media forms;
- enable teachers, students, and their parents to communicate and share information on-line;
- engage students in collaborative, project-based learning in which students work with other classmates on complex, extended, real-world-like problems or projects;
- provide students with individualized or differentiated instruction, customized to meet the needs of students with different achievement levels, interests, or learning styles;
- allow teachers and students to assess student and peer academic performance.

What is the significance of these role transformations? Although these changes in roles and technology-enhanced pedagogical practices can be linked with a number of factors, one stands out as noteworthy. The standards movement, which has resulted in schools throughout the U.S. adopting high performance standards, has had a significant impact on schools to prepare them to use technology. Coupled with the move toward challenging standards are the high expectations that schools have adopted, believing all children can achieve at high levels if given the necessary support. This environment has provided new opportunities for teachers and students to break out of old roles and patterns through the use of technology. Furthermore, technology has allowed teachers and students to adopt new behaviors and responsibilities consistent with the realities of a rapid technological society.

Unit 5   Materials & Test

Text A   Materials and Media

> 导读：随着社会进步和科学技术的发展，教材与教学媒体也经历着一次次重大的变革。承载于不同介质的教材具有不同的表意功能和各具特点的教学效用，传统媒体与现代数字媒体是传承、互补、扬弃的关系。从教材媒体的性状与教学主体的关系上来看，数字化、网络化教学媒体带来的本质意义上的变化是教育话语权的转移。教师和学生可以更多地、实质性地参与教学目的的设定、教材内容的选择、教学方式的确定，并享有信息科技从技术角度上提供的操作便利和平等权利。本文从教材与科学媒体的定义与分类、外语教学发展历程中教材与教学媒体的演变与改革以及为此教师面临的挑战几方面入手，呼吁教师在使用教材和教学媒体时要善于扬长避短，结合学习者的学习方式和学习需求，营造一个理想的教学情境。

Throughout the history of foreign language teaching, theorists and practitioners have tried to support the language learning process as best they can. To that end, foreign language teachers and material developers have introduced a variety of aids, materials and media. Whatever supportive means are chosen, their conception and format to a large extent determine the layout of a foreign language course.

Developments in the understanding of what foreign language competence implies and what is required to achieve it, combined with technological innovations and shifts in social demands on education, have entailed changes in the way in which the foreign language teaching process is conceived and supported. Materials and media that were believed to be effective learning tools at one point in time are supplemented with or even supplanted by others, which may in their turn become marginalized.

The gradual increase in and diversification of teaching materials and media, with the ensuing danger of overburdening teaching with them for their sheer availability, makes it an absolute necessity that teachers are able to perceive both strengths and weaknesses of available teaching aids, and can make well-considered judgments as to when, how and to what end they can most effectively be harnessed to particular learning or teaching tasks. Often such decisions are influenced by considerations beyond the control of the course designers and procedures. Questions of organization and coordination in any multimedia course will play an important role. In addition, materials and media deliberations must be made with respect to the abilities and needs of particular learner groups.

Definition and Classifications

Materials and media are everything that can be used to support the foreign language learning process. In many foreign language classes today, these aids will probably include a computer, a slide projector, a microphone, a blackboard or a whiteboard, the textbook, and a workbook. Many teachers will use additional worksheets, sets of task cards and objects (props, pictures, posters, food tins or labels, maps, wall charts and the like). Some teachers may also have an overhead projector with transparencies or even a video player with videotapes or films at their disposal. In some language classrooms reference materials, such as dictionaries, grammar or phrase books, may also be permanently available. Schools may have foreign newspapers, periodicals, magazines, cultural background books or supplementary readers in their library. Computers and the Internet are widely used as foreign language teaching aids, and many schools may have at their disposal a self-access centre, where a large variety of the above-mentioned media and materials are freely accessible to learners for self-study.

This broad spectrum of teaching aids can be classified according to various perspectives. An obvious way to do so is to distinguish between aural, visual and audio-visual aids, with the last category having the advantage of combining sound and image. Another common way to classify materials and media is to do so according to their function. Thus a distinction can be made between teaching and learning materials, or between data, instruction, process and reference materials. Data materials are chunks of language that are presented to learners for exploration. Instruction materials typically include workbooks, exercise books and other materials designed for language practice. Process materials are those parts of a language course that mediate to learners how the course is to proceed. Reference materials and media may be referred to as either basic or supplementary, with the first category comprising materials and media that are considered essential parts of a particular language course, and the latter that can but need not be used on top of the basic materials to assist students to meet the requirements of a particular course or to further improve their language competence. Whereas course books and workbooks are now typically considered basic course materials, computer packages, slides and transparencies, videos, additional listening materials, set of games, simplified readers and the like, tend to be considered supplementary, although many multimedia courses attempt to integrate a large variety of different media and materials, and, consequently, might consider these aids to be basic, not supplementary. Fourth, materials may either be designed for use in the classroom or for self-study. A final commonly used procedure is to classify materials and media according to the language components or skills they aim to practice. Thus, listening materials are distinguished from, for example, reading, writing, speaking or grammar practice materials. Some media are considered better suited to practice particular skills or deal with particular requirements of foreign language course than others. Thus, learners' listening skills may benefit most from aural aids, such as mobile phones, audio players on computers or stereos. Cultural background information, on the contrary, may best be presented over video, television, films, transparencies, posters or pictures, or it may be taught via the Internet.

Materials and Media in the History of Foreign Language Education

When looking at the history of foreign language education from the point of materials, a number of evolutions in their selection and design are noticeable. At various stages in the development of foreign language teaching, new media and teaching aids have been introduced, of which some have managed to establish themselves firmly, and continue to be used to date, whereas others have become marginalized or seem to have gradually disappeared from mainstream teaching altogether.

Shifts in the selection and conception of media and materials seem to have been dependent on a number of interrelated factors. Developments in the understanding of what competence in a foreign language entails and what is required to reach it, in theories about the nature of the language learning process and how it is best supported, combined with technological developments and the commercial exploitation of particular "teaching and learning machines", have to a large extent determined the way in which materials and media have been used in foreign language instruction. Thus, the need for the pupil to hear himself when practising pronunciation was recognized early. No effective way of meeting the problem was found until the tape recorder was invented. The popularity of drill exercises in the audio-lingual foreign language teaching can in part be explained by the commercialization of a machine that was capable of doing these monotonous, unnatural and inhuman activities, i.e. the language laboratory. Television and video were acclaimed by foreign language education theorists of the communicative era for their capability of bringing "real life" into the language learning classroom and of communicating the total situation of language to the learner. Insights from cognitive psychology, notably that people learn best when several senses are simultaneously addressed, triggered efforts of the teaching profession to introduce all kinds of visual, audio-visual and even tangible aids into foreign language teaching, so as to complement or replace the predominantly written and aural materials.

Teaching practice and teachers' and learners' experiences with particular materials and media, too, contributed to their refinement and adaptation to particular educational needs. Thus, following teachers' unsatisfactory experiences with films and videos which tended to be quite long when they were first introduced into the foreign language classroom, a clear evolution towards shorter films has been noticeably replacing the input of large amounts of aural and visual data with shorter sequences, say of about four minutes, followed by careful exploitation. Learners' frustrating experience with monolingual dictionaries containing long entries formulated in a language too far above their level of competence incited publishers and researchers to develop learner dictionaries with clear definitions written in simple language, highlighting active words to be learnt first, providing study pages and grammar help boxes focusing on vital grammar points, building in a workbook section to develop students' dictionary skills, providing colorful illustrations with corresponding vocabulary practice exercises or usage notes designed to help learners avoid common errors.

Teacher frustration at the impracticability of certain media and materials proposed by theorists further determined their lifecycle. Whereas textbooks are very user-friendly "packages" of materials, because they are light, easily scanned, easily stacked and do not need hardware or electricity. Slide projectors or video machines now are available to most teahers, which makes course planning easier. Some media can also be considered more flexible than others because they can be used for a variety of language practice activities, with various age groups and working arrangements. Thus, transparencies can not only be used by the teacher to capture class attention, they may also be used by pupils to report on group work results. They are easily wiped off and can be used in the context of almost any thinkable language practice activity. The language laboratory, on the contrary, in comparison, appears relatively static and limited in use, seeming suitable foremost for individual pronunciation and drill practice, albeit those communicative group activities are not wholly excluded.

The selection of teaching materials and media is also partly dependent on the demands made by society at a given period in time. Computer literacy is now put forward as one of the aims which all teaching should pursue. In view of the explosion of knowledge and the fastness with which it distributes, over the information highway and other media, society also demands that teachers and schools educate their children for independent, lifelong learning, providing them with the skills to find and evaluate information next to passing a body of well-structured knowledge on to them which can serve as a guiding framework. Since computers use language, it would seem logical to take advantage of them for language learning. Computers, moreover, enable independent individual work, since learners can progress at their own pace and many programs include a self-check facility, automatic contextualized feedback, the possibility to use reference materials on the screen, to listen to the spoken language, to watch pieces of video, to record one's own voice, or to interact on real time with native speakers of a foreign language, to name only a few advantages. The fact that young and adolescent learners in particular find the use of computers attractive and motivating is an added benefit.

These social demands urge a change in teachers' and learners' roles. Teachers have to become coaches rather than providers of information, since pupils can find their own texts and language data. Coaching entails the need to redesign many of the materials that have been developed for teacher-guided instruction and to consider seriously how individual differences in learning styles, needs, abilities and interests can best cater for in integrated powerful multimedia learning environments.

Debates and Perspectives

With the boom of teaching media, interdisciplinary groups of social scientists, psychologists, educationists and technically oriented researchers started studying "educational technology". One of their major concerns was to investigate the possible surplus value of particular media over others in particular learning environments. A major problem facing this field of study is the fact that it is next to impossible to prove empirically the excess value of one medium over another, since each language learning situation is shaped by a complex whole of situational, relational, educational, cognitive and affective variables, which are hard to control and make a reliable comparison of two groups of learners—one working with a particular media remain largely based on assumptions, not on general facts. It follows that authors, course designers and teachers alike have very little evidence upon which they can base any improvements to exciting media, materials or multimedia programs, or suggestions for new approaches in new materials.

It seems that, partly as a consequence of this, teachers have become skeptical and critical toward the hyperbole created around new teaching media. They tend to prefer to stick to what is familiar and most practicable, being ill-disposed toward devoting energy to changing teaching approaches that may well not lead to more effective learning. The fact that theorists and researchers often overlook the practical institutional or organizational constraints every teacher has to live with may further undermine teachers' belief in proposals made by non-practitioners.

On top of this, concerns over artificial intelligence coming to replace the role of teacher also exist. However, since it is only when media and materials are used in a meaningful and pedagogically well-considered manner that they may make the learning process more effective, and since the teacher best qualifies for designing appropriate learning environments, the chance that teachers will be replaced altogether is small. Certainly, if learners are to be provided with a large variety of learning experiences that promote independent learning, teacher's whole-class instruction time may well have to be reduced. Rather than supplanting the teacher and the textbook, however, newer teaching aids will supplement and support them.

In view of the challenges that await teachers, teacher training intuitions have the responsibility to prepare teachers for an informed selection, adaptation and integration of available media and materials. It will be vital for teachers to perceive both the strengths and weaknesses of new technologies, and to find ways to overcome shortcomings. The dangers that threaten teachers are those of over-burdening teaching with media for their sheer availability, and of falling prey to a naïve belief in media's inherent capacities, without devoting sufficient attention to the quality of data input and instruction and process materials, or carefully considering learners' needs, learning styles, abilities, interests and levels of competence in designing learning environments.

Note:

Cognitive psychology (认知心理学): A sub-discipline of psychology exploring internal mental processes. It is the study of how people perceive, remember, think, speak, and solve problems.

New Words and Expressions:

1. entail [in'teil]	v.	使必需；带来；限定继承
	n.	限定继承权
2. supplement ['sʌplimənt, 'sʌpləmənt]	n.	增刊；补充物
	v.	增补；补充
3. supplant [sə'plɑ:nt]	v.	取代；排挤
4. harness ['hɑ:nis]	v.	利用；管理；控制
5. periodical [ˌpiəri'ɔdikəl]	n.	期刊
	adj.	定期的
6. spectrum ['spektrəm]	n.	系列；幅度；范围；光谱
7. chunk [tʃʌŋk]	n.	厚块（片）；相当大的量
8. tangible ['tændʒəbl]	adj.	可触摸的；实际的；有形的；确凿的

9. surplus ['sə:pləs]	n.	过剩；顺差；盈余
	adj.	过剩的；多余的
10. empirically [im'pirikli]	adv.	经验主义地
11. prey [prei]	n.	猎物；受害者

Exercises:

I. Vocabulary.

Fill in the blanks with the most suitable words. Change the form when necessary.

| entail | supplement | harness | periodical | chunk |
| tangible | supplant | surplus | spectrum | prey |

1. The project would _____ a huge increase in defense spending.
2. He retired, and was free. Every day he spent the whole morning reading _____.
3. Nowadays, solar energy _____ to better serve us.
4. The policy of apartheid is only a political _____ to an economic policy that depends on cheap native labor.
5. Instead of falling a _____ to the enemy, he committed suicide.
6. To better pursue his dreams, he spent _____ of time studying and finally became a scientist.
7. An efficient government should serve the people and bring more _____ benefits to common people.
8. The Commercial Press published a wide _____ of books.
9. I hate this writer's writing because his works are always heavy with _____ phrasing.
10. Machinery has largely _____ hand labor in making shoes.

II. Comprehension of the text.

Decide whether the following statements are true (T) or false (F) according to the passage.

1. The broad spectrum of teaching aids can be classified according to various perspectives. ( )
2. At various stages in the development of foreign language teaching, some media and teaching aids have managed to establish themselves firmly, and continue to be used to date, whereas others seem to have gradually disappeared from mainstream teaching altogether. ( )
3. No valid facts have shown that people learn best when several senses are simultaneously

addressed. (　)

4. Computers support independent individual work because learners can progress at their own pace. (　)

5. If learners are to be provided with a large variety of learning experiences that promote independent learning, teacher's whole-class instruction time may well have to be reduced. (　)

III. Complete the following sentences according to the text.

1. An obvious way to classify teaching aids is to distinguish between aural, visual and audio-visual aids, with _____ _____ having the advantage of combining sound and image.

2. Because of _____ _____ _____ _____, listening materials are distinguished from reading, writing, speaking and grammar practice materials.

3. When looking at the history of foreign language education from the point of materials, a number of _____ in their selection and design are noticeable.

4. With the boom of teaching media, _____ _____ is studied by groups of social scientists, psychologists, educationists and technically oriented researchers.

5. Textbooks are very _____ "packages" of materials, because they are light, easily scanned, easily stacked and do not need hardware or electricity.

Text B　Test Anxiety and Academic Performance

> **导读**：考试焦虑，是指因考试压力过大而引发的系列异常生理、心理现象，包括考前焦虑、临场焦虑及考后焦虑紧张。心理学认为，心理紧张水平与活动效果呈倒U字曲线关系。紧张水平过低和过高，都会影响成绩。适度的心理紧张对人有种激励作用，产生良好的活动效果。但过度的考试紧张会导致考试焦虑，影响考场表现，并波及身心健康。本文在给出考试焦虑的定义、讨论造成这一现象的因素的基础上分析考试焦虑与学生考试成绩的关系，并强调了过度考试焦虑对学生身心的危害，最后呼吁教师应积极地帮助学生掌握减轻考试焦虑的策略。

Every attempt made hitherto in majority of the schools has been aimed at helping students score high marks in the public exams. These academic years are crucial for students because the marks they score determine their future path of education. One of the guaranteed ways of getting high marks is through rote-learning because the out-dated, rigid and narrow testing methods encourage such practices. Regrettably such methods keep schools away from any relevant innovations. In addition, school authorities pressurize teachers to train students to memorize rather than practise communication skills to better their scoring chances because these marks are used by the school authorities as advertisements to lure prospective students at the time of admission. Apparently, parents too insist on such marks-driven procedures. Willingly or unwillingly, teachers have to follow suit, for the expertise of the teachers is assessed primarily by the marks their students obtain.

The concern for high marks, as we know, has engulfed all the stakeholders alike; and this very concern eats into the development and happiness of the students who are at the receiving end. The students find it difficult to digest the fact that they are not trained for the practical use of the target language, instead are encouraged to memorize and ape responses. Also, the over-dependence on marks leads the students to adopt desperate measures sometimes even to manoeuvre unethical ways such as copying from the neighbors and from the "hidden" notes. We also come across shocking news ranging from students fainting inside the exam hall to the extent of taking their own lives after disappointing results.

Anxiety refers to affective factors that influence the way students learn a second language in classrooms. Psychologists have defined it as a combination of self perceptions, beliefs, feelings and behaviors that the students form in their minds regarding the language learning process. Studies suggest that language-anxiety is the best single correlate of achievement, therefore, the level of anxiety often determines the amount of learning. However, the intensity and longevity of it differ among individuals depending on personality traits.

Anxiety can be classified into three categories such as trait, state and situation specific anxieties; and test anxiety is part of situation-specific anxiety which is based on affective factors related to specific situations and events. Some educationists have considered test anxiety as a two-dimensional construct, consisting of worry and emotionality. Worry refers to the cognitive concern about the possibility of failure and the consequences of failure; and emotionality is the physiological change characterized by nervousness, tension, autonomic reactions and so on. Test anxiety, thus, is considered as a type of anxiety concerning apprehension over academic evaluation which emanates predominantly from fear of failure. Failure in this regard does not alone refer to the doubt over securing the required pass mark, but also to the failure related to meeting the future requirements, expectations of parents and so on.

It is not surprising that test has emerged as one of the most compelling anxiety-evoking stimuli, and thus has turned into a serious problem. The devastating impact of test anxiety on learning intake and output has a well-documented history. In fact, it has invited ample investigative attention since early 1950s. One of the earliest investigations is a series of study in which they have found a strong relationship between test anxiety and student performance. On the positive side, relevant researches have suggested that better performance is linked to encouraging levels of test anxiety among the students. On the negative side, findings reveal that academic failure has been more among high-anxiety students than low-anxiety counterparts. Eventually more of high anxious students have dropped out of college. All these studies point to the fact that test anxiety could not only impair test performance but also harm students' future.

Closely linked to anxiety level is the stage in which anxiety grips students' psyche, and it is a matter of concern because studies have reported that test anxiety starts as early as seven to ten years. Importantly, the first three of these studies have also identified that anxiety grows with age.

Apart from the level and the stage of anxiety, personality type of students is also important because the level of anxiety correlates with the personalities of the students. It is normal for students to be worried when they face life's challenges. However, intense and prolonged anxiety harms their performance. Some take exams lightly and others experience more intense levels of state anxiety when taking tests. Nonetheless, as mentioned elsewhere, anxiety is not always a deterrent to better learning conditions. Sometimes it functions as a base to better learning conditions because anxiety at a reasonable level can be beneficial. So, moderating the level of anxiety becomes imperative as the higher the anxiety level is, the lower the language performance of the students appear.

A number of variables is attributed to test anxiety. Firstly, inadequate test-taker qualities such as topical knowledge, language knowledge, personal trait, strategic competence, and effective schemata may cause anxiety. Secondly, unfamiliar content increases test anxiety. Thirdly, complicated and unfamiliar test format decreases test performance and increases anxiety. Fourthly, inadequate time allotment can pressurize test takers. Finally, the very thought of teachers being strict on assessment of answer scripts poses anxiety problems.

These five factors mentioned above impinge on the students as they cause psychological and physiological problems. At the psychological level, it affects motivation, decreases attention and increases the probability of language errors while using language and creates a negative attitude towards target language and towards self-concept. Physiologically too students experience difficulties. For example, their hands sweat and shiver, heads ache, hearts pound, memory falls short of expected recollection and so on. As a result, anxious students frequently fail to reach their potential. Their marks do not fully reflect their knowledge of second language.

In conclusion, theoretically speaking, testing has become more authentic, formative, developmental, ethical and user-friendly leading to student autonomy. But a three-hour paper-and-pencil exam can neither lend itself to accommodate these features, nor test language skills comprehensively and help classrooms benefit from positive washback. In fact, a major change in the present testing system does not seem be on the cards for some time now. Given the scenario, it is better that teachers do something about educating the students on the coping strategies to tackle test anxiety. This would at least reduce unwanted pressure which is looming large in the contemporary educational setup.

New Words and Expressions:

1. hitherto [ˌhɪðərˈtuː]	adv.	迄今；直到某时	
2. lure [lʊr]	v.	引诱；诱惑	
3. engulf [ɪnˈgʌlf]	v.	吞没，淹没；严重影响	
4. stakeholder [ˈsteɪkhoʊldər]	n.	（某组织、工程、体系等的）参与人；利益相关者	
5. ape [eɪp]	v.	（尤指笨拙地）模仿	
6. manoeuvre [məˈnuːvər]	v.	（使谨慎或熟练地）移动，转动；操纵，控制	
7. longevity [lɔːnˈdʒevəti]	n.	长寿；持久	
8. autonomic [ˌɔːtəˈnɒmɪk]	adj.	自主的；不受意志支配的；与自主神经系统有关的	
9. apprehension [ˌæprɪˈhenʃn]	n.	忧虑；恐惧；逮捕；拘押	
10. emanate from		发源于；从……发出	
11. stimulus [ˈstɪmjələs]	n.	（pl. stimuli）刺激（物）；促进因素	
12. psyche [ˈsaɪki]	n.	灵魂；心灵；精神；心态	
13. deterrent [dɪˈtɜːrənt]	n.	威慑因素；遏制力	
14. impinge [ɪmˈpɪndʒ]	v.	对……有明显作用（或影响）；妨碍；侵犯	

Notes:

1. **schemata (图式):** A form of knowledge representation as well as a whole information system of interrelated knowledge. To facilitate information storage and processing, the brain organically organizes new things with prior knowledge and experience.
2. **washback (反拨作用):** The effects of a test on teaching and learning and, on some occasions, restricted to impacts that will not occur if such a test does not exist.

Exercises:

I. Vocabulary.

Fill in the blanks with the most suitable words. Change the form when necessary.

| lure | engulf | ape | manoeuvre | longevity |
| autonomic | apprehension | emanate from | deterrent | impinge |

1. The strong smell of wood fires _____ the stove.
2. He was _____ by a crowd of reporters.
3. He prides himself on the _____ of the company.
4. Hopefully his punishment will act as a _____ to others.
5. _____ computing seems to be a feasible solution to these problems.
6. For years the British film industry merely _____ Hollywood.
7. Young people are _____ to the city by the prospect of a job and money.
8. She _____ the car carefully into the garage.
9. He never allowed his work to _____ on his private life.
10. There is growing _____ that fighting will begin again.

II. Comprehension of the text.

Decide whether the following statements are true (T) of false (F) according to the passage.

1. Anxiety refers to affective factors that influence the way students learn a second language in classrooms. ( )
2. Relevant researches have suggested that worse performance is linked to encouraging levels of test anxiety among the students. ( )
3. The thought of teachers being strict on assessment of answer scripts poses anxiety problems. ( )
4. Teachers should do something about educating the students on the coping strategies to tackle test anxiety. ( )
5. Closely linked to anxiety level is the stage in which anxiety grips students' psyche, and it is a matter of concern because studies have reported that test anxiety starts as early as three to seven years. ( )

III. Choose the word that has the similar meaning of the underlined word or expression.

1. These academic years are crucial for students because the marks they score determine their future path of education. ( )
   A. significant   B. efficient   C. valid   D. sufficient

2. In addition, school authorities pressurize teachers to train students to memorize rather than practise communication skills to better their scoring chances because these marks are used by the school authorities as advertisements to lure prospective students at the time of admission. ( )
   A. force   B. encourage   C. ignore   D. convince

3. The concern for high marks, as we know, has engulfed all the stakeholders alike; and this very concern eats into the development and happiness of the students who are at the receiving end. ( )
   A. benefits   B. repairs   C. restores   D. damages

4. In conclusion, theoretically speaking, testing has become more authentic, formative, developmental, ethical and user-friendly leading to student autonomy. ( )
   A. discipline   B. independence   C. consciousness   D. ambition

5. So, moderating the level of anxiety becomes imperative as the higher the anxiety level is, the lower the language performance of the students appear. ( )
   A. unnecessary   B. optional   C. vital   D. desperate

Supplementary Reading: Using Examinations and Testing to Improve Educational Quality

Academic achievement affects the eventual economic benefits of education. In industrialized countries, family socioeconomic background and other factors external to the school heavily influence the level of academic achievement. However, in low-income countries, the quality of the school influences student achievement as much as these factors, especially in science and mathematics. School quality includes the amount of instructional resources available per student and how these resources are used and managed. Rising population growth rates, slowed economic growth, and mounting foreign debt in developing countries mean that there are more children to educate and less money with which to educate them. The effect on the quality of schooling varies from region to region and from country to country. The poorest countries in the Third World have less money to invest in items that boost learning such as textbooks, instructional materials, good teachers, and teacher training. Although some middle-income countries in Asia, Latin America, and the Middle East are experiencing a slight increase in school quality, the gap between them and countries belonging to the Organization for Economic Cooperation and Development (OECD) continues to widen. As a result, educators and economists alike are intensifying the search for an inexpensive means of improving the quality of education in developing countries.

Examinations can be a powerful, low-cost means of influencing the quality of what teachers teach and what students learn in school. Examination agencies have an important role to play in increasing the effectiveness of schools. They can act not only as ex-post evaluators of educational achievement but also takes responsibility for making good teaching and learning happen. Examination agencies should improve the quality of the tests they design, in which an appropriate distribution of questions involving recall, application, synthesis, and evaluation is included.

The examinations rely heavily upon recall of factual, sometimes esoteric information. The emphasis in the classroom is on rote learning to pass classroom and the national examinations. There is very little incentive to pay attention to developing reasoning, imagination, and independent inquiry. Graduates thus are not usually prepared for the demands of reasoning ability and initiative in the workplace. The majority of students may not even achieve the basic literacy and numeracy skills needed to improve farming, family nutrition, or health practices.

Achievement also varies significantly from region to region within the same country depending on the type of community and school. Sometimes private schools are of higher quality and have higher achievement scores than public ones. Urban schools often score higher than rural ones, largely because scores are also higher in higher per capita income areas where classroom resources are more abundant.

When school performance is inadequate it weakens the future skills, adaptability, and competitiveness of a country's labor force. New pressures on already restricted education budgets have made making better use of scarce resources and maintaining acceptable standards of quality a high priority for educational officials in developing countries. Reforms in the area of examinations are valued as uniform mechanism for identifying talent and measuring achievement. Especially in environments where education resources are limited or unequally distributed among schools, examinations can help to ensure that society is investing in those who will in turn make the most useful contributions to society. A well-designed examination system can monitor and measure achievement and, occasionally, aptitude; provide performance feedback to individual districts, schools, and students; and inform education officials about the overall strengths and weaknesses of their education systems and suggest directions for change and improvement. However, the most important aspect of examinations is the degree to which teachers, administrators, students and parents think of them as important. Selection examinations are one of the most powerful motivational levers in the education sector. The question is whether their influence is positive or negative.

Deteriorating standards, high dropout and repletion rates, labor shortages in certain fields, high youth unemployment, and the demands of ambitious development plans are the main factors motivating educational and examination reform, Such reforms are usually aimed at making the curriculum more relevant to development needs or at redressing regional imbalances in the quality and opportunity for education. If reforms are contrary to public or parental aspirations, officials use the power of examinations to make reforms acceptable. However, if examinations do not fulfill parental aspirations for social and economic advancement, reforms are likely to fail.

Attitudes toward testing have changed. In the 1960s, many educators viewed tests as antithetical to creative thinking, as unreliable predictors of future academic success, and as unfair to disadvantaged groups. In the United States, many thought that teaching basic skills was only a part, and perhaps a lesser part, of schooling's mission. Schools, it was said, should respond to pupil interests and needs to make learning more attractive and productive. Those who held such views tended to deny the educational value of tests. Newly independent countries sometimes considered testing an unwanted colonial legacy, irrelevant to building new national identities. In some countries such as Tanzania, education officials replaced standardized tests with school-based assessments and experimented with other criteria for selection and certification such as political attitudes or quotas based on socioeconomic, geographic, and ethnic origins or on gender. Unforeseen problems arose. With school-based assessments, it is difficult to ensure that all teachers are judging on the same criteria. Since parents judge teachers on their ability to get their children ahead, teachers tend to inflate grades. Judging a child's potential on political attitudes is not reliable since attitudes can be faked. Though quotas are sometimes necessary to ensure equal utilization of facilities, making selection decisions solely on ethnic or geographic criteria can lead to abuse and can also create resentment among groups not selected. However, whether the criteria are academic or political, the need for some fair and efficient mechanism to recognize and reward ability is indisputable. Examinations are thus reemerging as instruments of educational and occupational selection. The challenge is how to make such a mechanism reinforce the teaching and learning of skills that are useful to society.

Especially in the context of scarce resources, with declining educational standards and the ever-increasing demand for better-qualified manpower, education officials are looking for low-cost ways to improve their education systems. What makes testing powerful is its use to allocate life's chances. This is especially the case in developing countries where rates of returns from education are higher and where in some instances high income-earning opportunities are available almost exclusively to those with access to postsecondary education.

When examinations determine a child's advancement through school and his or her later life's opportunities, parents understandably put pressure on teachers to ensure that their child succeeds. They hold the school system and particularly teachers accountable for their child's results on examinations. The consequence or backwash effect of his public expectation is that teachers adjust their teaching to what the examination will cover to ensure that their students score the highest marks. Teachers are less concerned with whether the test measures the full range of competencies set out in the official curriculum or whether the knowledge, concepts, and skills tested are of as much use to students who will enter the workforce as to those who will continue to be the next level of education. If examinations fail to test useful skills, teachers will have little incentive to teach them. The backwash effect of the examination thus restricts what is taught and learned in school. How can officials tell the extent to which their examinations measure the mastery of relevant skills and therefore have a positive impact on teaching and learning?

One means of making the backwash effects of tests positive is to improve the content of examinations. The content of examinations should correspond to the many functions they perform. In developing countries, one examination is often used to serve several functions. Examinations are used to select students for secondary and higher education and to certify mastery of the primary or secondary school curriculum. Rarely are they used to diagnose learning problems, place students at different levels of ability, or to help teachers plan what to teach. Usually, the content of the examination is determined much more by its function as a selection instrument. This enhances the importance of the knowledge tested in the examination and consequently of what is taught and learned in the classroom. Ideally one should test separately for selection, certification, and monitoring functions; however, resources do not permit this in many developing countries. Another means of making backwash effects positive is to set up a good feedback mechanism to analyze and interpret student errors. Explaining the thought processed behind wrong answers and making performance results public give school and testing officials incentive to do their jobs better. A third means is to make sure that the examination body is financed and managed in such a way that it can set questions and provide the necessary feedback on student performance.

What makes a good test item? Good examination questions should test more than the ability of the candidate to recall isolated facts. They should test the ability to observe, experiment, and interpret, to understand concepts and draw reasoned conclusions, to use knowledge and skills to solve problems, and to make decisions in new situations and contexts both in and out of school. Good test questions require the mastery of knowledge and skills that when applied in everyday life improve the quality of life and help families use their limited resources better. Anthony Somerset, who worked on improving the quality and relevance of test questions for the Kenya primary school-leaving examination, suggests eight criteria for enabling an examination agency to design the right balance of test questions:

1. Most questions should require students to restructure information rather than simply reproduce it.
2. Many questions should require candidates to understand and use information they have not seen before, in new situations and contexts.
3. Knowledge-based questions drawn from the official curriculum should test understanding of causes or consequences of interventions rather than familiarity with specific facts. Questions should ask "why" "how" rather than "who" "when" "where" and "what." Tests should emphasize understanding the world as a prerequisite to changing it.
4. The knowledge elicited should require integrating with a new knowledge explicitly related to the competent performance of some target behavior.
5. A high proportion of items, especially in science, health, agriculture, and geography, should draw upon both in- and out-of-school experience.
6. When an examination is given in languages other than the mother tongue, test designers should carefully monitor questions for language loading. Test questions should not contain idiomatic expressions or the use of "registers" not accessible to all. Good questions should measure mastery of knowledge and skills rather than mastery of the language of the test.
7. Though they are more expensive, some proportions of the questions should be open-ended. Candidates should generate answers as well as select them. In the world outside of school, one is rarely presented with possible solutions to a problem from which to choose the correct response.
8. Some questions should test the creative, imaginative skills of learners—that is, be based upon giving an unusual response, despite the problems associated with marking such responses.

If test questions measure the acquisition of knowledge useful to school leavers as well as to those continuing to the next level of education, the resulting positive backwash effects can benefit the entire school system. To tap these benefits, examination agencies must first inform teachers and students, well ahead of time, of changes in the content of examination questions and of the nature of the skills being tested. Second, they have to analyze performance on individual questions to determine what errors students are making and why. Third, the examination body has to suggest ways to improve the teaching of skills that require mastery of difficult concepts.

In addition to teachers and students, the audience for such feedback on test results includes teacher training institutes—so that future teachers will learn to teach difficult cognitive skills; curriculum development institutes and textbook designers—so that they can improve the way concepts and principles are identified and explained; and in-service training programs for inspectors, education officers, and head teachers—so that they can better focus their attention on managing the most crucial function of the education system.

Examination bodies can provide different levels and depths of feedback. They can report only individual performance as a general mean and standard deviation, or they can break mean scores and standard deviations down by subject, type of skill, and individual test item. They can report these, in turn, for the country as a whole, each region, each district, each school, and ideally, each classroom or each student. Any testing agency that can do all this has a strong feedback system. Unfortunately, few agencies even in OECD countries provide this level and depth of feedback. Most agencies see their task of explaining past performance as supplementary to their main function of grading individuals. Thus they rarely report more than general means and standard deviations for the country as a whole or for each region and seldom go into detail more specific than subject-by-subject results.

What are the aims of the feedback system? They help reduce performance gaps between different schools or districts by showing where differences in performance occur and why. They encourage better educational management by identifying specific cognitive skills that need to be strengthened. They also suggest what type of investments in schools—for example, more and better teachers, better textbooks, and better administrators—influences achievement.

A good examination body acts not only as an evaluator of educational achievement but also takes responsibility for making good teaching and learning happen. It does this by constructing tests that have a positive backwash effect on teaching and learning and by showing school systems the sources of children's learning problems. To provide high-quality feedback, an examination agency should analyze the pattern of errors made in past performance and break those patterns down to the lowest-possible unit of analysis—ideally, that may even be down to the level of specific questions and to the level of the individual school or classroom. However, a testing agency cannot design good test items and set up a good feedback system if it is not efficient, credible, and autonomous. To be efficient it must produce tests on time, within its budget, and within its competence. To be credible it must maintain professional standards when setting and marking tests and not succumb to political pressures to test inappropriately. To be autonomous it must be managed as an entire entity separate from the Ministry of Education and be able to hire the technical expertise necessary at competitive salary levels and to purchase the technical equipment necessary independent of public-sector regulations. It, therefore, requires a budget separate from the normal rises and falls typical of most public-sector enterprises—that is, it will most probably have to be self-financed. It must create a demand for its services, for which clients are willing to pay. Once self-financed, a testing agency can pursue its professional responsibilities without political interference.

Some issues in the area of examinations and testing have no hard and fast answers. They include dilemmas such as test coverage of the curriculum versus fairness of the examination, mother tongue versus metropolitan language as the language of testing, professionalism of examination bodies versus political influence, and well-constructed test questions versus socioeconomic advantages.

The content to which the national examination covers the official curriculum varies from country to country. Tests and the curriculum influence what teachers teach in the classroom and what students actually learn. Discrepancies between test content and the taught curriculum pose a dilemma since tests are supposed to choose and certify individuals on the basis of their knowledge of the common curriculum. If testing experts intend to conclude from test results about the quality of teaching and learning, then the match between what is actually taught and test content must be a close one. In Africa, for example, where schools are poorly equipped and learning materials scarce, teachers are typically able to cover only a small portion of the curriculum. The implications of this are particularly serious in countries where outside influences such as previous learning and home and social environment are less a factor and where achievement may be more directly traceable to school quality.

The amount of the curriculum covered varies enormously—rich schools cover more, poor schools less. What should the test designers do in the case where the quality of schools varies? Should they set questions on the intended curriculum even though some parts may have been taught in only 10 to 15 per cent of the schools? If that is done, the test will not reflect what has been learned but rather who had the opportunity to learn. Alternatively, should the test emphasize those parts of the curriculum for which it can be shown that a wide proportion of students had an opportunity to learn—non-laboratory sciences instead of laboratory techniques, for instance, since typically only wealthy schools can afford the laboratory materials to teach that portion of the science curriculum. If this is done, the test will be a truer reflection of what has been learned by the student population, but it will not accurately reflect the intended curricular objectives.

National tests are designed to measure commonly taught knowledge, and since the ability to teach that knowledge is shrinking, the portion that can be fairly tested is also shrinking. Schools that wish to do well must teach the knowledge and skills identified as important for pupils to learn. Better-equipped schools, with well-trained teachers and active headmasters, are more likely to cover the curriculum than poorer, ill-equipped schools. If test content is based on the official curriculum rather than on what is actually covered in the classroom, it will favor students from schools that are better able to cover the curriculum and thus will risk measuring students' opportunity to learn rather than what they have actually been taught. If tests measure more than what is covered in the classroom they can be unfair and unjust.

The language of assessment poses many questions for testing and instruction. In multilingual societies, the rationale for using international languages such as English, French or Spanish for teaching and testing is that they do not favor any particular linguistic group. How adequately is achievement measured in the second language? How does the tester of mathematics rather than what they understand of the English-based mathematics questions? Does the language of the test determine how exam items are constructed—that is, do test questions measure understanding of concepts and underlying principles or rather the language-based recognition of the correct answers? Tests in languages other than the mother tongue may be measuring the ability to understand the concepts themselves. There is more evidence of problem-solving and other higher-order abilities when students are tested in their mother tongue. Particularly in science subjects, testing in the second language may discourage the use of concepts and principles of modern science in everyday life. The existing literature suggests a larger role for indigenous languages in testing on the grounds that testing in an international language may confuse subject knowledge with comprehension of the language of the test.

The primary goal of learning should be understanding concepts and principles in order to make inferences from that knowledge and to apply it in daily life. Tests should accurately measure students' achievement of these competencies. Do tests in a second language elicit meaningful evidence of student achievement of competencies in a subject area? A good test should measure language in a particular subject area, not understanding of the language of the test. If a language other than the mother tongue is the medium of the test, children with more access to the language of the test will do better regardless of whether they know subject matter better. A testing agency must ensure that the language bias of test questions is minimized. In multilingual environments, testing agencies can handle the language question in two ways. They can make sure that tests are free of language experience and that test questions are accurately measuring subject-matter competence. In other words, they can pretest the language of the test item thoroughly and satisfy themselves ahead of time that there are no differences between the performance of mother-tongue and non-mother-tongue students. Alternatively, they can use the mother tongue in testing to ensure that those who perform poorly in the second or international language, but well in subject matter, are not discriminated against. A testing agency that chooses the second option will probably run into political problems with those who have a vested interest in testing in one or the other language. They will also face the high costs and logistical complexity of setting questions, administering, marking, and analyzing results of subject matter tests in several languages.

Unit 6　Educational Evaluation

Text A　Integration of Technology and Educational Assessment

> **导读**：随着科学技术的发展，教育评价也走上了现代化的道路，对学生的评价体系也由单一维度向多维度转变。广东省汕尾市2019年引入北京师范大学"智慧学伴"智能教育公共服务平台，平台将学生测试内容分为学习理解、实践应用、创新迁移3个层面。测试结果经平台智能分析后，自动生成学生解决问题、创新思维等高阶能力的学科素养评价数据。"大数据+人工智能+模拟技术"是未来实现全过程、多维、高效学生评价的重要手段和方法，技术的发展让设计复杂的评价体系成为可能。

Across the disciplines, technologies have expanded the phenomena that can be investigated, the nature of argumentation, and the use of evidence. Technologies allow representations of domains, systems, models, data, and their manipulation in ways that previously were not possible. Models of population density permit investigations of economic and social issues. This move from static to dynamic models has changed the nature of inquiry among professionals as well as the way that academic disciplines can be taught. Correspondingly, a new generation of assessments is well on its way to transforming what, how, when, where, and why assessment occurs and its linkages to teaching and learning. Powered by the ever-increasing capabilities of technology, these 21st-century approaches to assessment expand the potential for tests to both probe and promote a broad spectrum of human learning, including the types of knowledge and competence advocated in various recent policy reports on education and the economy.

Although early uses of technology in large-scale testing have focused on relatively straightforward logistical efficiencies and cost reductions, a new generation of innovative assessments is pushing the frontiers of measuring complex forms of learning. Computers' abilities to capture student inputs permit collecting evidence of processes such as problem-solving sequences and strategy use as reflected by information selected, numbers of attempts, approximation to solutions, and time allocation. Such data can be combined with statistical and measurement algorithms to extract patterns associated with varying levels of expertise. Research in the learning sciences is simultaneously informing the design of innovative, dynamic, interactive assessment tasks and powerful scoring, reporting, and real-time feedback mechanisms. When coupled with technology, such knowledge has propelled various advances in adaptive testing, including knowledge and skills diagnosis, the provision of immediate feedback to teachers and students accompanied by scaffolding for improvement, and the potential for accommodations for special populations. Technology also supports movement toward the design of more balanced sets of coherent, nested assessments that operate across levels of educational systems.

Information and communication technologies such as Web browsers, word processors, editing, drawing, simulations, and multimedia programs support a variety of research, design, composition, and communication processes. These same tools can expand the cognitive skills that can be assessed, including the processes of planning, drafting, composing, and revising. For example, the National Assessment of Educational Progress (NAEP) writing assessment in 2011 requires use of word processing and editing tools to compose essays.

In professional testing, architecture examinees use computer-assisted design programs as part of their licensure assessment. The challenge that such technology-based presentation and data capture contexts offers now lies in the design principles for eliciting complex learning, the analysis of complex forms of data, and their meaningful interpretation relative to models of the underlying components of competence and expertise. The area of science assessment is perhaps leading the way in exploring the presentation and interpretation of complex, multifaceted problem types and assessment approaches. In 2006, the Program for International Student Assessment pilot tested a Computer-Based Assessment of Science to test knowledge and inquiry processes not assessed in the paper-based booklets. The assessment included such student explorations as the genetic breeding of plants. At the state level, Minnesota has an online science test with tasks engaging students in simulated laboratory experiments or investigations of phenomena such as weather or the solar system.

Recently, a distinction has been made between assessments of the outcomes of learning, typically used for grading and accountability purposes (summative assessment), and assessments for learning, used to diagnose and modify the conditions of learning and instruction (formative assessment). Research has repeatedly shown the formative use of assessment to significantly benefit student achievement. Such effects depend on several classroom practice factors, including alignment of assessments with state standards, quality of the feedback provided to students, involvement of students in self-reflection and action, and teachers making adjustments to their instruction based on the assessment results. Technologies are well suited to support many of the data collection, complex analysis, and individualized feedback and scaffolding features needed for the formative use of assessment.

In addition to assessment of student knowledge and skills in highly structured problems with one right answer, technology can also support the design of complex, interactive tasks that extend the range of knowledge, skills, and cognitive processes that can be assessed. For example, simulations can assess and promote understanding of complex systems by superimposing multiple representations and permitting manipulation of structures and patterns that otherwise might not be visible or even conceivable. Simulation-based assessments can probe basic foundational knowledge such as the functions of organisms in an ecosystem, and, more important, they can probe students' knowledge of how components of a system interact along with abilities to investigate the impacts of multiple variables changing at the same time. When well designed and implemented, classroom assessments that are used during instruction to monitor and improve progress and that are also administered following instruction to document learning and identify remaining needs can become credible components of a multilevel state assessment system. Technology-enhanced formative assessments during instruction can provide immediate, contingent feedback and adaptive coaching for reteaching of problematic knowledge and skills. Benchmark assessments following instruction can provide summative classroom-based assessments with technical quality that could be aggregated into the state accountability system. Moreover, because simulations use multiple modalities and representations, students with diverse learning styles and language backgrounds may have better opportunities to demonstrate their knowledge than are possible in text-laden print tests.

It is an exciting time in the field of assessment for several reasons. First, individuals have realized that there are multiple roles for assessment to play in the educational process and that one of the most valuable roles is the formative function of assisting student learning. Second, cognitive research and theory have provided us with rich models and representations of how students understand many of the key principles in the curriculum, how students develop knowledge structures, and how to analyze and understand simple and complex aspects of student performance. Third, technology makes possible more flexible, tailored presentations to students of a much wider and richer array of tasks and environments where students can learn and where they can show us what they know and how they know it. Thus, there is an interesting and powerful confluence among theory, research, technology, and practice, especially when it comes to the integration of curriculum, instruction, and assessment.

In numerous areas of the curriculum, information technologies are changing what is taught, when and how it is taught, and what students are expected to be able to do to demonstrate their knowledge and skill. These changes in turn are stimulating people to rethink what is assessed, how that information is obtained, and how it is fed back into the educational process in a productive and timely way. This situation creates opportunities to center curriculum, instruction, and assessment around cognitive principles. With technology, assessment can become richer, timelier, and more seamlessly interwoven with multiple aspects of curriculum and instruction. As discussed earlier, the most useful kinds of assessment for enhancing student learning emphasize knowledge integration and extended reasoning, support a process of individualized instruction, allow for student interaction, collect rich diagnostic data, and provide timely feedback. The demands and complexity of these types of assessment can be quite substantial, but technology makes them feasible. Diagnostic assessments of individuals' learning, for example, must involve collecting, interpreting, and reporting significant amounts of information. No educator, whether a classroom teacher or other user of assessment data, could realistically be expected to handle the information flow, analysis demands, and decision-making burdens involved without technological support. Thus, technology removes some of the constraints that previously made high-quality formative assessment of complex performances difficult or impractical for a classroom teacher.

Clearly, we are just beginning to see how to harness technology to support the formative and summative functions of assessment. We still need to learn a great deal about the quality and efficacy of systems operating at both the large-scale level and the small-scale level. Not the least of the concerns facing us is the integration of assessment tools and practices into the educational system and teachers' practices. But we must also take note of the fact that extremely powerful information technologies are becoming as ubiquitous in educational settings as they are in other aspects of people's daily lives. Technologies are almost certain to continue to provoke fundamental changes in learning environments at all levels of the education system. Many of the implications of technology are beyond people's speculative capacity. Before the 21st century, for example, few could have predicted the sweeping effects of the Internet and social networking on education and other segments of society. The range of computational devices and their applications is expanding exponentially, fundamentally changing how people think about communication, collaboration, problem solving, connectivity, information systems, educational practices, and the role of technology in society.

We can therefore imagine a future in which the audit function of assessments external to the classroom would be significantly reduced or even unnecessary because the information needed to assess students, at the levels of description appropriate for various monitoring purposes, could be mined from the data streams generated by students in and out of their classrooms. A metaphor for such a radical shift in how one "does the business of educational assessment" exists in the world of retail outlets, ranging from small businesses to supermarkets to department stores. No longer do these businesses have to close down once or twice a year to take inventory of their stock. Rather, with the advent of automated checkouts and barcodes for all items, these enterprises have access to a continuous stream of information that can be used to monitor inventory and the flow of items. Not only can business continue without interruption, but the information obtained is far richer, enabling stores to monitor trends and aggregate the data into various kinds of summaries. Similarly, with new assessment technologies, schools would no longer have to interrupt the normal instructional process at various times during the year to administer external tests to students, nor would they have to spend significant amounts of time preparing for specific external tests peripheral to the ongoing activities of teaching and learning.

The design and deployment of even simple technology tools must ultimately rely on a technology infrastructure that connects the classroom to powerful database management and information retrieval systems that operate within and across schools and systems. This is especially true when the classroom assessment data are viewed as part of a coordinated system of assessment data that would potentially include curriculum-embedded assessment information, unit and end-of-course benchmark assessment data, interim cross-unit summative status checks, and state-level test data. Further work addressing issues of technology and the design of a comprehensive assessment system involves consideration of information and how it needs to flow through this system. For example, who needs to use assessment data? What questions need to be answered? In what timeframe do they need to be answered? What actions might they take based on these answers?

Extensive technology-based systems that link curriculum, instruction, and assessment at the classroom level might enable a shift from today's assessment systems, which use different kinds of assessments for different purposes, to a balanced design that would ensure the three critical features of comprehensiveness, coherence, and continuity. In such a design, for comprehensiveness, assessments would provide a variety of evidence to support educational decision-making, for coherence, the information provided at differing levels of responsibility and action would be linked back to the same underlying conceptual model of student learning, and for continuity, it would provide indications of student growth over time.

Technological advances will allow for the attainment of many of the goals that educators, researchers, policymakers, teachers, and parents have envisioned for assessment as a viable source of information for educational improvement. When we implement powerful technology-based systems in classrooms, rich sources of information about intellectually significant student learning will be continuously available across wide segments of the curriculum and for individual learners over extended periods of time. This is exactly the kind of information we now lack, making it difficult to use assessment to truly support learning. The major issue is not whether this type of innovative assessment design, data collection, and information analysis is feasible in the future. Rather, the issue is how the world of education anticipates and embraces this possibility, and how it will explore the resulting options for effectively using assessment information to meet the multiple purposes served by current assessments, and most important, to enhance student learning.

Notes:

1. **Summative assessment (or summative evaluation) (终结性评价):** The assessment of the learning and summarizes the development of learners at a particular time. After a period of work, e.g. a unit for two weeks, the learner sits for a test and then the teacher marks the test and assigns a score.
2. **Formative assessment (形成性评价):** A reflective process that intends to promote student attainment. Cowie and Bell define it as the bidirectional process between teacher and student to enhance, recognize and respond to the learning.

New Words and Expressions:

1. manipulation [məˌnipjʊˈleiʃən]   *n.*   操纵；控制
2. algorithm [ˈælgəriðəm]   *n.*   算法
3. simultaneously [ˌsaiməlˈteiniəsli]   *adv.*   同时地
4. propel [prəˈpel]   *v.*   推进；驱使
5. cognitive [ˈkɒgnətiv]   *adj.*   认识的；认知的
6. elicit [iˈlisit]   *v.*   引出；诱出；探出
7. alignment [əˈlainmənt]   *n.*   排成直线；（国家、团体间的）结盟
8. interactive [intərˈæktiv]   *adj.*   相互作用的；交互的
9. seamless [ˈsi:mləs]   *adj.*   不停顿的；无缝的
10. interwoven [ˌintəˈwəʊvn]   *adj.*   交织的；混合的（动词interweave的过去分词）

11. audit [ˈɔːdit]	n.	审计；审查
	v.	旁听（大学课程）；审计
12. aggregate [ˈægrigət]	adj.	合计的
	n.	总计；（可成混凝土或修路等用的）骨料
	v.	总计
13. envision [inˈviʒn]	v.	想象；展望
14. segment [ˈsegmənt]	n.	部分；弓形；瓣
	v.	分割

Exercises:

I. Vocabulary.

Fill in the blanks with the most suitable words. Change the form when necessary.

| manipulate | simultaneous | cognitive | alignment | interactive |

1. Hearing the good news, the crowds burst into applause _____.
2. Practice is based on the _____ elements of perception.
3. Intimate friends always have _____ effect on each other.
4. Having been in China for 4 years, Mr. Smith was able to _____ chopsticks with great dexterity.
5. A new _____ is rising in Middle East.

II. Comprehension of the text.

Decide whether the following statements are true (T) or false (F) according to the passage.

1. Planning belongs to the rank of cognitive skills, while revising is not. ( )
2. Assessment used to diagnose and modify the conditions of learning and instruction is called summative assessment. ( )
3. Technology can now support the design of complex and interactive tasks that can assess students' learning. ( )
4. Technology information is changing the way in which knowledge is taught and the content of teaching. ( )
5. Technology removes some of the constraints that previously made high-quality formative assessment of complex performances difficult or impractical. ( )

Unit 6　Educational Evaluation

III. Choose the word or expression that has a similar meaning to the underlined word or expression.

1. Chop the stalks into short <u>segments</u> so that the animals can digest them easily. ( )
   A. parts　　　　　B. sticks　　　　　C. circles　　　　　D. chunks

2. Though his plan is <u>seamless</u>, he still failed and got caught by the police. ( )
   A. good　　　　　B. plain　　　　　C. tight and close　　　　　D. clever

3. People in war all <u>envision</u> peace and a bright future. ( )
   A. desire　　　　　B. look forward to　　　　　C. call　　　　　D. fight for

4. <u>Propelled</u> by greed, he took away a large sum of money and went abroad. ( )
   A. Stimulated　　　　　B. Seduced　　　　　C. Tormented　　　　　D. Asked

5. The audience <u>aggregated</u> a million people. ( )
   A. were less than　　　　　B. were more than　　　　　C. totaled　　　　　D. added

Text B　Sustainable Assessment and Evaluation Strategies for Open and Distance Learning

> **导读：** 随着信息技术的飞速发展，远程教育应运而生并得到了空前的发展。远程教育质量一直是社会各界普遍关注的问题，质量已成为远程教育的"生命线"。教育评价成为保证远程教育质量，维护其"生命线"的重要依据。但与传统的教育评价相比，远程教育的评价则比较棘手。本文列出了远程教育评价的一些策略，如创建题库、设计电脑化的考试系统等。

Distance Learning (DL) is the fastest-growing form of domestic and international education today. In addition to the challenges of assessment in conventional institutions, distance learners are spread out geographically and physically from each other and from the instructor. Moreover, class sizes for DL courses are generally larger than those for traditional classes. These large numbers of students and numerous courses make assessment and evaluation very difficult and an administrative nightmare at DL institutions. Yet, given large class sizes and their physical separation from students, many distance learning instructors feel they have few options for assessing students' performance.

Assessment is a systematic basis for making inferences about the learning and development of students. It is the process of defining, selecting, designing, collecting, analyzing, interpreting and using information to increase students' learning and development. In education, assessment may be thought of as occurring whenever one person, in some kind of interaction, direct or indirect, with another is conscious of obtaining and interpreting information about the knowledge and understanding, or abilities and attitudes of that other person. There are two distinct interpretations of assessment. The first is interpretation of assessment in terms of the routine tasks that students undertake in order to receive feedback on their learning and a mark or grade signifying their achievement. The second interpret assessment is applied to processes at the institutional level, for example, program evaluation.

There are various methods of assessment. The commonly used ones are objective questions, short answer questions, long answer questions and presentations. The method of assessment named objective questions derives its name from objectivity employed in marking the answers to the questions. The marking which is a simple mechanical process can be done by an individual or by a computer. Examples of objective-type questions are true/false items; fill in the blanks item; multiple-choice items; completion items and matching items. Short answer questions may take different forms of answers such as one word/phrase; one sentence; completing a table/diagram; preparing a list or writing a paragraph. Long answer questions may also take various forms such as essay; reports or dissertations. The method of presentation is used to assess presentation skills. It requires appropriate assessment criteria for assessing the appearance of presenter; introduction of self; introduction of presentation; content of presentation; logic and order of presentation; eye contact; audibility; handling questions and use of visual aids. This method of assessment has high validity when the presentation is assessed by a group.

Assessment in Open and Distance Learning (ODL), unlike in the conventional system where students have a range of opportunities to demonstrate their learning periodically, depends on formal assessment tasks. The major characteristics of assessment in both settings are: for the conventional system, the learners are known through lectures, tutorials and individual consultations. They have a range of opportunities to demonstrate their learning—their interest, motivation, questioning and interaction. Moreover, they have opportunities to diagnose their errors before they go for formal assessment tasks and assessment activities have some flexibility.

On the other hand, ODL learners are at a distance, thus they rarely enjoy varied opportunities to communicate their learning depend much on formal task as they have less opportunity in which to diagnose their errors or mistakes before formal assessment task. Accordingly, assessment must be thoroughly planned, communicated and managed.

Validity is the extent to which an assessment measure does the job for which it is intended.

Unit 6 Educational Evaluation

The validity of an assessment can only be determined by reference to the assessment's stated purposes and its design specifications. For validity to be high the assessment must analyze student's performance on each objective and the assessment should provide the appropriate situation possible for measuring the specific abilities being measured. Reliability refers to consistency or precision or dependability of the assessment measurement and how consistent results are from one to another. The assessment is reliable if the results would be replicated on a subsequent occasion. Reliability is maximized when the assessment items are many, the items are not too easy or too difficult for the candidates and the marking is consistent.

Educators generally work with learners to review and support learning, and to make judgment regarding their merits and their achievements. In ODL, Self Assessment Questions, Tutor Marked Assessments and End of Semester Examinations are used. There is no immediate feedback or reinforcement. Self Assessment Questions embedded in the course material enable distance learners to evaluate their progress frequently. Tutor Marked Assessments serve as the continuous assessment and the marks obtained carry about 25% to 30% weight which count in the final result of the course. End of Semester Examinations carries about 70% to 75% weightage of the final results. Distance learners are usually free to appear at any of these examinations either for specific courses or for all the registered courses provided that the minimum period of study prescribed for the relevant course is completed. Like in the conventional system, assessment in ODL can be both formative and summative. Formative assessment takes the form of Tutor Marked Assessments. It helps to identify the weaknesses and strengths in learning. It also helps to improve upon the process and the attainment of learning. Grading or scoring may be done in formative assessment. Summative Assessment takes the form of End of Semester Examinations.

A question bank is a planned library of test items pooled through cooperative efforts under the protection and support of an institution for the use of evaluators, academics and students in partial fulfillment of the requirements of the teaching-learning process.

It is designed to fulfill certain predetermined purposes namely to enrich the instructional aspect and to judge the distance learner. It offers a utility service with an inbuilt feedback mechanism for improvement of its questions. The number of questions needed for a course or a program which runs for a number of years is very large in a distance education institution. The academic staff are accordingly supposed to prepare a large number of quality questions on different topics of the prescribed courses or programs for learners' self-assessment, Tutor Marked Assessments and End of Semester Examinations. Most of these academics lack the adequate skill in test development and the time at their disposal is limited and they cannot be expected to develop a question pool of reasonable magnitude and quality within a specific time.

In the absence of a stock of ready-made questions, the quality of question papers is liable to suffer. This necessitates the entrusting the preparation of quality items in different subjects to experienced teachers who are well conversant with the content and techniques of framing questions.

This strategy helps to build up ready-made stock of items for Learners' Self Assessment, Tutor Marked Assessments and End of Semester Examinations. Such pool of item is of immense use if developed according to predetermined objectives. The types of questions making up a question bank are to depend entirely on the total framework of reference envisaged at the planning stage.

Running a question bank efficiently to sustain assessment necessitates careful planning. The objectives of such a bank should clearly be visualized and include: To increase the value of measurement; to increase the pedagogical value of evaluation; and more detailed specific objectives on the special need for the question bank. The question bank should be located in such a place that it should be managed properly to provide utility services to all those who are interested. The planning of a question bank should take care of suitable place and equipment for storing, vetting and screening of items before depositing them in the bank, sorting and classifying items in the question bank, arrangement for subject wise assistance for efficient maintenance and an academic manager for question bank to direct the activities of the question bank. Carefully selected questions from the question bank can be used for instructional purposes. Various types of questions may be selected from the question bank for pre-testing, review and revision of a lesson. A question pool from a question bank can be utilized in the preparation of textual material and review exercises in course materials.

Learners can also use questions from question bank for self-assessment of their learning outcomes for specific units or modules of a course since outline answers are provided in such questions. A question bank is evaluated at regular intervals at least once in three years, the questions are screened and the obsolete ones are discarded. As old and obsolete materials are discarded, new materials are continually added in line with the revision of course materials. Enrichment of questions by updating, replacing, discarding, modifying, adding new ones, regrouping and classification is an ongoing process aimed at giving the question bank a dynamic look. A well-developed and efficiently used question bank is an asset to sustainable assessment.

Computer-based tests are defined as tests or assessments that are administered by a computer in either alone or networked configuration or by other technology devices linked to the Internet

Unit 6　Educational Evaluation

or World Wide Web (WWW). Computer-based testing is recognized as a sustainable strategy for sustainable assessment for ODL because it can be more responsive to the needs of both the test provider or institution and distance learners. Where "on-demand" testing of examinees is needed, the use of computer-based testing is more helpful. Computer-based testing works on a completely different model than paper and pencil administration and offers the benefits that the latter cannot match. A smaller number of candidates can be tested throughout the year rather than large numbers several times a year. Study centers can offer different tests at the same time since examinations may be delivered on personal computers using local area networks, and the computer selects test questions from a pool, so candidates taking the same examination will not be answering identical questions, which would enhance test security.

Computer-based assessment allows for a diverse range of question types which is a better test of candidates' competency. It can be offered at different times, locations or even different tests to different students. The computer selects test question from a pool, so candidates taking the same examination will not be answering identical questions. It eliminates the need for test booklets and answer sheets that increase the security levels. Self-paced tutorials show candidates how to use a mouse and other testing tools, ensuring that even those without computer experience are comfortable. Candidates can use either paper and pencil or word processing for essay questions depending on their own preference. It improves the link between instruction and assessment, providing a profile of candidates' strengths and weaknesses, and matches questions and the order in which they are presented to the ability of each test taker.

Computer-based examination system reduces the large proportion of workload on examination, training, grading and reviewing. The set of questions mostly used in computer-based examination system are multiple-choice tests that can be formally and easily evaluated online. Emphasis is now shifting to computer-based tests and on-screen marking of essay questions in the developed world. Computer based tests are scored immediately or shortly after administration, unlike the paper and pencil test result that takes several months to process. Fast scoring helps for publishing results quickly. It can be used to control inadequate examination halls.

Limitations of computer-based testing, particularly attempts to grade students' essays online, are now being explored. On-screen marking, which is already being practiced by Cambridge Assessment, is one such area. On-screen marking is much better than paper scripts. Although this process is already practised by some institutions in the developed world, it is still at the fundamental stage. It is necessary that the question bank should be large enough to prevent high levels of repetition. Computer crashes sometimes occur. Hence, there is a need for a contingency plan in case there are any technical faults in the middle of the examination period that may prevent student from completing the examination and disadvantage their results. Other limitations are related to the resources required—a sufficient number of computers, a room to install them, appropriate software and adequate technical expertise.

Note:

Cambridge Assessment (剑桥大学英语考评): Cambridge Assessment is the brand name of University of Cambridge Local Examinations Syndicate (UCLES), which is a non-teaching department of the University of Cambridge and is a not-for-profit organization.

New Words and Expressions:

1. replicate ['replikeit]　　　　　　v.　　复制；模拟
2. reinforcement [ˌriːinˈfɔːsmənt]　　n.　　（感情或思想等的）巩固，加强；援军
3. embed [imˈbed]　　　　　　　　v.　　（使）插入；（使）嵌入
4. magnitude [ˈmægnitjuːd]　　　　n.　　巨大；重要性；（地震）级数；（星星）亮度
5. entrust [inˈtrʌst]　　　　　　　v.　　委托；交托
6. immense [iˈmens]　　　　　　　adj.　巨大的；极大的
7. pedagogical [ˌpɛdəˈgɒdʒikəl]　　adj.　教学（法）的
8. configuration [kənˌfigəˈreiʃn]　　n.　　结构；布局；形态；[计算机]配置
9. responsive [riˈspɒnsiv]　　　　　adj.　反应敏捷的；反应热烈的
10. contingency [kənˈtindʒənsi]　　　n.　　偶发事件；可能发生的事

Exercises:

I. Vocabulary.

Fill in the blanks with the most suitable words. Change the form when necessary.

| replicate | magnitude | configuration | pedagogical | envisage |

1. The board of this company _____ that there will be a high profit in producing this kind of new product.
2. To be an excellent teacher, one should learn _____ techniques.

Unit 6 Educational Evaluation

3. Due to the lack of space, the designer has to reduce the _____ of the building.
4. Twenty-four _____ texts are carried out to obtain reasonable statistics.
5. Though it is a small business computer system in its simplest _____, it manages to produce large quantities of products efficiently.

II. Comprehension of the text.

Decide whether the following statements are true (T) or false (F) according to the passage.

1. Teaching assessment is the process of defining, selecting, designing, collecting, analyzing, interpreting and using information to increase students' learning and development. ( )
2. ODL learners enjoy varied opportunities to communicate their learning and have more opportunities to diagnose their errors or mistakes before formal assessment task. ( )
3. In the absence of a stock of ready-made questions in question bank, the quality of question papers is liable to suffer. ( )
4. Computer-based assessment can be offered at different times, locations or even different tests to different students. ( )
5. Computer-based testing is recognized as a sustainable strategy for sustainable assessment for ODL because it can be more responsive only to the needs of distance learners. ( )

III. Choose the word or expression that has a similar meaning to the underlined word or expression.

1. I have <u>reinforced</u> the elbows of the jacket with leather patches. ( )
   A. intensified   B. changed   C. minimized   D. beautified
2. Self Assessment Questions <u>embedded</u> in the course material enable distance learners to evaluate their progress frequently. ( )
   A. excluded   B. list   C. covered   D. included
3. I <u>entrusted</u> him to sign the contract for me. ( )
   A. authorized   B. asked   C. told   D. invited
4. China, as a trading market with <u>immense</u> potential and endless opportunities, has attracted many foreign funds. ( )
   A. profound   B. huge   C. extensive   D. little
5. In case of future <u>contingencies</u>, one should get well prepared. ( )
   A. problems   B. incidents   C. accidents   D. cases

Supplementary Reading: Online Diagnostic Assessment in Support of Personalized Teaching and Learning: The eDia System

With some deficiencies in conventional educational assessment arising (e.g. the long time between test administration and feedback, the limited usefulness of summative test results and the lack or limitations of student-level feedback), the focus of attention has shifted from summative to formative assessment or as it is often called, diagnostic assessment. Referring to a set of diagnostic procedures, diagnostic assessment attempts to pinpoint students' strengths and weaknesses in relation to their knowledge structures and processing skills in the target domain. The purpose is to help teachers identify students' problems with a certain instruction style and provide insights into potential improvement.

And the rapid development of online learning has also advanced technology-based assessment, including progress in adaptive testing and most recently in learning analytics, which broadens the possibilities of assessing students' learning and forms of feedback. Strategies based on several forms of computer-aided instruction and online learning designed for older students limit the role of teachers and teach students in specific domains. They open a different route for personalization and only partially overlap with the type of assessment-based differentiation for which the eDia system is devised.

Built in April 2007, the eDia system can be divided into two main parts: one is the hardware infrastructure (a server farm) and the software that operates the system. This has been developed and optimized for diagnostic assessment, e.g. being continuously accessible for the entire Grade 1–6 student population (up to 600,000 students), and for the management of large item banks (with tens of thousands of items). In addition, this infrastructure can also be used for several other assessment purposes. The other part is the main content of the system, the item banks prepared for the diagnostic assessment of reading, mathematics, and science. At present, there are more than 1,000 partner schools (about one-third of the primary schools in Hungary), where it is used on a regular basis. And the software has been continuously developed, with both the number of partner schools and the number of items available in the system growing.

Item Writing: The system contains an item builder module that makes the task of item writing as easy as writing multimedia documents. Items are written online, with the draft versions of items undergoing several phases of review (content, language, technical fitness, and format) before they are entered into the item pool for empirical testing. A number of tools are available to support item writing, including templates and scoring schemes.

Test Editing: Tests can be constructed with adaptive testing techniques, i.e., based on the answers given to all previous items or to items present in the last cluster, to minimize the difference between the students' ability level and the test difficulty level.

Online Test Delivery: Students complete the diagnostic tests as part of their school activity using the available school infrastructure. The tests can be done practically from any device equipped with an Internet browser, but the items are optimized for keyboard, mouse, and a large screen.

Automated Scoring: The items in the item banks that are prepared for the regular diagnostic assessments are scored automatically, with human scoring reserved for research and specific applications.

Built-In Data Processing and Statistical Analyses: The eDia system contains a statistical analytics module, which can perform every computation required by the assessment from descriptive statistics through classical test theory to IRT modeling.

Teacher-Assembled Tests: Participating teachers are granted access to the item banks, so they can assemble tests out of available tasks. These tests can then be administered to individual students, a group of students or an entire class, with the results made available immediately after testing.

Feedback: There are two basic forms of feedback: (1) the immediate feedback students receive right after the test has been completed in the form of percentage of total score of a particular test; (2) contextualized information based on normative reference data, available only after the central assessments. After the general assessments, both students and teachers receive detailed information about the results for each assessment dimension. Students may download a PDF file with a detailed description of the content of the assessment and their own achievement compared to the national norm and class mean. Teachers receive similar information on their students individually in each dimension as well as a comprehensive, contextualized picture of their class, comparing it to other members of the same age group in the entire school, school district, region, and country. This feedback is provided in graphic form as well to help teachers comprehend and use the data.

Unit 7　School Management

Text A　What Is School-based Management?

> **导读**：学校是一种特有的组织形式，而学校管理（School Management）是以学校作为管理对象的一种社会活动形式，是学校对本校的教育、教学、科研、后勤和师生员工管理等各项工作进行计划、组织、协调和控制的活动，由管理者、管理手段、管理对象这些基本要素构成，其核心是提高个人及整体的效率，及时完成任务，这是包括教育、服务、管理在内的多方互动的过程。学校管理决定着学校教育改革的方向和成果，更影响着学生的未来和成长。学校通过管理，把各项工作及其组成要素结合起来，发挥整体功能，以实现其对学生的培养目标和各项工作目标。

Despite the clear commitment of governments and international agencies to the education sector, efficient and equitable access to education is still proved to be elusive for many people around the world. Girls, indigenous peoples, and other poor and marginalized groups often have only limited access to education. These access issues are being addressed with great commitment in international initiatives, such as Education for All, in which resources are being channeled to low-income countries to help them to achieve the Millennium Development Goals for education. However, even where children do have access to educational facilities, the quality of education that is provided is often very poor. This has become increasingly apparent in international learning tests such as Trends in International Mathematics and Science Study (TIMSS), in which most of the students from developing countries fail to excel. There is evidence that merely increasing resource allocations will not increase the equity or improve the quality of education in the absence of institutional reforms. Governments around the world are introducing a range of strategies aimed at improving the financing and delivery of education services, with a more recent emphasis on improving quality as well as increasing quantity in education. One such strategy is to decentralize education decision-making by increasing parental and community involvement in schools—which is popularly known as school-based management (SBM). The argument in favor of SBM is that decentralizing decision-making authority to parents and communities fosters demand and ensures that schools provide the social and economic benefits that best reflect the priorities and values of those local communities. Education reforms in Organization for Economic Co-operation and Development (OECD) countries tend to share some common characteristics of this kind, including increased school autonomy, greater responsiveness to local needs, and the overall objective of improving students' academic performance. Most countries whose students perform well in international student achievement tests give local authorities and schools substantial autonomy to decide the content of their curriculum and the allocation and management of their resources.

An increasing number of developing countries are introducing SBM reforms aimed at empowering principals and teachers or at strengthening their professional motivation, thereby enhancing their sense of ownership of the school. Many of these reforms have also strengthened parental involvement in the schools, sometimes by means of school councils. Almost 11 per cent of all projects in the World Bank's education portfolio for fiscal years 2000–2006 supported school-based management, a total of 17 among about 157 projects. This represents $1.74 billion or 23 per cent of the Bank's total education financing.

The majority of SBM projects in the Bank's current portfolio are in Latin American and South Asian countries. In addition, a number of current and upcoming projects in the Africa region have a component focused on strengthening school-level committees and SBM. There are also two Bank-supported SBM projects in Europe and Central Asia and one each in East Asia and the Pacific (the Philippines), and in the Middle East and North Africa (Lebanon). The few well-documented cases of SBM implementation that have been subject to rigorous impact evaluations have already been reviewed elsewhere. In this passage, we focus on the concept of SBM and its different forms and dimensions and present a conceptual framework for understanding it. We define SBM broadly to include community-based management and parental participation schemes but do not explicitly include stand-alone, or one-off, school grants programs that are not meant to be permanent alterations in school management.

SBM programs lie along a continuum in terms of the degree to which decision-making is devolved to the local level. Some devolve only a single area of autonomy, whereas others go further and devolve the power to hire and fire teachers and authority over substantial resources, while at the far end of the spectrum there are those that encourage the private and community management of schools as well as allow parents to create schools. Thus, there are both strong and weak versions of SBM based on how much decision-making power has been transferred to the school.

The World Bank's World Development Report 2004 presented a conceptual framework for SBM. The WDR argues that school autonomy and accountability can help to solve some fundamental problems in education. While increasing resource flows and support to the education sector is one aspect of increasing the access of the poor to better quality education, it is by no means sufficient.

The SBM approach aims to improve service delivery to the poor by increasing their choice and participation in service delivery, by giving citizens a voice in school management, by making information widely available, and by strengthening the incentives for schools to deliver effective services to the poor and by penalizing those who fail to deliver.

SBM is the decentralization of authority from the central government to the school level. It is said that School-based management can be viewed conceptually as a formal alteration of governance structures, as a form of decentralization that identifies the individual school as the primary unit of improvement and relies on the redistribution of decision-making authority as the primary means through which improvement might be stimulated and sustained. Thus, in SBM, responsibility for, and decision-making authority over school operations are transferred to principals, teachers, and parents, and sometimes to students and other school community members. However, these school-level actors have to conform to or operate within a set of policies determined by the central government. SBM programs exist in many different forms, both in terms of who has the power to make decisions and in terms of the degree of decision-making that is devolved to the school level. While some programs transfer authority only to principals or teachers, others encourage or mandate parental and community participation, often as members of school committees (or school councils or school management committees). In general, SBM programs transfer authority over one or more of the following activities: budget allocation, the hiring and firing of teachers and other school staff, curriculum development, the procurement of textbooks and other educational materials, infrastructure improvements, and the monitoring and evaluation of teacher performance and student learning outcomes.

Good education is not only about physical inputs, such as classrooms, teachers, and textbooks, but also about incentives that lead to better instruction and learning. Education systems are extremely demanding of the managerial, technical, and financial capacity of governments, and thus, as a service, education is too complex to be efficiently produced and distributed in a centralized fashion. Hanushek and Woessmann (2007) suggest that most of the incentives that affect learning outcomes are institutional in nature, and they identify three in particular: (i) choice and competition; (ii) school autonomy; and (iii) school accountability. The idea behind choice and competition is that parents who are interested in maximizing their children's learning outcomes are able to choose to send their children to the most productive (in terms of academic results) school that they can find. This demand-side pressure on schools will thus improve the performance of all schools if they want to compete for students. Similarly, local decision-making and fiscal decentralization can have positive effects on school outcomes such as test scores or graduation rates by holding the schools accountable for the "outputs" that they produce. The World Development Report 2004, Making Services Work for Poor People, presents a very similar framework, in that it suggests that good quality and timely service provision can be ensured if service providers can be held accountable to their clients.

In the context of developed countries, the core idea behind SBM is that those who work in a school building should have greater control of the management of what goes on in the building. In developing countries, the idea behind SBM is less ambitious, in that it focuses mainly on involving community and parents in the school decision-making process rather than putting them entirely in control. However, in both cases, the central government always plays some role in education, and the precise definition of this role affects how SBM activities are conceived and implemented. SBM in almost all of its manifestations involves community members in school decision-making. Because these community members are usually parents of children enrolled in the school, they have an incentive to improve their children's education. As a result, SBM can be expected to improve student achievement and other outcomes as these local people demand closer monitoring of school personnel, better student evaluations, a closer match between the school's needs and its policies, and a more efficient use of resources. For instance, although the evidence is mixed, in a number of diverse countries, such as Papua New Guinea, India, and Nicaragua, parental participation in school management has reduced teacher absenteeism.

SBM has several other benefits. Under these arrangements, schools are managed more transparently, thus reducing opportunities for corruption. Also, SBM often gives parents and stakeholders opportunities to increase their skills. In some cases, training in shared decision-making, interpersonal skills, and management skills is offered to school council members so that they can become more capable participants in the SBM process and at the same time benefit the community as a whole.

Unlike in developed countries where SBM is introduced explicitly to improve students' academic performance, how school decentralization will eventually affect student performance in developing countries is less clear. This section tries to define the ways in which SBM can increase participation and transparency and improve school outcomes.

First, the SBM model must define exactly which powers are vested in which individuals or committees and how these powers are to be coordinated to make the plan workable within both the school culture and the available resources. However, the structure of authority needs to remain flexible enough to enable school managers to deal with any unexpected events, which always seem to emerge during implementation.

Second, the success of SBM requires the support of the various school-level stakeholders, particularly of teachers. Also vital to the success of SBM is for school principals to support the decentralization reform. This is not a foregone conclusion, as principals will remain personally accountable for the performance of their school but will no longer have complete control over its management. In effect, they are being asked to give up some authorities without a corresponding decrease in personal accountability. Once SBM is in place, principals can no longer blame the policies of the school district when things go wrong.

The support of both local and national governments is also required. SBM by definition requires these governments to surrender some power and authority to the school level, but they retain the right and ability to reverse their earlier decision in favor of SBM if they feel their power is being usurped.

The final and most important source of necessary support is from parents and other community members. It is important, however, to distinguish between parents and other community members. While parents are always part of the community that surrounds a school, school councils do not have to include parents as members. For instance, in the United States, many schools are locally controlled in the sense that a school board of local residents officially sets policy, but there may be no parental participation in these schools. In some cases, wealthy individuals in a community may be members of a school council simply because they financially support the school.

Particularly in developed countries, parental participation as members of school councils or of the group that is implementing SBM is distinct from community participation. However, in developing countries, in particular in isolated small or rural communities, parental participation tends to be synonymous with community participation, since in these small communities almost everybody has a family member in school.

The expectation underlying SBM is that greater parental involvement will mean that schools will be more responsive to local demands (for example, for better teaching methods or more inputs) and that decisions will be taken in the interests of children rather than adults. A further hope is that involved parents will become unpaid or minimally paid auxiliary staff who will help teachers in classrooms and with other minor activities. Furthermore, even if parents are too busy working to help in the classroom, they can still encourage their children to do their homework and to show them, in this and other ways, that their family really values schooling and academic achievement. Since parents are networked in various ways with community leaders, the further hope is that parental support for SBM will encourage local community leaders to put schools higher on their political agendas and thus provide the schools with more material resources.

Once the nexus of autonomy-participation and accountability has been defined and a realistic management plan has been drawn up that has the support of all stakeholders, then it becomes possible to expect better school outcomes. Thereafter, the hope is that the school climate will change as the stakeholders work together in a collegial way to manage the school. However, there is little evidence that this really happens in practice. Also, the possibility exists that teachers and principals will come to resent being constantly monitored by parents and school council members, which will cause relations within the school to deteriorate.

At the same time, the teaching climate of a school is predicated on, among many other factors, how motivated teachers are to teach well, whether they know how to teach well, how good the various curricula are, how eager pupils are to learn, and how much parents actually support their children's learning in whatever ways are practical for them. Any school that wants to improve its academic record will have to work actively on some or all of these factors. Sometimes, the obstacles to improve the quality of instruction are motivational, sometimes they are cognitive in the sense of what teachers know, and sometimes they are social in the sense of petty personal matters that can prevent teachers from behaving professionally. Ideally, under SBM, because those who run the school are intimately acquainted with the individuals who work there, they will be able to identify the specific problems that need to be fixed and use their authority to find and implement solutions.

Some caveats must be mentioned about SBM. Decentralization or devolution does not necessarily give more power to the general public because it is susceptible to being captured by elites. As for the relationship between decentralization, proper growth, and reduced corruption, the evidence is mixed. Bardhan and Mookherjee (2000 and 2006) and Bardhan (2002) suggest that there may be numerous reasons why local control over resource allocation or decision-making may not yield the desired outcomes. First, in more traditional and rural areas with a history of feudalism, the poor or minorities may feel the need for a strong central authority to ensure that services are delivered to them and not just to the more powerful local citizens. Second, and related to this, is the issue that there may be no culture of accountability within communities, meaning that no one would think to question any actions taken by the group running the school (De Grauwe, 2005). This can be a problem in places where the teacher is regarded as the ultimate authority by the virtue of being the only "highly" qualified individual in a community. Third, those given the responsibility for managing the school may not have the capacity to do so, which points up to the need to build the capacity of education stakeholders at the grassroots level to ensure that SBM reforms do not fail in their execution.

These caveats help to strengthen our understanding of the pattern of SBM in developing countries (as discussed above). In particular, the caveats strengthen the notion that the specific type of SBM introduced in any given country depends (or should ideally depend) on the political economy of the particular country. For instance, strong SBM reforms have been introduced, and have been quite successful, in those countries where communities have been forced by some calamity such as war or a natural disaster to come together as a group to find ways to deliver basic services, including education.

Notes:

1. **Education for All (全民教育):** The Education for All movement took off at the World Conference on Education for All in 1990. Since then, governments, non-governmental organizations, bilateral and multilateral donor agencies and the media have taken up the cause of providing basic education for all children, youth and adults.

2. **Millennium Development Goals (千年发展目标):** The Millennium Development Goals are eight international development goals that all 193 United Nations member states and at least 23 international organizations have agreed to achieve by the year 2015. They include eradicating extreme poverty, reducing child mortality rates, fighting disease epidemics such as AIDS, and developing a global partnership for development.

3. **Trends in International Mathematics and Science Study (国际数学与科学趋势研究项目):** Trends in International Mathematics and Science Study (TIMSS) is an international assessment of the mathematics and science knowledge of fourth- and eighth-grade (Year 5 and Year 9) students around the world. TIMSS was developed by the International Association for

the Evaluation of Educational Achievement (IEA) to allow participating nations to compare students' educational achievement across borders. The IEA also conducts the Progress in International Reading Literacy Study (PIRLS). TIMSS was first administered in 1995, and every 4 years thereafter. In 1995, forty-one nations participated in the study; in 2007, 48 countries participated. Another similar study is the Programme for International Student Assessment.

New Words and Expressions:

1. indigenous [in'didʒənəs]   adj.   本地的；土生土长的
2. marginalize ['mɑːdʒinəlaiz]   v.   使处于边缘；使无实权
3. portfolio [pɔːt'fəuliəu]   n.   投资组合；文件夹；系列服务
4. spectrum ['spektrəm]   n.   系列；范围；幅度；光谱；声谱
5. incentive [in'sentiv]   n.   刺激；鼓励
6. auxiliary [ɔːg'ziliəri]   adj.   辅助的；备用的
7. accountability [ə,kauntə'biləti] n.   负有责任；应作解释；可说明性
8. caveat ['kæviæt]   n.   警告；告诫

Exercises:

I. Vocabulary.

Fill in the blanks with the most suitable words. Change the form when necessary.

| marginalize | incentive | auxiliary | spectrum | caveat |

1. The _____ units are called in only when the main force has been overtaxed.
2. We must not _____ the poor in our society.
3. There is a wide _____ of opinions on this question.
4. But there is a crucial _____: how much worse might the politics get.
5. The child has no _____ to study harder because his parents cannot afford to send him to college.

II. Comprehension of the text.

Decide whether the following statements are true (T) or false (F) according to the passage.

1. Increasing resource allocations will increase the equity or improve the quality of education in

the absence of institutional reforms. (   )
2. Good education means merely physical inputs, such as classrooms, teachers, and textbooks. (   )
3. How school decentralization will eventually affect student performance in developing countries is apparent. (   )
4. In developed countries, parental participation as members of school councils or of the group that is implementing SBM is the same as community participation. (   )
5. The specific type of SBM introduced in any given country depends (or should ideally depend) on the political economy of the particular country. (   )

III. Read the text and answer the following questions.
1. What is School-Based Management?
2. What are the benefits of SBM?
3. What does SBM need to improve school outcomes?
4. Apart from the benefits, SBM may fail to achieve school outcomes. What's the major caveat about SBM?

Text B Data-informed Decision Making and Transformational Leadership

> **导读：** 近年来，基于数据的决策对学校管理和发展来说十分重要，将变革型领导效应引入数据团队则成为将数据应用于学校发展中的一项有效策略。校领导是学校数据团队的中流砥柱，他们的决策对学校管理和发展有着重大的影响。而作为目前领导者的主导理论模型之一，"变革型领导模式"对组建高效的学校数据团队至关重要。本文列出了变革型领导模式的三个关键因素，并分析了每个因素对建设高效学校数据团队的积极影响。

The concept of data-informed decision making (DIDM), a term used interchangeably with data-driven decision making (DDDM) and data-based decision making (DBDM), is relatively new to school planning process. In the past decade, educators have concentrated more on students' deficits than their assets, resulting in cheating on tests and teaching to the test. Thus, a new wave of data use is arising, where data cannot completely drive decisions, but inform decisions, which, combined with the professional knowledge of educators, can contribute to achievement and learning in schools. This type of data use does not focus solely on achievement on a narrow set of topics, but can be used to work on different sets of goals (e.g. literacy and numeracy, but also well-being, arts, critical thinking, and creativity). Moreover, data use does not include only standardized assessment data, but includes any type of data that can provide information on the functioning of schools, such as classroom assessment data, classroom observations, student focus groups, and so forth. Based on data, school leaders and teachers can assess to what extent changes are needed in the school and classrooms, and they can implement these educational changes accordingly. Emerging evidence suggests that under the right conditions, data use can lead to school improvement in terms of higher student achievement.

However, it is frequently reported that schools struggle with implementing data use effectively, principally because educators are lacking in the required knowledge and skills. A promising strategy for supporting the implementation of data use in schools is professional development for teachers and school leaders related to data use in teams. It is also of significance to take into account the role of the school leader, who can both enable and hinder the use of data in teams. For one thing, they occupy key positions in schools as far as, for example, implementing a culture of data use. For another, they can also hinder data use, for example by not facilitating teachers in time to meet, and by using data to "blame and shame" teachers instead of focusing on how to collaboratively use data to improve education. Moreover, although the role of the school leader is crucial in implementing interventions, how to apply these leadership behaviors in professional development interventions focused on data use hasn't been clarified.

Over the last few years, large-scale teacher professional development interventions for data use have been implemented in diverse contexts. The goal of the data team intervention is to scaffold data teams in the effective use of data for making informed decisions and solving educational problems. In this way (referred to as transformational leadership), data teams can be an avenue for professional development, with the ultimate goal of school improvement. As a key to building effective data teams, transformational leadership in educational settings can be operationalized as a construct comprised of three building blocks: (1) initiating and identifying a vision; (2) providing individualized support; and (3) providing intellectual stimulation.

The data team intervention aims at challenging the status quo in schools and wants to encourage greater data use for making informed decisions in schools. And the transformational leadership behaviors can support organizations in effectively implementing educational innovations. In addition, transformational leadership can lead to changes in teacher practice, cause commitment by teachers to the reform, and increase the effort they are willing to devote to such reform. Furthermore, the more school leaders engage in transformational leadership behaviors, the more likely teachers are to take risks in developing and implementing new knowledge.

Hence, transformational leadership behaviors and strategies could also be important for successfully implementing and sustaining data use in schools. The data team intervention can be described as an educational innovation that is being implemented in the school, for which the commitment and effort of teachers and school leaders are required. The data team is working together towards two organizational goals: implementing data use practices in the school, and solving a specific educational problem. Transformational leadership behaviors can support a team in achieving these goals. Therefore, the transformational leadership model was identified as a suitable framework to serve as the starting point for studying the role of school leaders in data teams.

Transformational Leadership Component 1: Initiating and Identifying a Vision

Initiating and identifying a vision refers to a leader's role in contributing to building a shared vision, norms, goals, and priorities in schools, as well as a more specific shared vision and norms for learning and improvement through data use. Thus, contributing to building a shared vision means that school leaders express and communicate goals and the approach for achieving these goals. In this way, transformational leaders may build teachers' emotional attachment to the school. This can increase teachers' commitment to the organization, their identification with their school's vision, and their internalization of school goals as personal goals, which may result in greater efforts of teachers towards realizing these organizational goals.

Related to the data team intervention, school leaders are expected to, for example, communicate school management's beliefs about data use, related goals and the approach for achieving these goals. In the data team intervention, learning and improvement through data use is an explicit goal, in addition to solving the school's problem based on data. By committing to these goals, school leaders provide direction for teachers for participation in data use. Moreover, together with the other data team members, norms and structures for safe data discussions should be developed, as well as a vision for data use in the school.

Transformational Leadership Component 2: Providing Individualized Support

Providing individualized support represents a leader's attempt to understand, recognize, and satisfy teachers' concerns and needs while treating each teacher as a unique individual. Mentoring and coaching of teachers plays an important role in this, for example by delegating challenging tasks to teachers, by providing feedback, and by recognizing and talking to teachers about their needs and concerns. Furthermore, by coaching, delegating challenging tasks, and providing feedback, school leaders may help to link teachers' current needs to the school's goals and mission and enhance teachers' sense of self-efficacy. Individual concerns, emotions and questions might impede collective learning. School leaders should recognize this and provide individual support to team members to overcome such concerns or negative emotions when they are present. Moreover, it is important that school leaders establish structures for collaboration, such as a systematic data team approach.

Regarding the data team intervention, school leaders are expected to pay attention to this aspect of transformational leadership by, for example, facilitating data use through scheduling time (including accessing, analyzing, and reflecting on data) and providing training related to data use. Leaders can also show that they recognize and are trying to satisfy teachers' needs related to implementation of data use by establishing structures that promote regular, consistent, and collaborative data use in schools.

Transformational Leadership Component 3: Providing Intellectual Stimulation

Transformational leaders who provide intellectual stimulation encourage teachers to challenge their beliefs and assumptions about daily practice; they collaborate with teachers, and increase teachers' ability to solve school-level problems. Transformational leaders stimulate creativity and professional development by encouraging teachers to question their own beliefs and values, and by enhancing their problem-solving abilities.

With regard to the data team intervention, leaders can challenge teachers' beliefs and assumptions about their daily practice, for example, by modeling data use practices. A skilled school leader who acts as a role model for data use can stimulate teachers in using data, lead discussions about data and data use, and engage teachers in those discussions. For example, in the context of data use, a school leader could ask questions when teachers make assumptions, such as "what (data) is your statement based on?" This helps teachers reflect on how their daily work is influenced by assumptions that might not hold up if investigated. Moreover, school leaders actively participate in the data team, and share and develop knowledge with the team.

Note:

Transformational leadership (变革型领导): Transformational leadership is a style of leadership that transforms followers to rise above their self-interest by altering their morale, ideals, interests, and values, motivating them to perform better than initially expected.

New Words and Expressions:

1. deficit ['defɪsɪt]   n.   [经济]亏损，赤字，逆差；不足额；缺少
2. numeracy ['nu:mərəsi]   n.   计算能力；识数；数学基础知识
3. hinder ['hɪndər]   v.   妨碍，阻碍
4. intervention [ɪntər'venʃn]   n.   干预；介入；调停；斡旋
5. scaffold ['skæfoʊld]   v.   给……搭脚手架；用支架支撑
6. internalization [ɪn,tɜrnələ'zeɪʃn] n. 内在化
7. delegate ['delɪgət]   v.   授权；把（工作、权力等）委托（给下级）；选派（某人做某事）
8. collaboration [kə,læbə'reɪʃn] n.   合作；协作；合作成果；通敌

Exercises:

I. Vocabulary.

Fill in the blanks with the most suitable words. Change the form when necessary.

| deficit | numeracy | hinder | intervention |
| scaffold | internalization | delegate | collaboration |

1. All students should be equipped with knowledge of _____ and literature when they leave school.
2. Military _____ will only aggravate the conflict even further.
3. The government worked in close _____ with teachers on the new curriculum.
4. Some teachers felt _____ by a lack of resources.
5. I've been _____ to organize the Christmas party.
6. Now you can run your migration and then _____ together the rest of the application.
7. The team has to come back from a 2-0 _____ in the first half.
8. Personality is the _____ of a group or a national culture.

II. Comprehension of the text.

Decide whether the following statements are true (T) or false (F) according to the passage.

1. Data-driven decision making does not focus solely on achievement on a narrow set of topics, but can be used to work on different sets of goals. (   )
2. Based on data, school leaders and teachers can assess to what extent changes are needed in the school and classrooms, and they can implement these educational changes accordingly. (   )

3. The data team intervention aims at challenging the status quo in schools and wants to encourage greater data use for making informed decisions in schools. ( )
4. By coaching, delegating challenging tasks, and providing feedback, school leaders may help to link students' current needs to the school's goals and mission and enhance students' sense of self-efficacy. ( )
5. School leaders shouldn't challenge teachers' beliefs and assumptions about their daily practice and educational values. ( )

III. Complete the following sentences according to the text.
1. Initiating and identifying a vision refers to a leader's role in contributing to building a shared _____, _____, _____, and _____ in schools, as well as a more specific shared vision and norms for learning and improvement through data use.
2. Providing individualized support represents a leader's attempt to _____, _____, and _____ teachers' concerns and needs while treating each teacher as a unique individual.
3. Transformational leaders stimulate creativity and professional development by encouraging teachers to question their own _____ and _____, and by enhancing their _____ _____ _____.
4. The goal of the _____ _____ _____ is to scaffold data teams in the effective use of data for making informed decisions and solving educational problems.
5. Individual _____, _____ and _____ might impede collective learning.

Supplementary Reading: Evaluating School-based Management

For more than 20 years, policymakers, educators, and academics have advocated participative leadership as a key ingredient in school improvement and reform. Two fundamental assumptions underlie the logic of participative leadership: (a) schools are most effective when stakeholders from across the school community are meaningfully involved in core school decision making, and (b) participative leadership reflects democratic practice and, as such, is justified as a valid management strategy. In practice, participative leadership can be referred to as school-based management, participative decision-making or democratic leadership. Although the practice of participative leadership can vary somewhat across different models, participative leadership typically revolves around a school-level management team comprised of administrators, teachers, staff members, parents and community members. These teams have articulated roles and responsibilities. They often are granted decision authority in core school decisions pertaining to learning and teaching, management, budget, and resources. Teams typically include elected members as well as non-elected representatives, who serve on various subcommittees. For example, teaching and non-teaching staff members, who are not elected as full members of the management team, typically are required (or are given the opportunity) to serve on one of several subcommittees. The subcommittee structure facilitates and maximizes the inclusion of all staff in school decision-making. This participatory structure is intended to distribute decision authority across the school community and is purported as a means to improve the quality of school-level decision-making. To this end, the potential benefits of participative leadership are difficult to refute and as such it has become a popular and widespread school management style.

The impetus for the current study came from the observation that, although prior research has provided substantial information on what constitutes effective teams as well as strategies for successful implementation, concomitantly, there is a paucity of research on team evaluation. Specifically, what strategies can teams use to self-monitor or evaluate their goals, outcomes, and overall effectiveness? Teams ultimately are accountable to their larger school community and to this end must be conscious of the degree to which their goals, objectives, and values align. The purpose of this study was to propose a practical evaluation tool—the values inquiry checklist—for management team self-review and evaluation. It is posited that the information derived from the checklist will enable teams to evaluate the degree to which their values align with those of the school community as a whole and as a result increase the transparency of team decision-making and improve team accountability.

The evaluation guide proposed in the current study is founded on values inquiry evaluation research (Mark 2001), which was posited as an appropriate melding of evaluation theory to the field of school management. As defined by Mark (2001), a values inquiry approach to program evaluation is one in which value positions important to social programs and policies are identified and incorporated into the evaluation plan. Values inquiry is intended to be transparent, with differing values acknowledged early in the evaluation process and included as evaluation findings. Such findings are believed to have an impact on the nature of the evaluation information and subsequent judgments regarding the merit of programs. For example, Mark (2001) uses the example of whether parents of young children in a preschool program would see the program as successful if it promoted academic outcomes but did not emphasize social skills. In such a case, in spite of the fact that academic achievement and social skills both are valid goals of preschool programs; differing values within the parent group would potentially impact judgments on program success. Acknowledging differences in values at the onset of the evaluation and incorporating this information into subsequent evaluation activities is the basis of values inquiry evaluation.

From the perspective of evaluation, school-management teams primarily are accountable to their constituents—the larger school community. Effective management teams are aware of their constituent needs. Therefore, team effectiveness should be gauged by the degree to which team decisions reflect and/or address constituents' needs. To this end, the purpose of values inquiry evaluation is to increase team accountability by increasing transparency in team decision-making. If teams are able to articulate the values that drive their decisions and align these articulated values with those of the larger school community, in theory, the teams will be more effective and more accountable. In practice, teams that perceive themselves as effective, competent, and cohesive, concomitantly can be perceived by the larger school community to be ineffective or even in opposition to the needs of their constituents. In such cases, it is likely that goals prescribed by the team either misalign with the expectations of the larger school community or are misunderstood. Such misalignment is the focus of values inquiry evaluation.

The values inquiry approach to evaluating team effectiveness outlined in the following section proposes that stakeholder values on all important issues related to team accountability should be identified, addressed, and incorporated into team decision-making. Based on findings from educational research on school-based management, a list of 30 questions was developed that represent core aspects of team functioning, operations, and decision authority (see Table 7-1). In theory, team values and individual team member values are reflected in the way these 30 questions are answered and, in turn, incorporated into team decision-making.

The list of questions in Table 7-1 has been organized like a checklist for use with individual team members and aggregated to the team level. Collectively, the questions address choices that teams must make. These choices reflect dominant team values. Conversely, answers to these questions gauge which values are tradeoffs. For example, in the case of the pre-school program and possible goals for the program being social versus academic outcomes, although both outcomes were valid for such a program, some parents might choose to trade off social skills in favor of academic achievement as an appropriate focus for the program. Tradeoffs are made in situations where more than one outcome is valued, but not to the same degree. In the case of school-based management, such tradeoffs are assumed to be commonplace. Due to the myriad of factors that can potentially impact school operations, teams most certainly make many decisions that involve tradeoffs. Subsequently, these decisions, or tradeoffs, reflect what is most valued by individual team members and by the team as a whole. The following scenario provides an example of how the values inquiry checklist might be used to identify, assess, and address a hypothetical values conflict experienced by a school management team.

Table 7-1   Values Inquiry Checklist

Does your school management team: 1 = yes, 0 = no
include budgets to facilitate new activities and training for participants?
include budgets to enable ongoing activities and training for participants?
create new administrative positions to administer school-based management?
involve a plan for the district decentralization of resources that is developed with input from various stakeholder groups?
enable teachers to identify problems and resources needed to solve them?
give the school rather than the district office authority over how school resources are allocated?
include group problem-solving strategies/training?
include conflict resolution strategies/training?
incorporate team building?
incorporate training in budgeting?
include interviewing/listening skills?
apply group consensus strategies such as delphi and nominal group techniques, force field analysis, and other brainstorming techniques?
employ data-driven decision-making?
offer training in communication skills for presentations and report writing?
offer training writing mission statements, goals, and objectives for curriculum and instruction?
clarify decision authority (versus influence) between the team and the administrator?

continued

Does your school management team: 1 = yes, 0 = no
clarify decision authority and influence within the team?
delineate team processes such as the roles, tasks, and responsibilities of team members?
clarify roles/tasks and responsibilities of the administrator?
clarify which decisions will be within the domain of the management team?
define team goals and identify measurable outcomes?
establish a consensus on the goals and outcomes?
define clear purposes for all students' learning?
take collective responsibility for student learning?
clearly delineate managerial policies?
safeguard against bureaucratic administrator control?
reflect the spirit of participation that views teachers as managing professionals?
encourage participation from non-management team staff members?
clarify the role of teacher unions?
include mechanisms that prohibit administrators from using teacher contracts as a means to exclude teachers from participating?

Most school-based management teams involve subcommittees which address particular school issues and report back to the primary team with recommendations. Within this structure, it is not atypical for subcommittee chairs to be selected by the management team chair. In turn, values held by the team chair are reflected, in part, by his or her choice of subcommittee chairs. For the current scenario, suppose the team chair chooses subcommittee chairs, who are personal friends or who are likely to align with and support the views of the team chair. In this case, it is probable that other team members would see the choice as transparent and perhaps even anticipated. In terms of possible repercussions, most team members likely would resent the favoritism, but accept it. For others, however, it might be reason enough to attempt to sabotage the efforts of the favored members. The team chair would most certainly be aware of ramifications such as this, but, nonetheless, would accept them as tradeoffs—the team chair chose to risk or tradeoff team cohesion in favor of having supporters head the subcommittees. The chair does not know if the possible negative impact on team cohesion will eventually outweigh the benefits of controlling who leads the subcommittees. However, this is the tradeoff. The team chair potentially has sacrificed team cohesion in favor of what he or she seems to be increased team capacity.

The fundamental problem in the scenario described here is that the chair's authority appeared to go unchecked and, as a result, team cohesiveness likely would be negatively affected. Further, distribution of authority within the team was unclear and consequently impacted not only team cohesion but team capacity as well. Some team members likely would not work cooperatively with the selected subcommittee chairs.

For the management team in this scenario, the values inquiry checklist would be introduced by the administrator as a tool the team could use to examine and to self-evaluate its internal decision-making process. The checklist would be administered, for example, to each team member. The structure of the values inquiry checklist is a simple dichotomous response format ("yes = 1" or "no = 0" to each question). Responses could be summed at the item level across team members and, as such, would represent areas of greatest and least value to the team as a whole. This simple analysis followed by some degree of structured group discussion on answers to the various questions would enable teams to also identify areas of greatest tradeoff. For example, for the questions on team training, it is probable that many teams do not put time and/or resources into team professional development (Turnbull & Mee 2003). As such, the checklist could be used to measure team member values on training and the data could be used as a platform to address the issue and possible associated tradeoffs. Through simple record-keeping and periodic application of the checklist, teams could revisit these issues and create benchmarks to gauge progress; all of which would be woven into the day-to-day functioning of the team in a relatively unobtrusive way.

In terms of using the checklist with established versus newly implemented teams, it is appropriate in both contexts. In the case of the team in the scenario, where issues of distribution of authority arose in the early implementation stages, the checklist would be useful as a means for teams to articulate and define decision authority, which ultimately is at the center of team functioning. Distribution of authority within the team and overall team decision authority ultimately impact the degree to which teams can achieve their goals and the expectations of their constituents. Therefore, established teams could use the values inquiry checklist as a means to review their goals and related values. Conversely, the checklist could be used by new teams as a tool to define goals, determine constituent needs and values, and to identify and align their own team values accordingly.

In an effort to move beyond school-based management as a symbolic gesture of democracy in practice, it is not unreasonable to expect that teams be accountable to their school community and the various constituent members. To achieve this, teams must be able to articulate their values and to assess their performance based on these values. The values inquiry checklist was developed to assist teams in achieving these important goals. The checklist is proposed as an unobtrusive and adaptable tool that principals and teams can use to evaluate overall management team effectiveness.

Unit 8　School & Family

Text A　School and Family Cooperation Models for Reducing Social Problems

> **导读**：作为重要的个体状态变量，社会排斥（social exclusion）是指个体处于被他人或群体孤立或拒绝而无法满足基本归属和人际关系需要的一种社会心理现象，影响到个体的认知、情绪和行为，会降低个体的归属感与控制感。社会排斥的表现形式很多，如排斥、拒绝、孤立、无视等。在拉脱维亚，社会排斥是七到十五岁的学生可能遇到的成长问题之一。本文的研究对象是寄宿学校的学生。寄宿学校的学生与综合学校的学生在团体关系方面是很不一样的，由于教师沟通不及时、情感教育措施缺乏合理性等问题，部分寄宿学校的学生甚至产生了严重的心理健康问题，引起了社会对寄宿学校制度的广泛思考。

Pupils' (7–15 years old) social exclusion is one of the contemporary problems in Latvia. The chosen target group for research is pupils living and studying in the boarding school. The membership of pupils in the boarding school highly differs from comprehensive schools in Latvia, because they usually are pupils from low-income and disadvantageous families, as well as children without parental care, those who have wandered for a long time, have not acquired education according to their age, children being left under relatives' supervision because their parents have left for working abroad and also children with many similar problems. A large part of these pupils have not only limited possibilities to adapt themselves to the social life, to have exciting spare time, to contact with equals in age, to identify and develop their skills, abilities and interests, but also lack socially meaningful experience regarding the conventionalities and a moral, ethic model for imitation of these norms. The micro-society, life conditions in families where pupils live, unfortunately, do not develop conventionalities, but encourage anti-social behavior.

Admittedly, pupils in boarding schools have fair intellect, they are physically fit, with sufficient potential of energy being impossible to put into practice within the pedagogical context that could help them socialize and express themselves. Education is regarded as a value in the family; however, the socially-psychological characteristics also affect the learning process, because we can often notice explicit Attention Deficit Syndrome lowering their working capacity. In order to facilitate the reduction of pupils' social exclusion in the boarding school and their incorporation into the social life, as well as to prevent critical situations, these pupils and their parents need special support, because the pupil's identity development begins in the family, but improves at school.

Along with the country's economic situation, the parents' socio-economic situation has sharply worsened. Therefore, as a result of such changes, many families have experienced stressful situations. Consequently, parents often are full of their own problems forgetting about the child's needs, interests and peculiarities of development. Parents often do not immerse into their child as an individual, do not perceive their child as a value, because in their own childhood, they had felt themselves unplumbed, troublesome, not cared for and pushed. Support for these children and their parents can be ensured by a complex of different educational measures and teamwork. One of the measures is the promotion of cooperation between the school and the family, because the priority of boarding school pupils is their family, family members' opinion which is taken into account. But this cooperation must be insistent and permanent as only in this case positive results can be expected.

The research was carried on within the framework of the Doctoral Thesis Holistic approach during the process of socialization of social risk group pupils.

The report contains the analysis of the issue within two levels: "the theoretical level", where the legislation of the Republic of Latvia related to social issues, children rights and parental duties as well as different models of school and family cooperation had been analyzed. Consequently, there was proposed a triangular model referring to direct cooperation between the school, NGO (non-governmental organization) and family; "the empirical level", where the approbation of the proposed cooperation model (SCHOOL—NGO—FAMILY) was developed by interviewing the parents of the pupils. By the content-analysis, there were analyzed the implementation of the cooperation model by the mediation of the NGO "Liepna Boarding School and Pupils

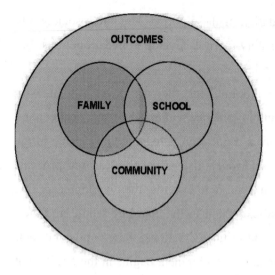

Support Families Union" in order to reduce social problems within the boarding school.

Each person is an individual system, which functions in interaction by surrounding environment, creates correlated and interacted system and aggregate of structures. It is an ecosystem approach and these conditions also refer to persons from social risk groups. In general, this thesis is basis for integrative and inclusive pedagogy. In accordance with scientific cognitions of U. Bronfenbrenner, microsystem is an aggregate of activities, roles and intermediate human relations, which is being experienced by the person with its characteristic physical and psychical features at some particular sphere of life by creating interaction with other persons. Accordingly, the child, his/her family and school are three microsystems.

In a child's upbringing, the family has an important role. However, the function of upbringing is also performed by the school and it means that for child's development the cooperation between school and family is important. It should be well-thought-out and organized, because every family has different resources, skills, desires and needs. One approach of cooperation does not fit to everyone. Pupils, their parents and teachers usually have different desires, aims, opinions, values; it sometimes leads to disappointment and misunderstandings between school and pupils' families. If these differences are not recognized and solved, there is developing lack of communication; consequently, there is impossible successful cooperation between school and family. This expression often is seen in boarding schools, where the parents of the pupils have different world outlook, because the majority of these families practice antisocial lifestyle. It is complicated to persuade and stimulate the parents to live more qualitatively; it creates necessity to include the parents:

- in active involvement into making decisions regarding school;
- in active school's activities as volunteers and members of parents' committee;
- leisure activities with their children;
- regular communication with school personnel regarding child's school and general progress;
- participation in opportunities of adults' education offered by the school.

Unit 8　School & Family

Families' involvement in school's activities can be one of the means by creating cooperative, tolerant community. Nowadays, as schools become more and more open to the society, communication between parents and teachers is becoming not only more intensive but also more complicated. Teachers tend to recognize that work out of classroom—in this case, community activities and communication with parents—involves both emotional and intellectual efforts. As a result of communication between school and family, pupils' achievements, behavior, attitude towards studies and school are improving. The cooperation depends on families' education, family and society members, who are working together for consummation of united aims.

The features of cooperation between the school and the family in Latvia had changed by historical course of time. A. Baldins and A. Razeva mention that the older generation teaching children has grown and developed their identities in other socio-economic and political relations to a great extent being typical to the conditions of a primitive society. The grounds for these relations were social and economic safety and absolutization of the country's interests. Government ensured a single educational system for all children where the school became a partial performer of the family's functions. This experience regarding the school is familiar to parents, but the contemporary school realizes only its educational functions making the family to realize its responsibility and importance of the upbringing function.

In its turn, the boarding school is an educational institution carrying out not only pupils' educating but also upbringing function. Pupils spend a majority of their life in boarding school; as a result, the school mainly takes responsibility for pupil's development as individuality, but parents' responsibility stays apart.

Basing on the *Children's Rights Protection Law* passed by Saeima of the Republic of Latvia prescribing children's rights to clean environment for life (Article 46); basic provisions for the protection of children from negative influences in social surroundings (Article 47); children's protection from smoking and the influence of alcoholic beverages (Article 48); children's protection from the use of narcotic, toxic and other intoxicating substances (Article 49); protection from negative influence of games, films and mass media (Article 50); restrictions for children's involvement into events (Article 501); safety requirements in children's supervisory services (Article 503); children's protection from unlawful activities (Article 51); a child—a victim of violence or other unlawful activity (Article 52); quite often the children at high risk are being sent to a boarding school and thus being isolated from their families. As a result, parents' rights to bring up their children are limited. The connection between the child and his family is broken, also the obligations of parents prescribed in Article 24 of the *Children's Rights Protection*

Law of the Republic of Latvia determining: "to take care of the child and his property and represent him within his private and property relations"; "to prepare the child for an independent life in the society, as much as possible respecting his/her individuality, taking into consideration his/her abilities and inclinations"; "to safe-guard the child's rights and interests protected by the law"; as well as "upon failure to discharge parental obligations, or for the malicious usage of parental authority, physical punishing of a child, as well as cruel behavior against him/her, parents shall be held accountable as determined by the law", etc.

A part of parents' obligations is performed by the boarding school, and exactly by the school support measures. It is possible to maintain and improve the existent relations between the child, parents and teachers, but positive moral concepts being acquired at school are not always supported by the families of the social risk group, because in most cases parents have transferred their own negative experience regarding school to their children. The majority of parents are unemployed at the moment due to the economic crisis and they are followers of the anti-social environment, quite often these parents, when bringing their children to grade 1, give them for school's care and upbringing for over nine years. However, the positive result of child's upbringing can be reached only in case school efforts are being supported by the family. Otherwise, a child acquires different skills and habits; but consequently, the positive influence in school often vanishes because of the lack of support in the family.

It creates the necessity to develop cooperation between the school and the family corresponding to school's intentions and motivating parents to arrive at school in order to see their child's growth. Frequently, the class teacher is the person informing parents about their children's interests, abilities, competences, needs, problems, friends, state of health. Usually it is quite difficult to involve parents into organization of the educational process, because there is a psychological barrier between the school and parents that is not easy to hurdle. The school visit mainly is connected to their child's bad behavior and insufficient success, the research shows that parents usually do not want to visit school and help its work due to the following reasons:

- they are not sure that their help is truly necessary;
- they are afraid to be mistaken;
- there is a lack of information regarding the form of the required support;
- low self-esteem, busyness;
- illness;
- alcoholism, drug addiction;
- they are undereducated and low-income people often with an inferiority complex.

Unit 8 School & Family

As V. Senko notes, the time of negative experience accumulating for pupils in junior grades is noticeably shorter than for youngsters, therefore the departure from the norm is not yet established. Their psyche is characterized by its flexibility and this feature facilitates the reformatory process. By the time when the child starts to attend school, a break of the dynamic stereotype happens and it goes quite easily, because the negative acquirements and habits have not become permanent. Therefore the initiative of the pedagogical cooperation between the school and the family should be taken by the school without waiting for parents' interest. But families having pedagogical neglect require special attention and approach, because it is necessary to practise both the educating and the reformatory or re-educating function at the same time. It requires energy to improve educational conditions in families, help parents change their attitude towards their children and achieve a single influence of the school and the family upon the child.

As part of its effort to build the capacity of schools, the Network facilitates linkages among schools and between schools and other key institutional players that can support schools. The support for schools includes education departments at the district and state level, as well as universities and organizations, communities, and national school reform movements.

Indication of effective cooperation between school and family is unity in accomplishing purposes. Cooperation process requires uninterrupted planning of works, their drafting and evaluation. Schools have to undertake the leading role in organizing the cooperation by providing environment and culture, helping families to perform their role of partnership.

Present situation in Latvian education, deep economic crisis and the living reality shows that the school's support team often does not work in a body, because due to the economic crisis and structural modifications of the Latvian education system, there is a lack of funding for wages of qualified employees—organizers of interest-related education, out-of-class activities, psychologists, social pedagogues, etc. wherewith the school has no opportunities to perform cooperation organizer's functions, as well as there is lack of funding for organizing of extra-curricular activities and promotion of collaboration.

As the economic situation in the country is becoming worse, the social crisis has also deepened, because at the moment a great part of families where children attend boarding school faces some difficulties increasing social exclusion and problems related to it. As a result, the support is necessary for both—the pupils and their families. It creates circumstances and necessity for searching for new ways of collaboration.

Notes:

1. **Social exclusion (社会排斥):** Social exclusion is a concept used in many parts of the world to characterise contemporary forms of social disadvantage. Dr. Lynn Todman, director of the Institute on Social Exclusion at the Adler School of Professional Psychology, suggests that social exclusion refers to processes in which individuals and entire communities of people are systematically blocked from rights, opportunities and resources (e.g. housing, employment, healthcare, civic engagement, democratic participation and due process) that are normally available to members of society and which are key to social integration.

2. **Latvia (拉脱维亚):** Latvia, officially the Republic of Latvia, is a country in the Baltic region of Northern Europe. It is bordered to the north by Estonia (border length 343 km), to the south by Lithuania (588 km), to the east by the Russian Federation (276 km), and to the southeast by Belarus (141 km). Across the Baltic Sea to the west lies Sweden. The territory of Latvia covers 64,589 square kilometers and it has a temperate seasonal climate.

3. **NGO (non-governmental organization) (民间组织，非政府组织):** A non-governmental organization (NGO) is a legally constituted organization created by natural or legal persons that operates independently from any government. The term is usually used by governments to refer to entities that have no government status.

New Words and Expressions:

1. contemporary [kən'temprəri]　　　　n.　　同时代的人；同辈人
　　　　　　　　　　　　　　　　　　　　adj.　　当代的；属于同一时期的
2. comprehensive [ˌkɒmprɪ'hensɪv]　　adj.　　综合性的（接受各种资质的学生）；全部的；详尽的
　　　　　　　　　　　　　　　　　　　　n.　　综合中学
3. parental [pə'rentl]　　　　　　　　　　adj.　　父母亲的；父亲的；母亲的
4. supervision [ˌsjuːpə'vɪʒn]　　　　　　n.　　监督；管理
5. ethic ['eθɪk]　　　　　　　　　　　　　n.　　道德标准；行为准则；伦理学
6. admittedly [əd'mɪtɪdli]　　　　　　　adv.　　诚然；无可否认
7. boarding ['bɔːdɪŋ]　　　　　　　　　　n.　　（学生的）寄宿；木板
8. incorporation [ɪnˌkɔːpə'reɪʃn]　　　　n.　　合并；编入；法人组织
9. priority [praɪ'ɒrəti]　　　　　　　　　n.　　优先；优先权；优先考虑的事

10. triangular [traiˈæŋgjələ]	adj.	三角的；三角形的；三人间的；三方面的	
11. implementation [ˌimplimenˈteiʃn]	n.	实施；履行	
12. mediation [ˌmiːdiˈeiʃn]	n.	调解；斡旋；调停	
13. in accordance with		依照；依据	
14. intermediate [ˌintəˈmiːdiət]	adj.	中间的；中级的	
	n.	中级学生	
15. necessity [nəˈsesəti]	n.	需要；必然性；必需品	
16. intellectual [ˌintəˈlektʃuəl]	adj.	智力的；聪明的；理智的	
17. consummation [ˌkɒnsəˈmeiʃn]	n.	完成；使完美	
18. provision [prəˈviʒən]	n.	规定；条款；准备；供应品	
	v.	为……提供所需物品（尤指食物）	
19. beverage [ˈbevəridʒ]	n.	（除水以外的）饮料	
20. intoxicating [inˈtɒksikeitiŋ]	adj.	醉人的；令人陶醉的	
21. supervisory [ˌsjuːpəˈvaizəri]	adj.	监督的	
22. prescribe [prisˈkraib]	v.	规定；开药方	
23. inclination [ˌinkliˈneiʃn]	n.	倾向；趋势；斜度	
24. accumulate [əˈkjuːmjəleit]	v.	积累；（数量）逐渐增加	
25. reformatory [riˈfɔːmətri]	adj.	改革的；感化的	
	n.	少年犯管教所	
26. stereotype [ˈsteriətaip]	v.	对……形成模式化的看法	
	n.	刻板印象；老一套	
27. wherewith [weəˈwiθ]	adv.	用什么；以其	

Exercises:

I. Vocabulary.

Fill in the blanks with the most suitable words. Change the form when necessary.

contemporary	comprehensive	parental	supervision	ethic
admittedly	priority	necessity	intellectual	prescribe

1. To pursue this vision, my administration conducted a _____ review of America's development programs.

2. "We cannot continue with costs that are out of control because reform is a _____

that cannot wait," he said.

3. The International Monetary Fund should strengthen its _____ of capital flows between countries.

4. I'm not prepared to _____ a drug to my patients that I wouldn't take myself.

5. The artist Michelangelo often stirred up the opposition of the _____ artists of his day.

6. The _____ is protecting the police and the public from their attacks.

7. The difference in _____ attitudes between first-borns and subsequent children is large and significant.

8. Optimism is an _____ choice.

9. Negativity gets on people's nerves and calls your work _____ into question.

10. _____, Mr. Yoon is no ordinary banker but a former engineer who designed the satellite communications network used in the US space shuttle program.

II. Comprehension of the text.

Decide whether the following statements are true (T) or false (F) according to the passage.

1. The membership of pupils in the boarding school is the same as that of comprehensive schools in Latvia. ( )

2. Each person is an individual system, which functions in interaction by surrounding environment, creates correlated and interacted system and aggregate of structures. ( )

3. Families' involvement in school's activities can be one of the means by creating cooperative, tolerant community. ( )

4. As a result of communication between school and family, pupils' achievements, behavior, attitude towards studies and school are improving. ( )

5. As the economic situation in the country is becoming worse, the social crisis has also deepened. ( )

III. Try to fill in the space with the suitable words.

1. In order to facilitate the reduction of pupils' social exclusion in the boarding school and their incorporation into the social life, as well as to prevent critical situations, these pupils and their parents need special support, because the pupil's identity development begins in the _____, but improves at school.

2. In a child's upbringing, the family has an important role. However, the function of upbringing

is also performed by the school and it means that for child's development the _____ is important.

3. Pupils, their parents and teachers usually have different desires, aims, opinions, values; it sometimes leads to _____ between school and pupils' families.

4. The positive result of child's upbringing can be reached only in case school efforts are being supported by _____.

5. The support for schools includes education departments at _____ level, as well as universities and organizations, communities, and national school reform movements.

Text B School-Family Partnership in Hong Kong, China

导读： 如何处理家校关系、加强家校合作一直是各地学校面临的难题。本文从家庭教养方式、家校沟通、家庭学习三个方面展开，梳理了中国香港近三十年来家校关系和合作的变迁，以期为未来的家校合作和家校关系发展提供经验与教训。

There has been a keen interest in studying parent involvement as an aspect of school reform in the past three decades. There are apparently two types of studies. The first type examines the family learning environments and parental roles, and the second type investigates the school role and programs. Despite some criticism, it has been widely agreed that parent involvement in school education is important in bringing about positive learning outcomes of children. Some outcomes were pointed out such as increased academic achievement, improved behaviour, increased readiness to do homework, a better sense of well-being and higher educational aspirations.

In Hong Kong, China, the roles of teachers and parents in educating the children were seen as separate in the past. The Government has increasingly given attention and support to home–school co-operation since 1990s. In 1993, the Government set up the Home–school Co-operation Committee to co-ordinate and promote the sustained efforts of home–school co-operation in the region.

Between 1993–1994 and 2000–2001, the number of activity funding applications increased from 450 to 1466. In 1997, the Government adopted "school links with parents and community" as one of the performance indicators for schools. In 2000, the Government further allocated HK$50 million and set up the Steering Committee for Parent Education to promote parent education in the region.

Parenting

Parenting is referred to as "assisting families with parenting skills and setting family conditions that support children, and assisting schools in understanding parents". There is a growing literature showing the general usefulness of parenting programs. In 1980s, parent education in Hong Kong, China was mainly provided by the non-government organizations (NGOs) in social welfare sector. In early 1990s, some Christian schools, with the support of their sponsoring bodies or the church situated at the school campus, have been organizing systematic parent education programs for parents of primary 1 and secondary 1 students with encouraging results. These programs are run on a weekly basis for 10–20 weeks in respective semesters, targeting at marriage enhancement as well as parenting. The speakers include the principal and senior teacher of the school, together with the helping professionals and pastors from the church or the sponsoring body. The facilitators or group leaders are chosen from parent participants and teachers.

Parents generally prefer to join school-based rather than community-based parent education programs for various reasons. It raises the question about the role of school and how much social/cultural capital that the school can draw from its school-sponsoring body (SSB). In 1990s, with the financial support of the Government, an increased number of schools and kindergartens have taken initiatives in organizing school-based parent education programs in collaboration with the NGOs. Hong Kong schools have become more aware of their role in parent education and see educating parents as a means for school improvement.

With the support of the Parent Education Fund set up in 2000, parent education has been extended to the community sector, including house estates and business organizations. Business companies have been supported to conduct parent education for their employees in the work place. Systematic parent education programs have also been organized by organizations. Some new NGOs were established for this purpose.

In the past three decades, the Government has developed various types of parent education resources in collaboration with NGOs. In the website of Education Manpower Bureau (EMB), the school parents have access to a variety of parent education materials for self-learning and for training purposes. They are in the forms of video, book, Parent-Teacher Association (PTA) newsletter, pamphlet article, weekly post and parent exchange. Other forms of non-web-based parent education are delivered through the mass media, talks, small group programs, family education camps, etc.

A review of the contents of parent education shows that it mainly covers areas like parent–child communication/relationship, children learning, parent–child reading, handling emotion, stress management, marital relationship and understanding education system and education reform. While the school can address "parenting children" with the support of the NGOs, it is doubtful how far the school should render itself for the other two missions, i.e., "adult learning" and "empowerment".

Despite the increasing importance that the Government and local schools have given to parent education, it was found that the programs are not very well attended, especially in the non-elite schools. One of the reasons is that the emphasis of the Hong Kong parents on materialistic values, which had perpetuated parents to work long hours, leaving them little energy and time to participate in parent education. Research has shown that parent education programs were less successful with low socioeconomic status (SES) families, single parent families, and families with marriage discord. Its main consumer was said to be the middle-class parents. In Hong Kong, China, while the marriage institution is declining and the numbers of single-parent family, family of new arrivals and family with violence are increasing, it occurs that schools need to determine how to effectively implement parent education programs for the disadvantaged population. Perhaps the programs need to be designed in an inclusive way and to suit the interests of the low SES and aberrant forms of family, for example to integrate the program with parent–child activities, visits and interest groups. Besides making reference to their time available, parents may need to be provided some support of child care, traffic and financial assistance.

Communicating

Communicating appears to be the most common type of partnership between schools and home in Hong Kong, China. Communicating refers to the school-to-family and family-to-school communication about school programs and student progress.

In early 1990s, home–school contacts in local schools were rare and typically one-way. Like those practices in Japan and South Korea, they were "crisis triggered", i.e., when students had academic, behavioral and emotional problems. Parents' lack of time, teachers' high workload, and the mismatch of time for teachers to meet parents were seen by school personnel as major difficulties in enhancing family–school cooperation. About 57% of the class teachers of primary schools indicated that they had difficulties reaching at least some students' parents.

The frequency of teacher communication practices was in the descending order of student handbook, telephone call, teacher–parent conference, informal chatting with parents and verbal message through students. Unlike the Japanese practice, family visits were seldom used in Hong Kong, China. Similar to some Asia–Pacific regions and the United States, the school–family communication in Hong Kong regions tends to decrease as the child grows up. In communicating with parents, a primary school class teacher was found to spend about 0.69 h per week on average, compared to 0.91 h for kindergarten teachers and 0.55 h for secondary school teachers. Despite the increased importance given to home–school co-operation, the contacts between class teachers and parents have not increased much in late 1990s. This is no surprise, as teachers and parents have become more occupied owing to the education reform and the changing economy.

In late 1990s, as more PTAs are set up in schools and more financial support from Government is available, there has been an increased variety of home–school contacts. Teachers and parents have more chances to meet each other in PTA activities and school functions. A significant number of schools have established parent resource rooms via the support of the Quality Education Fund. This provision of a base for parents implies that parents could play a more active role in school–family communication. The change of means of school–family communication is also due to the use of new technologies, including e-mail, mobile phones and websites. Perhaps also owing to efforts of teacher training and parent education, sunshine calls—telephone calls informing parents of school success, have been used more often and teacher–parent conferences have become less threatening to parents. Overall, teacher–parent communication is becoming more informal and two-way. The teacher–parent contacts have become less focused on problems.

In recent years schools have made efforts to increase its transparency. On the one hand, this is a move in response to the Government policy of school-based management, which requires schools to release more information to the public, such as newsletter, school plan, school inspection report, teacher qualification, students' performance in public examination, and how schools perform against various benchmarks. On the other hand, owing to the dropping birth rate and the significant decrease of student population, schools wish to publicize themselves to attract students for survival purpose. This is best represented by the common use of banner outside school building in recent years to impress the public on its special features and achievements. In both cases, parents were seen by schools as customers. Despite that parents have increased in their understanding of school, it is sceptical that this kind of accountability-driven communication has any impact on students' learning. It occurs that schools need to provide parents with more information about classroom learning, about their own child, and how to help their children to enhance children's learning.

Learning at Home

Learning at home is defined as "involving families with their children learning at home including family work and curriculum-linked activities". Learning at home is perhaps one of the less explored areas of partnership in Hong Kong, China. The school parents generally care about the academic work of their children. For example, two-third of the parents of primary schools always reminded their children to do homework and checked their homework. Ninety-two percent of the primary school parents insisted that their children finished their homework even if they thought that the homework was excessive. While the majority parents recognize their important role in reinforcing their children's learning, there has been little co-operation between individual parents and teachers on children's learning in the past. The working relationship between parents and teachers was depicted as "division of labour" but not "co-operation".

In the past three decades, there has been some partnership in learning at home developed. In 1994, an NGO called Greenfield set up the Parent–child Reading Association to promote parent–child reading. The Government reinforced the activity in recent years. In 2001, a pamphlet called "parent–child reading with pleasure" was published for parents with children of 4–6 years, which includes skills of reading and how to find books for children. In the last 5 years, with the support of the Quality Education Fund, a few parent–child reading projects were launched by schools and kindergartens. Parents were provided with training of storytelling and reading with their children. In other subject areas, IT workshops were organized for parents and children to learn together in individual schools. English classes have also been organized for newly arrived parents. Despite the progress made by parents in English proficiency is slow, it was reported that such learning experience helps parents to be more considerate towards their children who feel difficult in learning the language. The developments of shared learning experience in reading, IT and English are consistent with the implementation of the concept of learning family in the community. This concept, which has been broadly promoted in Taiwan, China, stresses upon the self-development, shared learning, and communicating among family members. A series of television programs have been produced by the Radio Television Hong Kong on this theme.

Another aspect of learning at home is project work. Project making has become more popular in junior secondary schools and primary schools in recent years. This is in response to the curriculum reform and is probably facilitated by the removal of the Aptitude Test for secondary school entrance. In such subject like General Studies, owing to their integrated and relevant nature, parents are encouraged to involve in their children's learning.

An extreme type of learning at home is "home-schooling." Despite this practice has experienced a rapid growth in some regions, it is still not permitted under the current policy for children under 15 in Hong Kong, China to undertake home-schooling.

Though the concept of involving parents in children's learning has been experimented with in some schools, most teachers have not yet realized the importance of such joint venture and that they have a role in it. Further, the partnership attempt may be hampered by the increasingly long working hours of parents and the exceedingly high workload of teachers in the era of education reform. The low teacher perception of parent efficacy is also expected to discourage teachers from involving parents in their children's learning.

In conclusion, since 1990s, the educators and the Government have made efforts to enhance home–school co-operation and expect parents to play a greater role in the school education of their children. This is evidenced by the Government's support in funding home–school programs, and the increased variety and quantity of programs that schools have provided to parents. In the past three decades, the school and the family have enhanced their interactions, and there is an increase in shared experience among various stakeholders. Schools and parents have become more convinced than before that they have a shared responsibility rather than the separate responsibility in educating children.

Notes:

1. **Socioeconomic status (SES) (社会经济地位):** It is an economic and sociological combined measure of a person's work experience and of an individual's or family's economic and social position relative to others. It is based on income, education, and occupation. When analyzing a family's SES, factors such as household income, earners' education, and occupation are examined. This is distinct from assessing an individual's SES when their own attributes are assessed.

2. **Parent-Teacher Association (PTA) (家长—教师协会):** A formal organization composed of

parents, teachers and staff that is intended to facilitate parental participation in a school. PTAs are prevalent in countries such as the United States, the United Kingdom, and Japan, and can be found in other nations as well.

New Words and Expressions:

1. aspiration [ˌæspəˈreɪʃn]	n.		渴望；抱负；志向；[语音]发送气音
2. facilitator [fəˈsɪlɪteɪtər]	n.		诱导者；促进（或推动）……的事物
3. pastor [ˈpæstər]	n.		（尤指英国国教的）牧师
4. reinforce [ˌriːinˈfɔːs]	v.		加强；使更强烈；使更结实；加强力量（或装备）
5. estate [ɪˈsteɪt]	n.		（通常指农村的）大片私有土地；住宅区；工业区；[律]个人财产；遗产
6. pamphlet [ˈpæmflət]	n.		小册子；手册
7. render [ˈrendər]	v.		使成为，使处于某种状态；给予，提供；（以某种方式）表达，表现；粉刷，往（墙上）抹灰；将（脂肪）熬成油，熔化；提交，呈报
8. marital [ˈmærɪt(ə)l]	adj.		婚姻的；夫妻关系的
9. discord [ˈdɪskɔːrd]	n.		意见分歧，不和；[音]不协和和弦
10. aberrant [æˈberənt]	adj.		异常的；违反常规的
11. transparency [trænsˈpærənsi]	adj.		透明，透明性；易懂，清楚；幻灯片
12. benchmark [ˈbentʃmɑːrk]	n.		基准
13. publicize [ˈpʌblɪsaɪz]	v.		宣传；推广
14. hamper [ˈhæmpər]	v.		阻碍；妨碍

Exercises:

I. Vocabulary.

Match the word in Column A to the correct definition in Column B.

Column A	Column B
1. aspiration	A. to make a feeling, an idea, etc. stronger
2. reinforce	B. not usual or not socially acceptable
3. discord	C. to prevent sb. from easily doing or achieving sth.
4. aberrant	D. a strong desire to have or do sth.
5. hamper	E. disagreement; arguing

II. Comprehension of the Text.

Decide whether the following statements are true (T) or false (F) according to the passage.

1. There are two types of studies on parent involvement. The first type examines the family learning environments and parental roles, and the second type investigates the school role and programs. ( )
2. Parents generally prefer to join community-based rather than school-based parent education programs. ( )
3. Despite that parents have increased in their understanding of school, it is sceptical that accountability-driven communication has any impact on students' learning. ( )
4. Home-schooling has experienced a rapid growth in some regions, and it is permitted under the current policy for children under 15 in Hong Kong, China to undertake it. ( )
5. Since 1990s, the educators and the Government have made efforts to enhance home–school co-operation in Hong Kong, China. ( )

III. Try to fill in the space with the suitable words.

1. Parenting is referred to as "assisting families with _____ and setting family conditions that support children, and assisting schools in understanding parents".
2. Communicating refers to the school-to-family and family-to-school communication about _____.
3. Learning at home is defined as "involving families with their children learning at home including _____".
4. In recent years schools have made efforts to increase its transparency. On the one hand, this is a move in response to the Government policy of school-based management, which requires schools to _____ to the public.
5. Schools and parents have become more convinced than before that they have _____ rather than the separate responsibility in educating children.

Supplementary Reading: Parent-Teacher Communication : Tips for Creating a Strong Parent-Teacher Relationship

Parent-teacher communication is essential to your child's success in school. Below are some important suggestions to help you create a strong parent-teacher relationship that will serve your child's best interests. The hidden perk is that it will also make things easier and more enjoyable for you and your child's teacher.

Parents and teachers must agree to serve the same purpose which means serving the best interests of the child and the class as a whole. For instance, if a child's behavior disrupts the class, the parent and teacher can work together (from different fronts) to help the child express his needs in a way that serves him, the teacher and the class.

Parent-teacher communication should be focused on the best interests of the child.

Parents and teachers must make a commitment to know the child. Socrates said, "Know thyself." I say, "Know the child." A child is much more than the sum of his behavior, his test scores or the grades on his report card. A child is a living being who has needs, hopes, interests and dreams. In order for parents and teachers to bring up a well-rounded individual, they must take the time to see who the child is, to draw forth what is inside and treat him with respect.

Parents must give teachers insights into their child's character, strengths, interests, needs and areas of concern. After all, the parent should know the child better than the teacher. To achieve this end, a teacher may send home a questionnaire at the beginning of the year which is designed to elicit this information. The answers help a teacher get to know the child, while revealing how the parent views her child and whether she acknowledges his strengths and is aware of areas of concern. Although this information can be helpful, the teacher needs to create her own relationship with the child that is based on her observations and interactions with the child.

Parents should discuss answers on the questionnaire with their child and set goals together, particularly with regard to pursuing areas of interest and improving skills that will help their child succeed in school and in life.

Parent-teacher communication depends upon mutual disclosure. A parent must be willing to mention when there are struggles at home that might affect the child's ability to get along with others or dampen his enthusiasm for learning. Although parents may not choose to disclose personal details, it is important to alert the teacher when a child is experiencing undue stress at home. Teachers can use this information to provide empathy, support and guidance to a child who may not be getting all his needs met. Of course, disclosures should not be viewed as excuses for poor child behavior, but as a way for parents and teachers to work together for the benefit of the child.

Parent-teacher communication is dependent upon mutual disclosure.

In the same vein, teachers must keep parents informed about what is happening at school. For instance, if a child is humiliated in front of the class while giving a report or is often taunted by his peers, parents need to know, so they can give the child support at home and teach him coping strategies and comebacks. (Of course, parents should create an open dialogue with their children, so they already know what is going on.) Keeping the lines of communication open so that parents and teachers can have a bigger perspective about what is happening in the life of the child creates a supportive network that benefits everyone involved.

The parent-teacher relationship is dependent on establishing a regular means for communication. Many teachers are accessible at school (and some even give out their home numbers), via email or school websites. Find a way to communicate with your child's teacher on a regular basis. If your child is struggling at school, either with homework or relationships with peers, be proactive and work with the teacher to create a two-pronged approach which encourages the child to discover ways to solve the problem using the guidance at home and school.

Establish a regular means of parent-teacher communication.

Familiarize yourself with the school policies and rules specific to a teacher's class. Talk these over with your child, so he has a clear understanding of expectations for performance and guidelines for acceptable behavior. Although I have encountered a few school policies that were designed less to protect the children than to protect the school against a lawsuit, help your child understand the rules and how they contribute to a safe environment in which students can learn and interact positively with others. If your child understands how a rule benefits everyone, he is more likely to respect it.

Parent-teacher communication tip: send your child's teacher a note of appreciation for all she does.

Teachers often hear from parents only when there are complaints or conflicts. On occasion, send your child's teacher a note or email to tell how much you value his or her influence in your child's life. Since teacher's office can be flooded with unwanted gifts during the holidays and on Teachers' Day, I think a note is more appropriate. Although teachers are paid for what they do, the best among them contribute far more to the children than their job description requires. Acknowledge and inspire teachers with your recognition and support.

Parent-teacher communication is paramount to your child's success at school.

Create a strong parent-teacher relationship by volunteering. Although many parents have to work, ask your boss if you can have some flex time once per month to volunteer or chaperone on field trips. If your children are anything like mine, they'll be tickled when you help out at school. In addition to supporting the teacher, you'll get to observe the dynamics of the class and get to know the cast of characters.

Unit 8　School & Family

It takes a village to raise a child who is healthy, caring, and responsible. In school, this village starts with the network formed by parents, teachers and administrators who understand that their job is to work together to support and guide the development of each child.

Unit 9 Extra-curricular Activities

Text A Extra-curricular Activity and the Transition from Higher Education to Work

> **导读**：课外活动是对课内活动和课堂教学的有效补充和延伸，以培养学生的探究意识、提升其自主探究能力为主要目标，是丰富学生精神生活的重要组成部分，也是培养全面发展人才所不可缺少的。根据一份针对英国毕业生的大规模调查，课外活动对毕业生从学校走向工作岗位这一过程的转变有着重大的影响，从中可以总结出两种情况：一种是频繁的课外活动使毕业生在转变期的表现比平均水平好，另一种是比平均水平差。这种现象值得深入研究。

The reason why extra-curricular activity is important is that it has the potential to reinforce and market the outcomes of the education system. Any particular involvement in a certain type of extra-curricular activity may affect the transition process of graduates to labor market, for instance, by speeding up or slowing down access to employment. Therefore, students and graduates must understand the impact of extracurricular activities and appraise the role it may play in their strategies for transition from higher education to employment.

The results of a study suggest that extra-curricular experience has a twofold influence on the outcome of the transitional process. On the one hand, participating in extra-curricular activities will create advantages in professional status. As compared with graduates who were involved in extra-curricular activities, those who did not participate were almost three times more likely to begin their careers as office employees rather than as managers. On the other hand, graduates without extra-curricular experience had been unemployed for a significantly shorter period of time before getting their first jobs. These findings show that participation in extracurricular activities makes a difference. In the following part, this article will further demonstrate that within the group of the graduates who decided to be involved, the nature of the extra-curricular experience matters, including the 5 parts: job security, occupational status, access to large firms, wages, and unemployment.

Unit 9　Extra-curricular Activities

Job Security

Within the group of graduates with extra-curricular experience, 93.75% obtained an open-ended employment contract before the end of the transitional period. The most important factor favoring job security is participation in cultural activities.

Compared to other respondents, those who participated in cultural and spiritual activities were more likely to get open-ended contracts. Conversely, three characteristics were strongly linked with job insecurity: (1) the depth of the involvement. Graduates who engaged in an activity for a long period of time or at the leadership level had fewer chances of getting open-ended contracts. (2) participation in the social sector. It led to fixed-term rather than open-ended contracts. (3) participation with their families or as clients. The graduates who practiced with their families or as clients were less likely to be employed under open-ended contracts within the transitional period.

Occupational Status

Of the respondents with extra-curricular experience, 71.87% held management positions during the transition period. The opportunity to obtain a management position mainly depends on the depth and length of participation and the background of practice. Leadership experience will give you more opportunities to hold management positions. However, the whole extra-curricular experience should be kept in reasonable limits: the longer the experience, the fewer the chances of reaching managerial positions. Practice with family or with friends is also significantly correlated with becoming a manager. The types of activity play a role too.

Access to Large Firms

Of the respondents with extra-curricular experience, 51.56% were employed in large firms during the transitional period.

When starting a career in a large company, participation in sports activities is less efficient extracurricular activity. Compared with participating in sports activities, participating in student associations, social departments or cultural activities has a better chance to join a large company from the beginning of your first job. Graduates with an experience in citizenship activities also began their careers in larger firms. And at the end of the transitional period, graduates who had been participating in student associations or in citizenship activities were working in larger firms than those who participated in sports.

Wages

Wages are influenced by the context of practice and by the type of activity. Two observations may be made: (1) as compared with practice within associations, practice with family seems to be more closely linked with better wages at the end of the transitional period. (2) the graduates who participated in student associations or in the social sector had lower first-job wages than those who participated in sports.

Unemployment

50% of the surveyed graduates with extracurricular experience were unemployed at some time during the transition period. The risk and length of unemployment depend on the four extra-curricular factors. On one hand, two characteristics lower the risk and length of unemployment: (1) The graduates who had been leaders in their extra-curricular activities had a lower risk of experiencing unemployment before the first job. (2) as regards the length of unemployment, the graduates who had practiced their activity with their family were unemployed during a significantly shorter period of time than others both before and after the first job. On the other hand, other characteristics increase the risk and length of unemployment: (1) participation in cultural activities and long-term involvement increase the risk of experiencing unemployment before the first job. (2) practice with friend or as a client lengthens the spells of unemployment.

Extra-curricular Profiles

Therefore, it can be seen that among the graduates with extracurricular experience, the nature of extracurricular activities has an impact on entering the workplace. Although most extra-curricular factors have a twofold influence, three clear-cut profiles could finally be distinguished.

Profile 1 comprises "Leaders and Citizens". The graduates who engaged at the leadership level had better access to managerial positions and the lowest risk of unemployment before the first job. Those who participated in citizenship activities had access to large firms right from the first job on, and all along the transition period. Their spells in unemployment also seem to have been shorter.

Profile 2 represents the "Sportspersons". This profile corresponds to the most frequent extra-curricular behavior, which consists in practicing sports as simple participant within associations. Profile 2 appears to be generally associated with average transition outcomes.

Profile 3 comprises "Activists and Clients". This profile features long-term participation and practice as a client. It could be observed that the graduates who practiced for a long period or as clients had fewer chances of getting open-ended contracts or managerial positions, and were at more risk of unemployment.

These results highlight the strategic potential of extracurricular activities for students and graduates who want to make a better transition to the labor market. Of course, extracurricular activities are not only about career development, but also have a lot to do with personal development. But in so far as employers take account of the non-market involvement of job applicants, neither students nor education and guidance institutions should ignore the professional dimension of extra-curricular activity. Thus, for instance, it might be suggested to graduates to highlight in their resumes their "Profile 1" features. The recognition of the strategic potential of extracurricular experience should also encourage guidance institutions to investigate employers' extracurricular preferences at the local level, so as to help graduates formulate transition strategies from college to work, including effective extracurricular participation. Furthermore, reconsidering the position and recognition of extra-curricular activities within higher education and their links with regular curricula might be of advantage to educational institutions facing competition in the higher education market. However, these results also raise the question of the way employers derive turnover and resignation probabilities from the nature of any extra-curricular activity. Why should employers unanimously appreciate involvement in citizenship activities but have diverging perspectives regarding participation in the social sector or in cultural and spiritual activities? To better understand the reasons and preferences of employers about extracurricular experiences, further investigation is definitely needed.

New Words and Expressions:

1. involvement [ɪn'vɒlvmənt]   n.   参与；加入；插手；耗费时间；恋爱
2. transition [træn'zɪʃn]   n.   过渡；转变；变迁
3. appraise [ə'preɪz]   v.   估量；估价；（对某人的工作）作出评价
4. contract [kɒntrækt]   n.   合同；合约
5. respondent [rɪs'pɒndənt]   n.   （尤指）调查对象；[律]被告
6. twofold [tuːfəʊld]   adj.   两倍的；由两部分组成的
7. correspond [kɔːrə'spɑːnd]   v.   符合；相一致；类似于；通信
8. in so far as   在……范围；到……程度
9. derive sth. from sth.   （从……中）得到，获得；（从……中）提取

Exercises:

I. Vocabulary.

Fill in the blanks with the most suitable words or expressions. Change the form when necessary.

involvement	in so far	derive	correspond	appraise

1. Your account of events does not _____ with hers.
2. _____ as I can see, the representatives are all satisfied with the arrangement.
3. Her _____ in the fraud has left a serious blot on her character.
4. She _____ great pleasure form painting.
5. This prompted many employers to _____ their selection and recruitment policies.

II. Comprehension of the text.

Decide whether the following statements are true (T) or false (F) according to the passage.

1. Any particular involvement in a certain type of extra-curricular activity may speed up or slow down the process of graduates to labor market.
2. The graduates who participated in student associations or in the social sector had higher first-job wages than those who participated in sports.
3. Graduates who engaged in an activity for a long period of time or at the leadership level had more chances of getting open-ended contracts. (　)
4. The graduates who engaged at the leadership level had better access to managerial positions and the lowest risk of unemployment before the first job. (　)

III. Translate the following sentences into Chinese.

1. Therefore, it is essential that students and graduates understand the impact of extra-curricular activity and appraise the role it may play in their strategies for transition from higher education to employment.
2. As compared with graduates who were involved in extra-curricular activities, those who did not participate were almost three times more likely to begin their careers as office employees rather than as managers.
3. However, the whole extra-curricular experience should be kept in reasonable limits: the longer the experience, the fewer the chances of reaching managerial positions.
4. But in so far as employers take account of the non-market involvement of job applicants, neither students nor education and guidance institutions should ignore the professional dimension of extra-curricular activity.
5. Furthermore, reconsidering the position and recognition of extra-curricular activities within higher education and their links with regular curricula might be of advantage to educational institutions facing competition in the higher education market.

Text B Extra-curricular Physical Activity and Socioeconomic Status in Italian Adolescents

> **导读**：课外体育活动是指学生在体育课以外所从事的各种体育活动，既包括学生在校内外有目的、有计划、有组织地参加的体育活动，又包括学生自发参与的一切校内外体育活动。课外体育活动不仅使学生的课外文化生活得到丰富与发展，更能够帮助提高他们坚韧的素质和良好的集体精神，对促进学生身心健康和培养其终身体育意识有着极其重要的作用。体育活动和健康状况之间的关系已经被人们深入研究过。然而，关于体育活动和社会经济状况之间的关系的研究较少。本文以对意大利几个地区高中生展开问卷调查的形式，来探讨青少年的体育活动和他们家庭的社会经济地位之间的关系。调查结果对教育管理者及政治家们缩小贫富家庭之间的差距提供了思路。

The intricate relationship between physical activity and health has been extensively explored in numerous studies. Active lifestyles are commonly linked to improved health status and enhanced quality of life. However, a notable gap exists in research examining the intricate interplay between socioeconomic status (SES) and sports activities, particularly among adolescents. This article endeavors to fill this void by investigating the relationship between extra-curricular physical activity among adolescents and the SES of their families.

A comprehensive survey was conducted anonymously by distributing questionnaires to randomly selected junior high school students across various regions of Italy from 2002 to 2003. A robust sample of 2411 students willingly participated in the study. The questionnaire, previously validated through a pilot study, encompassed various domains:

—Scholastic physical activity

—Extra-curricular physical activity

—Physical activity attitudes

—Lifestyle habits

—Parents' physical activity, education and work activity

—Students' socio-demographic data

In the realm of adolescents' physical activity, the questionnaire scrutinized the existence of extra-curricular physical activity, the type of physical activity chosen, and the weekly time commitment to such activities. Attitudes towards physical activity were explored, probing its perceived utility in preventing obesity, fostering socialization, and contributing to character-building. Furthermore, lifestyle habits such as cigarette smoking, coffee consumption, and alcohol drinking were collected as dichotomous variables (yes/no).

Critical data pertaining to students' parents were also collected, including: (1) weekly physical activity levels categorized as intense, regular, scarce, or absent; (2) educational levels attained, classified as degree, senior high school, junior high school, or primary school; (3) work activities, employing a classification system from a prior study: managers/professionals, office workers/skilled workers, non-skilled workers, unemployed, and pensioners.

Unfortunately, information regarding family income was challenging to acquire directly from students. Consequently, SES was estimated by considering parents' educational levels and work activities. The families' socioeconomic levels were subsequently classified as very high, high, middle, middle-low, and low.

The survey's findings unveiled intriguing insights. The socioeconomic status of students' families was notably influenced by variables such as parents' education level and work activities. A compelling revelation was the substantial impact of the father's educational attainment on the physical activity levels of students. Compared to students with fathers having lower educational backgrounds, those whose fathers held degrees engaged in more frequent and intensive extra-curricular sports activities.

The educational level of mothers similarly played a significant role in shaping adolescents' sports activities. Offspring of mothers with degrees were more inclined to participate in extra-curricular physical activity and dedicated more than three hours per week to such activities compared to those with mothers of lower educational levels.

Moreover, extra-curricular physical activity demonstrated correlation with parents' work activities. Students with fathers in managerial or professional roles, as well as office workers or skilled workers, exhibited significantly higher levels of engagement in extra-curricular physical activity compared to those with fathers categorized as non-skilled workers, unemployed, or retired.

The impact of the mother's work activity on students' extra-curricular physical activity was also pronounced. Adolescents with mothers classified as non-skilled workers/housewives or unemployed were found to undertake less extra-curricular physical activity than their counterparts with mothers in managerial or professional roles, or office workers/skilled workers. A similar trend was observed in the weekly hours dedicated to extra-curricular physical activity.

Several studies have consistently demonstrated a connection between socioeconomic status and health outcomes. A study revealed that higher family income is associated with lower alcohol and cigarette consumption, as well as reduced sedentary behavior. Individuals with low family income and those in non-skilled or unemployed positions are less likely to engage in adequate physical activity.

The results of this study reaffirm the intricate relationship between family socioeconomic status, parents' educational levels, and the physical activity of adolescents. These findings align with international surveys conducted in the USA, South Africa, and Canada. The conclusion drawn is that socioeconomic status plays a pivotal role in determining extra-curricular physical activity among students. Specifically, higher educational levels and more remunerative work activities are directly linked to increased sports participation among adolescents.

In the USA, evidence suggests that among ethnic minorities and low-SES teenagers in high school populations, the prevalence of vigorous exercise often diminishes with age or when participation in school physical education becomes discretionary. In South Africa, children in the highest quartile of SES exhibit higher physical activity levels, reduced television viewing, and more lean tissue compared to their counterparts in the lower quartile. Similarly, in Canada, adolescents from low-income families are 30% more likely to be inactive than their counterparts from high-income families.

Families with high socioeconomic status view physical activity as crucial for preventing chronic and degenerative diseases, facilitating socialization, and ensuring the proper physical and psychological development of adolescents. In contrast, individuals with low socioeconomic status, characterized by low parental education and low-paid work activities, face barriers to their children's participation in extracurricular sports activities.

The study emphasizes the pervasive lack of knowledge regarding the benefits of physical activity, particularly among individuals with low socioeconomic and cultural levels. This knowledge gap serves as an additional hurdle inhibiting participation in physical activities.

Within the scope of this study, parents' physical activity emerges as a robust predictor of adolescents' extra-curricular physical activity, aligning with findings from previous studies. A recent review underscores the significance of parental factors in shaping the physical activities of children. For children, factors such as parents' overweight status, physical activity preferences, willingness to engage in activities, and access to projects/facilities are statistically linked to physical activities.

Among adolescents, variables consistently associated with physical activity include perceived activity competence, intentions, involvement in community-level sports, parental support, sibling physical activity, direct parental assistance, and opportunities for exercise. The study further elucidates that social, cultural, and economic deprivation exert a tangible influence on participation in extra-curricular physical activities.

The study advocates for schools to play a pivotal role in addressing these disparities. In Italy, where the majority of scholastic buildings and infrastructures belong to municipalities and provinces, these resources are currently underutilized. A potential solution to enhance adolescents' participation in physical activities could involve integrating extra-curricular activities within schools. For instance, initiatives targeting the prevention of childhood obesity could leverage interventions implemented in preschool institutions, schools, or after-school care services, utilizing these natural settings to influence diet and physical activity positively.

In conclusion, the study's outcomes provide valuable insights for school administrators aiming to bridge the gap between the most and least deprived children. By understanding the multifaceted interplay between socioeconomic factors, parents' education levels, and adolescents' physical activities, targeted interventions can be devised to promote inclusivity and equal opportunities for all students, irrespective of their socioeconomic background.

Words and Expressions:

1. remunerative [rɪ'mju:nərətɪv]	adj.	报酬丰厚的
2. variable ['veərɪəbl]	n.	变量；可变因素
3. validate ['vælɪˌdeɪt]	v.	证实；确证；使生效；使有法律效力；批准
4. degenerative [di'dʒenərətɪv]	adj.	（随着时间的推移）变性的，退化的
5. sedentary ['sednteri]	adj.	（人或动物）定居的，定栖的；（工作、活动等）需要久坐的；（人）惯于久坐不动的
6. anonymous [ə'nɒnɪməs]	n.	匿名的；没有特色的
7. quartile ['kwɔ:taɪl]	n.	[统计]四分位数；四分位值
8. chronic ['krɒnɪk]	adj.	（尤指疾病）长期的，慢性的；长期患病的；糟透的
9. deprived [di'praɪvd]	adj.	贫困的；贫穷的；穷苦的

Unit 9 Extra-curricular Activities

Exercises:

I. Vocabulary.

Fill in the blanks with the most suitable words. Change the form when necessary.

| anonymous | degenerative | validate | sedentary | chronic |

1. People in _____ jobs need to take exercise.
2. The ticket has to be stamped by the airline to _____ it. I'm sorry I can't help you more.
3. The money was donated by a local businessman who wishes to remain _____.
4. _____ changes of the myocardium occur in many diseases.
5. _____ fatigue is also one of the salient features of depression.

II. Comprehension of the text.

Decide whether the following statements are true (T) or false (F) according to the passage.

1. The relationship between socio-economic status and physical activity has been extensively investigated in numerous studies. ( )
2. Students with mothers graduated with a degree are more likely to practice extra-curricular physical activity and undertake physical activity for more than three hours per week. ( )
3. Higher family income is associated with higher alcohol and cigarette consumption and a higher level of sedentary behavior. ( )
4. Families with high SES consider physical activity useful both in preventing chronic and degenerative diseases and for socialization, essential for the correct physical and psychological development of adolescents. ( )

III. Translate the following sentences into Chinese.

1. Attitudes towards physical activity were explored, probing its perceived utility in preventing obesity, fostering socialization, and contributing to character-building.
2. The educational level of mothers similarly played a significant role in shaping adolescents' sports activities.
3. In conclusion, the study's outcomes provide valuable insights for school administrators aiming to bridge the gap between the most and least deprived children.
4. In contrast, individuals with low socioeconomic status, characterized by low parental education

and low-paid work activities, face barriers to their children's participation in extracurricular sports activities.
5. For instance, initiatives targeting the prevention of childhood obesity could leverage interventions implemented in preschool institutions, schools, or after-school care services, utilizing these natural settings to influence diet and physical activity positively.

Supplementary Reading: Discussion and Conclusion of Correspondence Hypothesis

According to the correspondence hypothesis: the persuasive effectiveness of democratic rather than authoritarian influence styles is affected by the initial position of the targets of influence. We need to stress that the targets' position was not expressed in terms of social status or competence, but as an attitudinal position, as expressed at the beginning of the interaction, as regards the very object of discussion: i.e., the presumed advantage of completing one's academic training with the attainment of the European Computer Driving License (ECDL).

More specifically, results confirm that the predicted interaction affects the direct agreement with the message statements. As expected, students who have previously elaborated an autonomous orientation toward the proposed extra-curricular activity are more likely to concur with the source when this latter adopts a flexible, rather than a coercive, influence style. The complementary effect is not verified, as we expected, but we do not find that the rest of the students, initially less inclined to attain the ECDL, are persuaded more by a coercive rather than by an obliging approach.

When we turn from the evaluative agreement with the source, to the behavioral intention to act as the source suggests, single planned contrast show a complementary influence pattern.

For instance, authoritarian style is proved to increase students' intention to attain the ECDL when this intention has not been previously elaborated by students themselves. Anyway, when students' position is already coherent with the subsequent source request, i.e., when they are already inclined to undergo the ECDL exams, a flexible approach does not enhance their commitment to the task more than an authoritarian one. For instance, this effect might be due to a measurement artifact, since these latter students might not have perceived a need to increase their agreement with the source, as their behavioral intentions are already adequate to meet the source's expectations.

A theoretical explanation of the difference between direct and indirect influence patterns could refer to the Conflict Elaboration Theory, from which the correspondence hypothesis is drawn. This postulates that direct or indirect persuasive outcomes are the consequence of the processes by which the target solves their conflict with the source. Briefly, the acceptance of the source's point of view at a direct level allows the targets to work out superficially, without any further message elaboration, its relational conflict with the source; in this case, a socio-cognitive paralysis prevents any indirect or deeper influence to appear, in particular for those subjects who are already close to the source's position. On the contrary, the rejection of an explicit direct agreement with the source leaves the conflict unsolved, thus compelling the target to elaborate the conflicts at a deeper level; in this case, an indirect change could appear, as a consequence of the more profound socio-cognitive activity.

What we observe here is that a democratic style produces the highest message acceptance, at a direct level, by targets who are attitudinally closer to the source, and that this explicit agreement is not followed by any indirect change in behavioral intentions. In a complementary way, an authoritarian style gives rise to a shift in behavioral intentions to attain the ECDL (indirect influence) only by students who were not previously orientated to act as the source demanded, despite (or thanks to) the fact that these targets show no significant direct agreement with the source's statements. What is new, and is predicted by the correspondence hypothesis, is that both authoritarian or democratic styles prove to be effective, the former at a direct and the latter at an indirect level of influence, only when they are appropriate to the specific relational context, i.e., when they are addressed to targets who actually expect that kind of communication style to be used. If this condition is not satisfied, any influence outcome is definitely prevented.

In this study, we proposed an application of the correspondence hypothesis to the negotiation of innovative conducts in educational settings, following recent interest in the ecological implications of social influence models to the innovation fields.

Here, evidence confirms that communication rhetoric may affect the outcome of these situated negotiation processes: for our purpose, different influence styles prove to facilitate or to prevent students' orientation toward innovative academic practices, depending on the students' positions in the influence interaction.

Interestingly, the correspondence hypothesis predicts that under some circumstances authoritarian styles may eventually induce a greater consensus by the targets, despite the social value normally devoted to respectful communication behaviors. In fact, it is stated that some interactions require coercive rhetoric, owing to the communication rules (i.e., the communication contract) that partners expect to be used in that context. This is the case of highly asymmetrical relationships between targets in a low social position and sources provided by much higher psychosocial resources. Under similar conditions, it is hypothesized that targets themselves expect sources to recur to assertive rhetoric, and perceive the use of a more obliging style as inconsistent, as regards the ruling communication contract.

It may easily be guessed that empirical findings supporting the correspondence hypothesis need to be discussed at different explanation levels. Contrary to Moscovici's first studies about influence style, whose predictions result from attributional processes, i.e., from an inter-individual level of explanation, the correspondence hypothesis refers to positional aspects (the psychological and/or social distance between the source and the target/s), and most of all to the level of representations (shared expectations about the context and the partner's role) and norms (the activation of specific communication contracts and rules).

Alternative explanations to our main findings may be found in the reactance theory, which states that an assertive persuasive effort, limiting the targets' perceived freedom of choice, motivates the targets themselves to restore their threatened autonomy. One of the easiest ways to restore one's threatened freedom is often to shift away from the source's request, although this shift may induce the devaluation of a response that was previously considered desirable. Maybe this is what happens, in our study, to students already orientated to the ECDL achievement: when the source addresses them with an authoritarian message, they evaluate the ECDL itself in less positive terms, despite the fact that they were previously inclined to attain the certificate.

Nevertheless, it seems difficult to explain, in terms of reactance, why students who define themselves as farther from the source position are eventually persuaded more by an authoritarian rather than by a respectful style. Despite the fact that these students may not perceive a threat to their freedom neither under a coercive nor under a flexible persuasive attempt, as the source is legitimated to suggest an extra-curricular task, it seems difficult to account for their authoritarian preference (at least at the level of declared behavioral intentions).

What the correspondence hypothesis suggests is that such "paradoxical" preference has to do with the significance that people attribute to relationships they are involved in, rather than to the influence style itself; both acceptance of the sources' proposal, and activation of counter-persuasive reactance or defensive motivations, arise from situated representations of the social context in which persuasive information is delivered.

It has to be underlined that the correspondence hypothesis predictions were not unequivocally and fully fulfilled, as it was in similar previous studies. Quiamzade points out that

Unit 9　Extra-curricular Activities

the correspondence hypothesis was studied in various socio-cultural contexts (France, Suisse, Romania, and Italy in our case), so that a reference to the different cultural backgrounds could help to explain the diverse extent to which students submit to authority, or alternatively valorize their decisional autonomy. In fact, a systematic cross-cultural approach to the influence style issues seems to be essential.

A possible limitation of this study lies in its purposely academic connotation: the setting and object of influence are explicitly related to academic tasks and to the relational conditions which enable university teachers and students to engage in educational innovations. A prominent academic connotation as this increases our findings' ecological validity, even though it reduces their extensive generalization to different relational and institutional contexts.

Research development should eventually explore the relational conditions under which authoritarian communication contracts are used in influence exchanges, possibly avoiding any reference to school and educational settings. Renewed interest in authoritarianism may provide useful links with the study of coercive influence styles in many contexts of daily life, such as in public communication campaigns (information, prevention, social marketing, and so on), influence attempts in different organizational settings (enterprises, institutions, etc.), and also informal face-to-face interactions outside of educational bounds.

Unit 10　Moral Education

Text A　Education as a Moral Enterprise

> **导读**：道德教育是指对受教育者有目的地施以道德影响的活动，内容包括提高道德觉悟和认识，陶冶道德情感，锻炼道德意志，树立道德信念，培养道德品质，养成道德习惯等。道德教育是素质教育的核心内容，良好的道德教育对于学生身心健康发展、良好思想品德的形成以及正确三观的树立具有重要影响。杜威在《民主主义与教育》一书中指出："教育上合乎需要的一切目的和价值，它们自身就是合乎道德的。"可以说，道德教育已然成为一个国家在意识形态上维持其存在和独立的根本。国家的发展和社会的进步都需要有相应的道德教育，道德教育的缺失将会对社会造成严重的负面效应。

It is uncontroversial to say that schooling is inevitably a moral enterprise. In fact, schools teach morality in many ways, both implicitly and explicitly.

Schools have a moral ethos embodied in rules, student government, styles of teaching, extracurricular emphases, among other factors. Schools convey to children what is expected of them, what is normal, what is right and wrong. It is often claimed that values are caught rather than taught; through ethos of the school, schools socialize children into patterns of moral behavior.

Textbooks and courses often address moral issues and take moral positions. Literature inevitably discusses moral issues, and writers take positions on those issues—as do publishers who decide which literature goes in the anthologies.

The overall shape of the curriculum is morally loaded by virtue of what it requires, what it makes available as electives, and what it ignores. For example, for more than a century, there has been a powerful movement to make schooling and the curriculum serve economic purposes. In contrast, religion and art are largely ignored. As a result, schooling encourages a rather more materialistic and less spiritual culture—a matter of moral significance.

Educators have devised a variety of approaches to values and morality embodied in self-esteem, community service, civic education, sex education, drug education, Holocaust education, multicultural education, values clarification, and character education programs—to name but a few. We might consider two of the most influential of these approaches briefly.

In the past few decades, values clarification programs have been widely used in public schools. In this approach, teachers help students "clarify" their values by having them reflect on moral dilemmas and think through the consequences of the options open to them, choosing that action that maximizes their deepest values. It is unreasonable for teachers to "impose" their own values on students; this will be an oppressive behavior that deprives students of their individuality and autonomy. Values are ultimately personal; indeed, the implicit message is that there is no right or wrong values. Needless to say, this is a highly controversial method, which is now widely rejected.

The character education movement of the last decade has been a response, in part, to the perceived relativism of values clarification.

Finally, we note that its shortcomings are obvious: although all universities offer courses in ethics, very few public schools have such courses. Unlike either values clarification or character education programs, the major purpose of ethics courses is usually to provide students with intellectual resources drawn from a variety of traditions and schools of thought that might orient them in the world and help them think through difficult moral problems. Although we all believe that morality is important, it is shocking that the school does not believe that moral curriculum is a worthwhile option.

We believe that socialization is to cultivate students into a tradition, a way of thinking and behavior without criticism. Education, by contrast, requires critical distance from tradition, exposure to alternatives, informed and reflective deliberation about how to think and live.

Not all, but much character education might better be called character training or socialization, for the point is not so much to teach virtue and values by way of critical reflection on contending points of view, but to structure the moral ethos of schooling to nurturing the development of those moral habits and virtues that we agree to be good and important, that are part of our moral consensus.

This is not a criticism of character education. Children must be morally trained. But there are limitations to character education as a general theory of moral education; it was not designed to address critical thinking about those "ideologically charged" debates that divide us. Character education does appeal, as *The Communist Manifesto* makes clear, to a heritage of stories, literature, art, and biography to inform and deepen students' understanding of, and appreciation for, moral virtue. Often such literature will reveal the moral ambiguities of life, and discussion of it will encourage critical reflection on what is right and wrong. But if the literature is chosen to nurture the development of the right virtues and values, it may not be well suited to nurture an appreciation of moral ambiguity or informed and critical thinking about contending values and ways of thinking and living.

In contrast, one of the presumed advantages of the value clarification movement is that it takes advantage of moral dilemmas and split issues. In addition, when students are asked to consider the consequences of their actions, it requires them to think critically. But the values clarification movement never required students to develop an educated understanding of moral frameworks of thought that could inform their thinking and provide them with critical distance on their personal desires and moral intuitions; it left them to their own inner resources.

Let us put it this way. Character education is an essential aspect of moral education, but a fully adequate theory of moral education must also address those morally divisive ("ideologically charged") issues that are sufficiently important so that students must be educated about them. Of course, one of these issues is the nature of morality itself; after all, moral education was not designed to address critical thinking about those "ideologically charged" debates that divide us. If students are to be morally educated—and educated about morality—they must have some understanding of the moral frameworks civilization provides for making sense of the moral dimension of life. After all, morality is not intellectually free-floating, a matter of arbitrary choices and merely personal values. Morality is bound up with our place in a community or tradition, our understanding of nature and human nature, our convictions about the afterlife, our experiences of the sacred, our assumptions about what the mind can know, and our understanding of what makes life meaningful. We make sense of what we ought to do, of what kind of a person we should be, in light of all of these aspects of life—at least if we are reflective.

For any society to exist, its members must share a number of moral virtues: honest, responsible, and respectful of one another's well-being. We agree about this. Public schools have a vital role to play in nurturing these consensus virtues and values, as the character education movement rightly emphasizes; indeed, a major purpose of schooling is to help develop good persons.

If we are to live together peacefully in a pluralist society, we must also nurture those civic virtues and values that are part of our constitutional tradition: we must acknowledge responsibility for protecting one another's rights; we must debate our differences in a civil manner; we must keep informed. A major purpose of schooling is to nurture good citizenship.

What shape moral education should take depends on the maturity of students. We might think of a K–12 continuum in which character education begins immediately with the socialization of children into those consensus values and virtues that sustain our communities. As children grow older and more mature they should gradually be initiated into a liberal education in which they are taught to think in informed and reflective ways about important, but controversial, moral issues.

Character education and liberal education cannot be isolated in single courses but should be integrated into the curriculum as a whole. We also believe, however, that the curriculum should include room for a moral capstone course that high school seniors might take, in which they learn about the most important moral frameworks of thought—secular and religious, historical and contemporary—and how such frameworks might shape their thinking about the most urgent moral controversies they face.

Note:

K-12 (pronounced "k twelve", "k through twelve", or "k to twelve", 基础教育的年龄段): It is a designation for the sum of primary and secondary education. It is used in the United States, Canada, Australia, and New Zealand where P–12 is also commonly used. The expression is a shortening of Kindergarten (K) for 4–6-year-olds through twelfth grade (12) for 16–19-year-olds, the first and last grades of free education in these countries.

New Words and Expressions:

1. ethos ['i:θɒs]		n.	（某团体或社会的）道德思想，道德观
2. initiate sb. into sth.			使了解；传授；教……开始尝试
3. holocaust ['hɒləkɔ:st]		n.	（尤指战争或火灾引起的）大灾难；（20世纪三四十年代纳粹对数百万犹太人的）大屠杀
4. orient ['ɔ:rient]		v.	使适应；朝向；确定方位
5. arbitrary ['ɑ:bitrəri]		adj.	任意的；武断的；专制的
6. pluralist ['plʊərəlist]		adj.	（社会）多元化的；多元论的
7. capstone ['kæpstəʊn]		n.	拱顶石；（使事业等臻于圆满的）顶点
8. secular ['sekjələ]		adj.	世俗的；非宗教的；教区的
9. continuum [kən'tinjuəm]		n.	（相邻两者相似但起首与末尾截然不同的）连续体
10. nurture ['nɜ:tʃə(r)]		v.	养育；培养；扶持；滋长

Exercises:

I. Vocabulary.

Fill in the blanks with the most suitable words. Change the form when necessary.

> nurture   ethos   secular   arbitrary   capstone

1. These plants should be _____ in the greenhouse.
2. I guess we're not used to your _____ standards, and you'd better change your plan.
3. Ours is a _____ society.
4. The day could not be far distant when naturalism would dominate the _____ of American literature.
5. He stood at the _____ of his political career.

II. Comprehension of the text.

Decide whether the following statements are true (T) of false (F) according to the passage.

1. It is often claimed that values are taught rather than caught; through their ethos, schools socialize children into patterns of moral behavior. (　)
2. For the past several decades values clarification programs have been widely used in private schools. (　)
3. The major purpose of schooling is to develop good persons and nurture good citizenship. (　)
4. Character education and liberal education should be integrated into the curriculum for a moral capstone course in which school seniors learn about the most important moral frameworks of thought. (　)
5. Moral education was supposed to address critical thinking about those "ideologically charged" debates that divide us and whose moral character we should hold onto. (　)

III. Discussion.

1. Do you think your school teaches morality in different ways, both implicitly and explicitly?
2. What are the other major purposes of schooling in your view? Try to name some.
3. One of the supposed virtues of the values clarification movement, by contrast, was its use of moral dilemmas and divisive issues. Do you think this method can be adopted in China? Can it really work?

Unit 10　Moral Education

Text B　Moral Education of Youth in the Information Age

> **导读**：道德教育应与时俱进，着眼于人的全面发展，最大限度地调动人的积极性，发挥人的潜能，满足学生实现自身价值的合理需求。传统的道德教育无外乎正确道德观和价值观的反复灌输，而在当下的网络信息时代，道德教育的环境与对象发生了很大的变化，使得学生的道德教育工作既存在机遇又充满挑战。因此，如何利用网络信息时代的优势实现有效的道德教育，已成为学生道德教育工作的重要课题。

In the dynamic landscape of the Information Age, the realm of moral education undergoes a profound transformation, evolving into a multifaceted project of increasing complexity. The amalgamation of diverse values within our community institutions and life situations, coupled with the relentless pace of change characteristic of this era, presents formidable challenges to the general and uniform applicability of moral principles that have long been regarded as unquestionable truths. As we navigate the uncharted waters of this technologically advanced age, the need for a robust and enduring intellectual and moral basis in moral education becomes increasingly pronounced.

The escalating anxiety among moral educators finds its roots in the current cultural diversity and social dynamics. Cultural diversity, once confined within national boundaries, has transcended its limits through the Internet's quiet yet effective dissemination of ideas, images, and cultural artifacts. This interconnectedness brings with it a unique set of challenges, particularly in the realm of online interactions. The "cyber world" presents an environment where physical contact is replaced by anonymity, distorting our perceptions of moral obligations. Immoral behaviors, shielded by online anonymity, have found refuge behind the scenes of the "cyber world".

Cultural diversity and social change, hallmarks of the Information Age, warrant a comprehensive reevaluation of the foundations of moral education. The diversity and constant flux provide an opportunity for reflection on the objectives of moral education and the exploration of ways to achieve these goals. In the face of contextual values and perpetual change, succumbing to moral relativism may seem tempting. However, maintaining a moral stance becomes imperative for the vitality of moral education, ensuring it remains a principled exercise that engages both hearts and minds. In schools, adherence to defensible moral principles becomes particularly crucial, determining whether moral education can fulfill its educational purposes.

Fortunately, schools often encapsulate these moral principles in their missions. While continuous interpretation and refinement support these efforts, there may be resistance to deviating from established norms. Moral educators must strive to identify and uphold simple and lasting principles that resonate with all stakeholders.

One such enduring principle is "respect for oneself and respect for others". This universal maxim, embraced by both Chinese and Western educators, goes beyond idealizing others to acknowledging one's own value, dignity, and rights. The principle of "do not do to others what you do not want done to yourself" serves as a simple yet powerful constraint on desires and actions. "Respect for others" provides a crucial reference for attitudes and conduct, especially towards unfamiliar individuals. By magnifying the worth of a person, it establishes a value perspective recognizing the needs and values of others.

Rooting moral education in respect for others enhances students' ability to navigate relationships. Socially, moral conduct manifests in interactions with others, making the "I-other" relationship the epistemological and axiological basis for effective moral education. Considering the dignity, rights, and welfare of others before acting minimizes harm to individuals and public interests. Additionally, fostering positive feelings like compassion and empathy contributes to holistic moral development.

The role of moral education is to guide students in handling relationships with others adeptly. Moral educators must lead students in appreciating others, understanding their needs, empathizing with their plight, and respecting their rights and values. This approach gradually steers students beyond self-interest towards a consideration of public interests. Participation in promoting common interests becomes natural.

Many educational scholars and practitioners believe that schools are the only place suitable for moral education. In fact, as a social institution responsible for educating children's basic literacy and social skills, schools seem to be the natural place for them to conduct moral education.

Unit 10 Moral Education

However, today's formal schooling has lagged behind the developmental needs of the Information Age. This is especially true in terms of its requirements for human development. The examination-oriented pedagogy that is so prevalent in Chinese schools leaves little time and intellectual space for students to develop their social awareness and skills. The only focus of school education today is the verifiable and measurable results of education. To a large extent, our school has neglected the exploration of the inherent value of education; and, if such values are needed for ornamental purposes, the schools pay lip service to them and to moral education which embodies and expresses them.

Actually, the most natural site for moral education is the family. The family is considered to be the unit that consists of the most significant "others" in the lives of children and youths—their parents. The parents' influence on the moral development of their children is strong and lifelong. It is in the family where parental devotion to the well-being of the child can be considered a given, and where adult-child ratio in the educative process is definitely more favorable than that of the school. In addition, the family environment provides an environment in which parents and children can easily share intimate thoughts and feelings without the social pressure and camouflage that often occur in a more formal social environment. Therefore, family provides a more relaxed environment for moral education, ensuring the exchange of ideas and the instillation of personal values. Among educators, the common concern about the family as a site of moral education is whether parents can truly understand the developmental needs of their children, and whether they are ready to engage their offspring in a knowledgeable and sensible way. In fact, children's needs for parental guidance and support vary at different stages of moral development. The manners of engagement, whether restrictive or supportive, actually reflects the psychological basis of moral education in the family.

Other websites that can serve as moral education platforms are educational activities carried out outside the framework of the formal school system. Rich in diversity, these activities afford a broad educational avenue through which the interests of growing children and adolescents can be served. Out-of-school programs which constitute what is known as "non-formal education" include a large variety of organized social and cultural activities that are organized by institutions and agencies such as youth palaces, cultural stations and museums, and by children and youth groups such as the Boys Scouts and Young Pioneers. Compared with classroom teaching, these off-campus courses are less rigid, but more informal, and equally effective in instilling ideal values and attitudes into students. However, their efficacy still needs to be explored by moral educators.

Another possible site for moral education is the neighborhood. Compared to the schools and non-formal education programs, the neighborhood is much less structured. We should not underestimate the potential of children to explore and understand the "I-others" relationship in the neighborhood. In addition to family and school, this neighborhood is where children and teenagers spend most of their time. Unlike some highly controlled sites such as homes and schools, neighborhoods are much less restrictive on behaviors. Thus, whether neighborhoods are sites of opportunities for exploration and discovery or danger zones for indulgence and debauchery depends very much on the kind of activities that children and youths participate in. This in turn depends on the kind of peers that they choose to keep. Research shows that young people in poor communities prefer adventure activities compared with those who are in densely populated urban areas. What's more, it is found that because adolescents "live in the middle of the transition between childhood and adulthood", they are excluded from many physical and social spaces in the community. For the purpose of moral education, the neighborhood can be a site where "respect for others" can be understood and practiced. If appropriate activities can be arranged, children and youths can practice neighborliness through participation in community service and observe first-hand the effects of their own contribution to the well-being of others.

The unique moral education website in the Information Age is "cyber world", which contains many networks and can promote instant communication between information technology users. For moral educators, the emergence of the "cyber world" can be unsettling because of all the "demons" that lurk within a world that we cannot see. If the influence of corruption cannot be easily identified from the behavior of young people, the protection for them will be minimal. This kind of disorientation caused by the existence of the "cyber world" poses the most serious challenge to moral education, regardless of its sites of application. This is because the "multi-directional network" is changing the structure of our economic and social institutions and our established system of beliefs and values would have to be able to maintain its validity and relevance in order to survive. The challenges to the established system will be multidimensional, intense and swift, because the global onslaught of axiological persuasions is projected through so many powerful lenses of informational technologies. Our world is now connected in global networks of the information and images that travel throughout the world instantly. Without a clear and strong epistemological and axiological anchor, moral education will drift in the sea of contentious ideas and values.

If we accept that moral education is an enterprise that should undergo constant review and revival, then the waves of new information that are generated from the multi-directional networks should not be feared. In fact, it is in this newly discovered wisdom that we can find the driving force for the continuous revival of moral education. New information and ideas challenge us to reflect on our own values, and if we can develop new notions of justice, rights, fairness, equity and harmony that we can uphold, and then we can confidently use them to guide our children and youths through the stages of their development with renewed interest and relevance. Moral educators should accept the current uncertainty and try to negotiate new concepts of morality and education, so that they will not fall behind the development needs of our children and adolescents. In fact, educators in other fields are trying to do so.

New Words and Expressions:

1. warrant ['wɒrənt]	v.	使有必要；使正当；使恰当
2. axiological [æksɪɒ'lɒdʒɪkl]	adj.	价值论的
3. epistemological [e‚pistiːmə'lɒdʒɪkəl]	adj.	认识论的
4. plight [plait]	n.	困境；苦境
5. lip service		空口的应酬话；口惠
6. debauchery [dɪ'bɔːtʃəri]	n.	道德败坏；淫荡；沉湎酒色（或毒品）
7. anchor ['æŋkə(r)]	n.	锚；精神支柱；顶梁柱
8. confined [kən'faɪnd]	adj.	狭窄而围起来的
9. dissemination [dɪ‚semɪ'neɪʃn]	n.	传播，散布（信息、知识等）

Exercises:

I. Read the following phrases and put them in the blank in this text appropriately. Each phrase should generalize the main idea of the next several paragraphs.

a. The "Cyber World" as a Site of Moral Education

b. Respect as a Guiding Principle for Moral Education

c. Sites of Moral Education

d. Whither Is Moral Education Drifting?

II. Comprehension of the text.

Decide whether the following statements are true (T) or false (F) according to the passage.

1. The conception of cultural diversity is limited in a nation, for people immigrate and emigrate

more often than before. (　)

2. Lofty ideas that defy common wisdom should not be fully acknowledged by students, so educators labor to uphold some simple principles. (　)

3. Home and neighborhood are two ideal places for children to cultivate and nurture moralities. (　)

4. Due to measures taken by the government and serious policies devoted to the protection of young minds when they are online, we totally don't have to worry about "demons", which lurk in a virtual world. (　)

5. We need to develop new notions of justice, rights, fairness, equity and harmony that we can uphold, and then we can confidently use them to guide our children and youths through the stages of their development with renewed interest and relevance, because they need various help during different steps. (　)

III. Discussion.

1. What are some of the methods you can think of that your parents help you to cultivate moralities in different developmental steps? Do you think they are helpful?
2. Why do you think it is very important for us to focus on "cyber world" morality?
3. In what other ways do you suggest we can take full advantage of the Internet to serve the purpose of morality?

Supplementary Reading: The Role of Moral Education in Students' Value Development

Exploring the terrain of moral education raises fundamental questions: What defines moral education, and why is it indispensable for students? Furthermore, what prompts the integration of moral education into the academic curriculum? These are recurrent queries that underscore the importance of this educational facet. Moral education serves as a vehicle for teachers to steer students toward assimilating values and virtues crucial for evolving into exemplary human beings over the long haul. These virtues not only play a pivotal role in individual development but also cast an enduring influence on societal well-being. Recognizing the paramount significance of moral education, researchers delve into its role in shaping students' values and character.

A notable initiative in this realm emanates from the University of Salamanca, where a research team conducted an experimental study, leveraging Information and Communication Technologies (ICTs) to deliver moral education. This novel approach aimed to not only impart values but also assess its tangible impact through a meticulously designed quasi-experimental methodology. This methodology involved non-equivalent groups, pre- and post-test assessments, and variable manipulation and control to enhance experimental precision. The program, known as VES (Values in Situation, "Valores En Situación"), spanned nine weeks, each dedicated to instilling a different value. The methodology involved acknowledging positive actions in secondary school life through blog posts, triggering reflections and encouraging participation through blog comments.

The team worked with a cohort of 50 students, with 12 selected for the experimental group based on their performance in program activities. Post-test evaluations revealed that actively engaged participants demonstrated a greater capacity to recognize their own success. This outcome underscored the positive influence of the program on fostering social-personal values, affirming the potential of ICTs in moral education.

Parallel research conducted in the United States echoes the efficacy of employing ICTs for teaching conflict resolution, emphasizing its relevance as a viable alternative. Post-program assessments demonstrated qualitative and quantitative improvements in adolescents' abilities to solve and prevent conflicts. Other studies, such as the one conducted by Ryan, Sweeder, and Bednar (1998), underscore the effectiveness of educational technology in developing values like solidarity, responsibility, equity, and self-control. Goldworthy, Schwartz, Barab et al's (2007) research further supports this notion, indicating that ICTs can be instrumental in transmitting knowledge that leads to conflict resolution. Collectively, these studies highlight how these mediums foster cognitive development and impactful learning experiences, influencing personality and sociability.

The overarching objective of these research endeavors is to substantiate that implementing a moral education program through new technologies has the potential to enhance the socio-personal values of adolescents. The values that govern coexistence, solidarity, honesty, equality, responsibility, freedom, love, respect for life, difference, human rights, cooperation, and peace and justice must not merely be theoretical concepts but actively promoted in the daily life of educational institutions and within curricular areas.

Recognizing the urgency of instilling moral and attitudinal education, a collaborative effort is deemed essential. The values underpinning this educational endeavor are not confined to the classroom; they extend to coexistence and societal harmony. Therefore, a concerted effort is warranted to cultivate individuals committed to upholding these core values, transcending the boundaries of traditional education.

In conclusion, the convergence of research initiatives from institutions like the University of Salamanca and analogous studies in the United States underscores the global acknowledgment of the transformative potential of moral education through ICTs. As we navigate an increasingly interconnected world, the importance of fostering values that extend beyond personal gain becomes ever more apparent. The dynamic interplay of technological advancements and moral education holds promise in sculpting a generation cognizant of their social responsibilities and committed to a harmonious coexistence. The future of education lies not just in the acquisition of knowledge but in the cultivation of ethical frameworks that endure the test of time.

Unit 11   Education & People's Overall Development

Text A   Importance of Early Childhood Education

> **导读**：人的全面发展首先是指人的"完整发展"，即人在个性、道德、能力等方面的和谐、自由、全面的发展和完善，最根本是指人的劳动能力的全面发展，即人的智力和体力的充分、统一的发展；同时，也包括人的才能、志趣和道德品质的多方面发展，即德、智、体、美等方面的完整发展。人的全面发展是全面发展教育的目的，全面发展教育又是实现人的全面发展的教育保障和教育内涵。而幼儿时期是幼儿大脑发育最快、智力开发的最佳时期；幼儿教育作为教育的起始阶段，对于儿童的成长及日后的全面发展至关重要。

Why do child care professionals emphasize early childhood education? What is the impact of early childhood education in a child's life? It plays a significant role in the brain and the overall development of a child. It's not just a series of activities to fill a child's time. The conditioning that a child receives from 0 to 5 years of age leaves a lasting imprint in their adulthood.

A brain begins to take shape when it's as small as a fetus. And babies enter this world with a keenness to explore all that it has to offer. A child begins to establish brain connections right from their birth. The working of the brain depends on the genes and the environment a child grows in. In these tender years a child's brain molds easily, hence brain development is the fastest in this age. A baby's brain has over 100 billion nerve cells that begin to acquire knowledge by establishing connections either with each other or with neurons. These connections are more easily formulated in childhood and babyhood rather than in any other stage of life. It is these spurts of development that lay the foundation for characteristic attributes like resilience, problem-solving, motivation, and communication.

Young children need safety, love, conversation and a stimulating environment to develop and keep important synapses in the brain. During the first 3 years of life, children experience the world in a more complete way than children of any other age. The brain takes in the external world through its system of sight, hearing, smell, touch and taste. This means that infant social, emotional, cognitive, physical and language development are stimulated during multistory experiences. Infants and toddlers need the opportunity to participate in a world filled with dominating sights, sounds and people.

Before children are able to talk, emotional expressions are the language of relationships. Research shows that infants' positive and negative emotions, and caregivers' sensitive responsiveness to them, can aid early brain development. For example, shared positive emotion between a caregiver and an infant, such as laughter and smiling, engages brain activity in good ways and promotes feelings of security. Also, when interactions are accompanied by lots of emotion, they are more readily remembered and recalled.

The primary giver, when providing consistent and predictable nurturing to the infant, creates what is known as a "secure" attachment. This is accomplished in that rhythmic dance between infant and caregiver—the loving cuddles, hugs, smiles and noises that pass between caregiver and infant. Should this dance be out of step, an unpredictable, highly inconsistent or chaotic "insecure" attachment is formed. When attachments are secure, the infant learns that it is lovable and loved, that adults will provide nurture and care, and that the world is a safe place. When attachment is insecure, the infant learns the opposite. As the child grows from a base of secure attachment, he or she becomes ready to love and be a friend. A secure attachment creates the capacity to tort and maintain healthy emotional bonds with another.

Education begins at home and continues in the preschool. Every pre-designed activity of the preschool curriculum leads to development in different domains like physical, social, emotional cognitive, and language. To begin with, playtime is not just another activity to keep a child entertained but it is an alternate approach to learning. Every game and every activity have a nugget of wisdom or a lesson accompanying it. And preschools have a multitude of play options to feed a child's mind.

Early childhood education is an interactive experience encouraging peer interactions and conversations between the teacher and child. Encouraging their questions, providing descriptions, and modulating your tone all contribute significantly to language development. Additionally, physical activities play a crucial role in children's overall development. When children physically exert themselves, the resulting increase in heart rate acts as a mood lifter, generating chemicals that enhance the mind's receptiveness to grasping new concepts. Activities like art and craft further encourage cognitive thinking.

Another impact of early childhood education is the life lessons it offers a child. A structured routine instills in children security, self-control, and focus. The daily activities and interactions create a sense of awareness about the emotions of those around them. The carefully chalked out

Unit 11 Education & People's Overall Development

curriculum nurtures in children a love for learning. The environment is conducive to encourage a child to take on new challenges without giving up.

Modern brain and child development research supports the need to provide nurturing, educationally stimulating, safe environments and experiences in the early years. A strong and nurturing relationship between children and adults is the most basic ingredient for growing up healthy. Supporting the whole child—physically, socially, and emotionally—provides a baseline for positive experiences from which the child can learn, grow, and thrive. These experiences shape a child's life and create a strong, foundational web of support that positively contributes to their future.

New Words and Expressions:

1. conditioning [kən'dɪʃənɪŋ]	n.	训练；熏陶；条件作用
2. fetus ['fi:təs]	n.	胎儿；胎
3. keenness ['ki:nnəs]	n.	渴望；热切；兴趣；敏锐
4. neuron ['njʊərɒn]	n.	[生]神经元
5. attribute [ə'trɪbju:t]	v.	把……归因于；认为…是由于；认为……是所为（或说、写、作）
	n.	属性；特征
6. synapse ['saɪnæps]	n.	（神经元的）突触
7. caregiver ['keəɡɪvə(r)]	n.	照料者；护理者
8. attachment [ə'tætʃmənt]	n.	依恋，爱慕；信念，信仰；（机器的）附件，附属物；连接，连接物；附件
9. nugget ['nʌɡɪt]	n.	天然贵重金属块；（某些食品的）小圆块；有价值的小东西；有用的想法（或事实）
10. modulate ['mɒdjuleɪt]	v.	调节（嗓音的大小、强弱等）；[音]变调；控制

Exercises:

I. Vocabulary.

Fill in the blanks with the most suitable words. Change the form when necessary.

keenness	attribute	caregiver	fetus	nugget
synapse	conditioning	neuron	attachment	modulate

1. Is personality the result of _____ from parents and society, or are we born with it?
2. Her _____ for sport soon yielded place to an interest in music.
3. Information is transferred along each _____ by means of an electrical impulse.
4. Pregnant women who are heavy drinkers risk damaging the unborn _____.
5. Patience is one of the most important keen _____ in a teacher.
6. Our brain cells communicate by sending signals to one another across a small gap called a _____.
7. While we all have this need for _____, the way we show it differs.
8. My mother-in-law is the 24-hour _____ for her sick husband.
9. Here is a small _____ of butter.
10. These chemicals _____ the effect of potassium.

II. Translate the following phrases into English.

幼儿教育 _____
教育环境 _____
形成 _____
特性 _____
情绪表达 _____
安全感 _____
安全型依恋 _____
学前教育课程 _____
同伴交往 _____
认知思维 _____

III. Comprehension of the text.

Decide whether the following statements are true (T) or false (F) according to the passage.

1. A child begins to establish brain connections before his or her birth. ( )
2. A child's brain molds easily in tender years. Hence, brain development is the fastest in this age. ( )
3. A baby's brain has over 100 billion nerve cells that acquire knowledge by establishing connections either with each other or with neurons. ( )
4. The primary giver, when providing inconsistent and unpredictable nurturing to the infant, creates what is known as a "secure" attachment. This is accomplished in that rhythmic dance

between infant and caregiver—the loving cuddles, hugs, smiles and noises that pass between caregiver and infant. ( )

5. Every activity of the preschool curriculum leads to development in different domains like physical, social, emotional cognitive, and language. ( )
6. Encouraging children's questions, offering descriptions contribute to their language development. ( )
7. Providing inconsistent and unpredictable nurturing is the most basic ingredient for growing up healthy. ( )
8. Playtime is not just another activity to keep a child entertained but it is an alternate approach to learning. Every game and every activity have a nugget of wisdom or a lesson accompanying it. ( )
9. During the first 5 years of life, children experience the world in a more complete way than children of any other age. ( )
10. Physical activities lead to the generation of a chemical which makes the mind all the more receptive to grasping new concepts. ( )

Text B Social Skills Development in Primary Education

> **导读**：初等教育即小学教育，或称基础教育，是使受教育者打下文化知识基础和作好初步生活准备的教育，是教育系统中最基础的部分，被联合国教科文组织称为第一级教育。在我国，初等教育是当前九年义务教育的第一阶段，是对全体公民实施的基本的普通文化知识的教育，是培养公民基本素质的教育；教育对象为6—12岁的儿童，教育场所一般为全日制普通小学，具有全民性、义务性、全面性等特点。初等教育是整个教育事业的基础，对提高国家民族文化水平极为重要，因此各国在其经济文化发展的一定历史阶段都把它定为实施义务教育或普及教育的重要阶段。

The aim of the present research is to survey the views of teachers regarding social skills development in primary school students. The research was carried out using the qualitative research technique. A questionnaire prepared by the researcher was used to collect data. The results show that there are four main factors that play an important role in the development of primary school students' social skills: family, school, environment and the personal characteristics of individual students.

Family

The effect of family, which starts in the prenatal period and continues its influence until the end of an individual's life, is of great importance in a child's development. That a child is supported in the primary school period by his parents and spends sufficient and quality time with them is one of the important factors that substantially determine how a person will adapt during the lifelong socialization process.

Unconditional love exhibited by parents, regular care and support develop a child's basic sense of confidence. Positive communication between children and their parents in the primary school period is reflected in the children's social behaviors. Positive social relations and model parental behaviors may set patterns that children can repeat. As stated by the teachers, the children who are accepted by their families as they are can express themselves easier in social environments and develop their social skills. Families should not only focus on the academic successes of their children but also support their social and emotional development. Parents should cooperate with schools and teachers in this area.

School

Primary schools are of great importance in a child's socialization process. Elementary school years constitute the most important period in which children develop attitudes and behaviors. In this period, children learn how to live with others in the same environment, how to share, how to communicate and how to express themselves. In the present research, teacher's views support the idea that primary school has an important role in the development of young children.

Attaching importance to social activities at schools is one of the sub-themes that educators focus on most. Teachers emphasized that one of the most important aims of primary schools is to prepare children for a healthy social life.

It is also important that activities directed at enabling students to gain social skills are shown in primary school curricula. Educators emphasize that lessons should be prepared in a way that enables an individual to develop his social skills, to realize himself and to actively participate in social activities. Again, the results of the present study show that the preference of student-centered teaching methods and techniques by the teachers is very important for developing children's social skills.

Primary school is the place where students' tendency to see their teachers role models reaches its highest level. It is known that at these ages the attitudes and behaviors of teachers significantly influence the social development of the child. Teachers also understand that their positive attitudes and behavior in school and the classroom environment will further encourage students to take part in social activities.

The democratic attitudes of teachers in classroom management and positive communication with students can enable students to have more self-confidence and to take part in social activities more voluntarily. The relationship between teacher and student in the classroom forms the basis of learning and education. Teachers who are conscious of their profession try to furnish their students with the necessary knowledge and skills on one hand; they can be a good model for children with their exemplary characters on the other hand.

It is understood from teacher's views that the exams for passing from primary school to secondary school cause stress on primary school students and therefore students cannot spare time for and be directed to social activities. As the educators, even if it is obligatory to test students for admission to secondary education, the necessary precautions should be taken in order to prevent this situation from negatively affecting the social development of students by way of causing pressure and stress on them.

Environment

According to the teachers, the environment is one of the factors which play an important role in the development of elementary school children's social skills. The environment may be much more dominant than the family and the school in some cases; for example, children may acquire a great deal of information and skills from their close groups of friends. According to Hartup (1996), a child needs to make friends and participate in groups of friends in order to be able to adapt to his social environment. Friendship provides children with the necessary environments and conditions for learning and development, supports children in emotional and cognitive terms and helps them to learn how to take responsibility, how to protect their own rights and how to respect the rights and responsibilities of others. Therefore, children adopt the methods and the rules of social life. Children can develop the skills of working together in a group, struggling for the common goal and group success, obeying rules, leadership and communication thanks to the social and sporting activities in which they participate together with their peers.

One of the most important environmental factors for the social development of primary school students is children's playing games with their peers. Children recognize their own bodies, realize their abilities, get in the habit of taking responsibility and study regularly by way of learning how to share with their peers and help each other.

According to the teachers who participated in this project, some problems may occur in the social development of the children who spend a long time in front of television, computers and the Internet rather than spending time together with their peer groups in their close environments. Moreover, studies show that the children who watch television for a long time, addict to computer games and surf on the Internet for a long time cut off communication with their close environments, exhibit anti-social behaviors and become passive individuals. However, it should be known that the use of these technologies in a controlled manner and relevantly would contribute to the child's social development, knowledge and skill development. For example, some studies emphasize that using a computer plays a quite significant role in the cooperation of primary school students, problem-solving, accessing information and the development of primary school students.

Children's Personal Characteristics

Teachers declared that children's personal characteristics play an important role in the development of their social skills as well as other factors in primary school. The characteristics such as developing language and communication skills in children, building personal characteristics such as self-confidence, self-discipline and expression of personal abilities are actually among the most important aims of primary education.

Language and expression skills play a key role in the development of the social skills such as starting relations between individuals, expressing oneself, giving information and joining a group. The children who have communication skills can easily join groups of friends and improve their self-confidence. The most important aim of social skill education is to enable individuals to be aware of their feelings and thoughts, express their feelings, deal with undesired behaviors and develop behaviors which allow for positive social interaction.

Consequently, based on teacher's views, the present research shows that family, school, environment and children's personal characteristics play an important role in the development of the social skills of primary school students.

Notes:

1. **Social skills (社交技能):** Social skills are any skills facilitating interaction and communication with others. Social rules and relations are created, communicated, and changed in verbal and nonverbal ways. The process of learning such skills is called socialization. The rationale for this type of approach to treatment is that people meet a variety of social problems and can reduce the stress and punishment from the encounter as well as increase their reinforcement by having the correct skills.

Unit 11 Education & People's Overall Development

2. **Primary education (初等教育)**: Primary education is the first stage of compulsory education. It is preceded by pre-school or nursery education and is followed by secondary education. In most countries, it is compulsory for children to receive primary education, though in many jurisdictions it is permissible for parents to provide it. The transition to secondary school or high school is somewhat arbitrary, but it generally occurs at about eleven or twelve years of age. Some educational systems have separate middle schools with the transition to the final stage of education taking place at around the age of fourteen. The major goals of primary education are achieving basic literacy and numeracy amongst all pupils, as well as establishing foundations in science, mathematics, geography, history and other social sciences. The relative priority of various areas, and the methods used to teach them, are an area of considerable political debate.

3. **Secondary education (中等教育)**: Secondary education is the stage of education following primary school. Secondary education is generally the final stage of compulsory education. However, secondary education in some countries includes a period of compulsory and a period of non-compulsory education. The next stage of education is usually college or university. Secondary education is characterized by transition from the typically compulsory, comprehensive primary education for minors to the optional, selective tertiary, "post-secondary", or "higher" education for adults.

New Words and Expressions:

1. prenatal [ˌpriːˈneitl]	adj.	产前的	
2. socialization [ˌsəʊʃəlaiˈzeiʃn]	n.	社会化；适应社会的过程	
3. elementary [ˌeliˈmentri]	adj.	基本的；初级的	
4. preference [ˈprefrəns]	n.	偏爱；最喜爱的东西	
5. exemplary [igˈzempləri]	adj.	典范的；惩戒性的；可仿效的	
6. obligatory [əˈbligətri]	adj.	义务的；必须的；随大溜的	
7. precaution [priˈkɔːʃn]	n.	预防；预防措施	
8. peer [piə]	v.	凝视	
	n.	身份（或地位）相同的人	
9. addict [ˈædikt]	n.	瘾君子；对……入迷的人	
	v.	使上瘾；使沉溺	

10. access ['ækses]　　　　　　v.　　使用；进入；存取（计算机文件）
　　　　　　　　　　　　　　　n.　　（使用或见到的）机会，权利；入径；通路
11. interaction [ˌɪntərˈækʃn]　　n.　　相互作用；交流

Exercises:

I. Vocabulary.

Match the word in Column A to the correct definition in Column B.

Column A	Column B
1. elementary	A. the people who are the same age as you or who have the same status as you
2. preference	B. the mental process involved in knowing, learning, and understanding things
3. obligatory	C. occurring, existing, or performed before birth
4. cognitive	D. very simple and basic
5. precaution	E. a way of entering or reaching a place
6. peer	F. binding in law or conscience
7. access	G. mutual or reciprocal action or influence
8. interaction	H. a greater interest in or desire for sb. or sth. than else
9. addict	I. an action that is intended to prevent something dangerous or unpleasant from happening
10. prenatal	J. to cause to become physiologically or psychologically dependent on a habit-forming substance

II. Translate the following phrases into English.

社交技能　　　　　　　　＿＿＿＿＿＿＿＿＿＿＿＿＿＿＿＿＿＿＿＿＿
执行，完成（任务）　　　＿＿＿＿＿＿＿＿＿＿＿＿＿＿＿＿＿＿＿＿＿
无条件的爱　　　　　　　＿＿＿＿＿＿＿＿＿＿＿＿＿＿＿＿＿＿＿＿＿
以学生为中心的教学模式　＿＿＿＿＿＿＿＿＿＿＿＿＿＿＿＿＿＿＿＿＿
觉察，意识到　　　　　　＿＿＿＿＿＿＿＿＿＿＿＿＿＿＿＿＿＿＿＿＿
中等教育　　　　　　　　＿＿＿＿＿＿＿＿＿＿＿＿＿＿＿＿＿＿＿＿＿
为……努力　　　　　　　＿＿＿＿＿＿＿＿＿＿＿＿＿＿＿＿＿＿＿＿＿
遵守规则　　　　　　　　＿＿＿＿＿＿＿＿＿＿＿＿＿＿＿＿＿＿＿＿＿
自律，自我约束　　　　　＿＿＿＿＿＿＿＿＿＿＿＿＿＿＿＿＿＿＿＿＿

Unit 11 Education & People's Overall Development

III. Comprehension of the text.

Decide whether the following statements are true (T) or false (F) according to the passage.

1. There are four main factors that play an important role in the development of primary school students' social skills: family, school, environment and the personal characteristics of individual students. ( )
2. The effect of family starts in the postnatal period and continues its influence until the end of an individual's life and it is of great importance in a child's development. ( )
3. Families play an important role in children's development of social skills. Parents should not only focus on the academic successes of their children but also support their social and emotional development. ( )
4. Elementary school years constitute the most important period in which children develop attitudes and behaviors and in which children learn how to live with others in the same environment, how to share, how to communicate and how to express themselves. ( )
5. Preparing children for a healthy social life is the most important aims of primary schools, according to the teachers. ( )
6. Teachers who are conscious of their profession try to furnish their students with the necessary knowledge and skills on one hand; they may not be a good model for children with their exemplary characters on the other hand. ( )
7. According to the teachers, the stress on primary school students caused by the exams for passing from primary school to secondary school make those children have no spare time for social activities. ( )
8. The environment is one of the factors which play an important role in the development of elementary school children's social skills, which may be much more dominant than the family and the school in some cases. ( )
9. Although some problems may occur in the social development of the children who spend a long time in front of television, computer and the Internet rather than spending time together with their peer groups in their close environment, it should be known that the use of these technologies in a controlled manner and relevantly would contribute to the child's social development, knowledge and skill development. ( )
10. The characteristics such as developing language and communication skills in children, building personal characteristics such as self-confidence, self-discipline and expression of personal abilities are actually the most important aims of primary education. ( )

Supplementary Reading: Importance of Education in Human Development

Education can be defined as the procedure of acquiring skills, values, knowledge, habits, and beliefs. There are also many experts who believe that education can also be defined as the procedure of facilitating learning. There are many educational methods which are often employed, including teaching, discussing, training, storytelling, and directed research. It is important to note that in the majority of the situations, education takes place under the guidance of an educator. However, there are also many conditions in which an individual might educate himself or herself without any help from others. Human development, on the other hand, is a field of science which has the main aim of understanding the changes which take place in people of all ages and circumstances. It is important to remember that the field of human development is not just concerned with physical changes; in this field, the focus also relies on other types of changes, including psychological changes. Many experts also suggest that education plays a very important role in the development of human beings. In this essay, readers will learn about the definition of education, the importance of education in the development of human beings, among many other points.

Understanding Education

Before discussing how education plays a key role in shaping various aspects of an individual, it is essential to understand what education truly entails and the meaning of the term "human development". In this subtopic, readers will learn about the importance of education, which can be defined as the process of facilitating learning and acquiring different skills, beliefs, values, habits, and knowledge. According to experts, education can take place in either a formal or informal setting. However, it is often observed to be most effective when children are provided with a comfortable environment that allows them to focus solely on the information they are receiving.

Many government bodies worldwide recognize the right to education. In numerous countries, the formal education process comprises various stages, including kindergarten or preschool, primary school, secondary school, and university or college. In many regions globally, education is compulsory for children up to a certain age. Several philosophers have offered their own definitions of education, but most of them tend to agree that recognizing the importance of education at the right time is crucial for leading a healthy and happy life.

Unit 11 Education & People's Overall Development

Understanding Human Development

In this section, readers will gain an understanding of the process involved in the development of human beings. According to many experts, to comprehend the process of human development, it is important to study the concept of the human condition, which primarily focuses on a capability approach. Organizations use various scales and indexes to measure an individual's progress in terms of overall development, and one of the most commonly used indexes is the inequality-adjusted human development index. The United Nations Development Programme has also provided a precise definition of education. According to them, human development can be defined as the process of expanding the choices of an individual. These expanded choices can further enable an individual to have a better, longer, healthier, and more educated standard of living.

The Importance of Education

It is widely agreed that education plays a crucial role in the development of any individual. Below are some reasons why education is considered highly important:

➢ Getting Rid of Social Prejudices

One of the significant challenges in human societies is social prejudice, defined as negative beliefs held by members against certain castes, tribes, or social groups. Studies have shown that education can successfully eliminate many social prejudices. Educated minds are less prone to biases and often use logic and reason to form conclusions.

➢ Pursuing Dreams

The definition of education emphasizes knowledge acquisition. Pursuing education helps individuals identify their true passion and dreams. This enables them to have a better future spent doing something they genuinely love or care about.

➢ Enhanced Imagination and Creativity

While everyone has the potential for creativity, research suggests that education enhances this potential, providing individuals with more resources. This is one reason why the education definition is often linked with creativity and imagination.

➢ Contribution to Larger Growth

Education often leads to a better quality of life, enabling individuals to look beyond personal concerns. Educated individuals frequently contribute to the larger growth of society as a whole.

➢ Better Exposure to Wisdom and Knowledge

Education opens various channels of knowledge and wisdom. By pursuing education, individuals can unlock these different channels, becoming more experienced and intelligent in the long run. These are significant ways in which education aids in the development of individuals.

Conclusion

Education can be defined as the process of acquiring knowledge, skills, habits, and values. It is widely acknowledged that education facilitates more efficient individual development, offering various benefits. These advantages include gaining better exposure to knowledge and wisdom, pursuing dreams, fostering enhanced creativity and imagination, eliminating social prejudice, contributing to society, and many others. It is crucial to recall the key points discussed in this essay on education to motivate individuals to pursue their dreams and attain a higher quality of education.

Unit 12　Education & Social Development

Text A　Open and Distance Education: A Better Way of Competence Building and Sustainable Development

> **导读**：远程开放教育是当今信息时代的发展趋势，它以一种新型的、多元化的、互动的方式传播教育，其初衷是为教育均衡发展提供更多可能，让教育技术真正为广大渴望知识的人才谋福利。远程开放教育模式在本质上秉承终身教育的基本理念，借助最新的传播媒体和信息技术，通过灵活有效的教学方式满足学生随时随地、人人参与的学习需求，适应了时代发展的需要，体现了人才培养的目标。它不仅是对现行学校教育的补充，而且与学习型社会的内在需求具有高度的契合性，是建设学习型社会的重要力量。

　　Globalization as a phenomenon influences all disciplines of life, particularly education. The increasing demand for highly educated people is the cause of permanent education, calling for newer, better, faster, and more convenient ways of learning. In view of the present situation, Open and Distance Learning (ODL) is gaining currency, serving as a system where a student cannot go to the traditional institution due to distance, resource limitations, time constraints, physical disability, age, etc.

Competence Building

　　Competence includes education and skills acquired through technical and social behavior, an aptitude for initiatives, and a readiness to take risks. Building competence lies in strengthening the identity and foundation of emotional stability and self-esteem, which is important for physical and mental health, as well as financial performance. Therefore, competence building should be viewed in a much more comprehensive and deeper way.

　　In the present era of globalization, there is much need for sustainable development and the competence-building process. Sustainable development is a pattern of resource use that aims to meet human needs while preserving the environment so that these needs can be met not only in the present but also for future generations. Besides, sustainable development was formally defined for the first time in the "Brundtland Commission report" published in 1987 as "development that meets the needs of the present without compromising the ability of future generations to meet their own needs." This definition encompasses the ideas of limitations imposed by the state of technology and social organization on the ability of the environment to meet present and future needs. It further suggests that the needs of the future depend on how well we balance social, economic, and environmental objectives or needs when making decisions today. Sustainable development ties together concerns for the carrying capacity of natural systems with the social challenges facing humanity.

Education for Sustainable Development

An important prerequisite for sustainable development is the issue of equity—equity for future generations and equity for those of the present generation who have little or no access to natural resources and economic goods. Education and training appear to be dominant factors for increasing creativity and rational thinking, problem-solving capacities, and competitiveness needed to foster the increasingly complex cultural, social, and technological decisions involved in sustainable development. Therefore, education and training for sustainable development are not only social issues but also matters of economic policy. Decision-makers today face two major challenges in reshaping education for sustainable development. One is devising institutional educational strategies and programs, taking into account all the educational actors and communication channels available. The other is increasing the quality and usefulness of the various educational and training processes aimed primarily at citizens, economic partners, and young people.

Strengthening worldwide cooperation in education should help each country devise the most effective ways and means of enabling its people to contribute to improving the material and spiritual living conditions of the present generation without denying life for future generations. Education for sustainable development stresses the achievement of continuous well-being by searching for an optimal balance in the formation and use of different resources and capital types—human capital, physical infrastructure and tools, natural resources, financial means, technology and decision system, the world of work and that of the media. ODL plays a very important role in achieving these goals regarding sustainable development and competence building.

The Role of ODL in Sustainable Development and Competence Building

The role of ODL in sustainable development and competence building is mainly to develop human capital and encourage technical progress, as well as to foster the cultural conditions favoring social and economic changes. This is the key to creative and effective utilization of human potential and all forms of capital ensuring rapid and more equitable growth. Empirical evidence demonstrates that education is positively correlated with productivity and technological progress because it enables companies to obtain and evaluate information on new technologies and economic opportunities.

ODL is especially well-suited to deliver learning outcomes consistent with sustainability goals. Its emphasis on access, the service of personal needs, and supporting lifelong learning mirrors the way in which environmental values are best inculcated into personal and professional life. Meanwhile, ODL can't be ignored in the role of facilitating environmental sustainability. Technologies in e-learning distance education are helping the environment. Online courses showed a 20% reduction in energy and a 12% reduction in CO_2 emissions compared to printed-based courses. There is less carbon pollution in online delivery in the ODL system, so it truly results in "dematerialization." In the ODL system, students have to travel less for going to their study center, which is mostly near to their residence. So consumption of petroleum oil becomes less, contributing to fostering environmental sustainability and encouraging sustainable management. Thus, it can be called "Green Distance Education."

ODL is very helpful in "Inclusive Education," which is based on the aspects of human rights, equal opportunities, social justice, and participation. Inclusive education is very complex and multifaceted, recognizing that there is not just one inclusion but rather it is seen by children in schools, inclusions according to disable activists. It has multiple interpretations. Poverty, ethnicity, disability, gender, or membership of a minority group may limit access to or marginalize. Within education, inclusive education appreciates every learner's fundamental rights to learn and knows that each child has unique abilities and needs. If given the right opportunity, all children can develop their potential. Inclusive education considers differences in the learning and physical abilities of children. ODL is very helpful in achieving these goals of inclusive education.

Authorities of the universities running distance education courses should sharply ensure that distance education centers do not get reduced to degree distribution institutions. So universities and distance institutions' higher authorities keep ensuring that only quality education should be provided through ODL. Proper libraries, laboratories, and required study materials, essential equipment, and materials for students should be in coordination with other related universities running similar courses located in the same area. Open and distance learning has been improvised upon by integrating various other methods that are successfully followed in other countries, such as Virtual Education, Alternative Education, and E-learning.

The need of the hour is to pool such innovative experiences and disseminate the same effectively. The exchange of experiences within and outside the country would surely help to promote and transfer knowledge to the masses and benefit society in the long run.

Notes:

1. **Open and Distance Learning (开放远程教育)**: Open and Distance Learning is a field of education that focuses on teaching methods and technology with the aim of delivering teaching, often on an individual basis, to students who are not physically present in a traditional educational setting such as a classroom. It has been described as "a process to create and provide access to learning when the source of information and the learners are separated by time and distance, or both." Its courses that require a physical on-site presence for any reason (including taking examinations) have been referred to as hybrid or blended courses of study.

2. **Brundtland Commission (布伦特兰委员会)**: Brundtland Commission, formally the World Commission on Environment and Development (WCED), known by the name of its Chair Gro Harlem Brundtland, was convened by the United Nations in 1983. The commission was created to address growing concern "about the accelerating deterioration of the human environment and natural resources and the consequences of that deterioration for economic and social development." In establishing the commission, the UN General Assembly recognized that environmental problems were global in nature and determined that it was in the common interest of all nations to establish policies for sustainable development.

3. **Inclusive Education (全纳教育)**: Inclusive Education is an approach to educating students with special educational needs. Under the inclusion model, students with special needs spend most or all of their time with non-disabled students. It is about the child's right to participate and the school's duty to accept the child. A premium is placed upon full participation by students with disabilities and upon respect for their social, civil, and educational rights.

4. **Virtual Education (虚拟教育)**: Virtual Education refers to instruction in a learning environment where teacher and student are separated by time or space, or both, and the teacher provides course content through course management applications, multimedia resources, the Internet, videoconferencing, etc. Students receive the content and communicate with the teacher via the same technologies. This term is primarily used in higher education where so-called Virtual Universities have been established.

5. **Alternative Education (选择性教育)**: Alternative Education, also known as non-traditional

education or educational alternative, includes a number of approaches to teaching and learning other than mainstream or traditional education. It is often rooted in various philosophies that are fundamentally different from those of mainstream or traditional education. While some have strong political, scholarly, or philosophical orientations, others are more informal associations of teachers and students dissatisfied with some aspect of mainstream or traditional education. Alternative Education, which include charter schools, alternative schools, independent schools, and home-based learning vary widely, but often emphasize the value of small class size, close relationships between students and teachers, and a sense of community.

6. **E-learning (在线学习，电子化学习或网络化学习)**: E-learning comprises all forms of electronically supported learning and teaching. The information and communication systems, whether networked or not, serve as specific media to implement the learning process. The term will still most likely be utilized to reference out-of-classroom and in-classroom educational experiences via technology, even as advances continue in regard to devices and curriculum. E-learning is essentially the computer and network-enabled transfer of skills and knowledge. E-learning applications and processes include Web-based learning, computer-based learning, virtual classroom opportunities and digital collaboration. Content is delivered via the Internet, intranet/extranet, audio or video tape, etc. It can be self-paced or instructor-led and includes media in the form of text, image, animation, streaming video and audio.

New Words and Expressions:

1. aptitude ['æptitjuːd]   n.   天资；天生的才能
2. initiative [iˈnɪʃətiv]   n.   倡议；主动性；主动权
3. comprehensive [ˌkɑːmpriˈhensiv] adj.   全部的；所有的；综合性的
                                n.   （英国为各种资质的学生设立的）综合中学
4. compromise [ˈkɑːmprəmaiz]   v.   妥协；违背（原则）；（尤指因行为不明智）使陷入危险
                                n.   妥协；妥协方案
5. encompass [inˈkʌmpəs]   v.   包含；包围；环绕
6. optimal [ˈɑːptiməl]   adj.   最佳的；最理想的
7. empirical [imˈpirikl]   adj.   经验主义的；以实验（或经验）为依据的
8. inculcate [ˈinkʌlkeit]   v.   谆谆教诲；反复灌输

9. interpretation [in,tɜːpriˈteiʃn]   n.   解释；翻译；演绎；演奏方式
10. marginalize [ˈmɑːdʒinəlaiz]   v.   使处于边缘；使无实权
11. integrate [ˈintigreit]   v.   （使）合并；（使）加入
12. disseminate [diˈsemineit]   v.   传播，散布（知识、信息等）

Exercises:

I. Vocabulary.

Fill in the blanks with the most suitable words. Change the form when necessary.

| aptitude | comprehensive | encompass | integrate | interpretation |
| initiative | compromise | optimal | inculcate | disseminate |

1. He was educated at the local _____ school.
2. How can local communities work with planners and decision-makers to find some _____ solutions for the future?
3. If a child shows any musical _____ or interest, get an instrument into his/her hand early.
4. These so-called solar-energy zones _____ about 680,000 acres of land owned by the federal government.
5. It's hard for a state-run program to _____ ideals like thinking out of the box.
6. I wanted to go to Greece. However, my wife wanted to go to Spain. After a little talk, we _____ on Italy.
7. Can we _____ his silence as a refusal?
8. It has been very difficult to _____ all of the local agencies into the national organization.
9. This publication has been prepared to _____ the lessons learned to a wider audience.
10. Charles is shy and does not take the _____ in making acquaintances.

II. Translate the following phrases into English.

人力资源　　_____
可持续发展　_____
自然资源　　_____
理性思维　　_____

Unit 12　Education & Social Development

考虑	_____
生活条件；居住环境	_____
有形基础设施	_____
符合；与……一致	_____
终身学习	_____
社会公正	_____

III. Comprehension of the text.

Decide whether the following statements are true (T) or false (F) according to the passage.

1. Distance education is a system where teacher and students are integrated by physical distance and where they use technology like print, voice, data and video to convey the learning material through postal services, countries, Internet, CDs, etc. (　)
2. Sustainable development was formally defined for the first time in the "Brundtland Commission report" published in 1978 as "development that meets the needs of the present without compromising the ability of future generations to their own needs." (　)
3. Education and training for sustainable development is not only a social issue but also matters of economic policy. (　)
4. Online courses showed a 12% reduction in energy and 20% reduction in CO_2 emission compared to printed-based courses. (　)
5. Proper libraries, laboratories, and required study materials, essential equipment, and materials for students should be in coordination with other related universities running similar courses located in the same area. (　)

Text B　Higher Education Within a Knowledge-based Society

导读：1994年，美国管理学家德鲁克在《后资本主义社会》中指出，人类社会正在进入知识社会。知识社会是一个以创新为社会主要驱动力的社会，也是一个大众创新、共同创新、开放创新成为常态的社会。在知识社会，知识、创新成为社会的核心，人民的受教育水平成为经济和社会发展的基础，知识资本成为企业最重要的资源，受过良好教育的人成为社会的主流，财富的累积、经济的增长、个人的发展，均以知识为基础。知识社会以知识经济为主体，强调借由知识的不断创新、

> 累积、应用与分化，促进产业进步，引导个人、组织和社会的成长与发展；这也使得创新不再是少数科技精英的专利，而成为更为广泛的大众参与，推动了创新的民主化进程。知识社会带来了人与知识关系的深刻变化，并由此对教育提出了新的挑战：人如何与知识相处？这是教育不能回避的问题。

Research in higher education is a quite new field of interest and can be seen as a multidisciplinary subject. Researchers from different fields of study are interested in learning about the complexity of higher education. They are looking on higher education from different angles as for instance, educational or political sciences, psychology, sociology, history, economy or law—different fields of research are interested in bringing light into the complex system of higher education (educational, management and social science approach). Nevertheless, the term higher education is relatively new and became popular in the 1970s because universities lost their exclusive right to provide higher education. From the middle age to the 60s, the main and often the only post secondary institution have been the university. After that time other forms of tertiary education emerged and higher education came up to include universities as well as vocational and professional institutions.

Before World War II, university education was a domain of the elite. But this changed dramatically. The following figure (Figure 12-1) illustrates phases of higher education developments with a clear tendency towards diversification and internationalization of higher education in a knowledge-driven economy. In the last phase especially research in higher education is emphasized "as primary differentiator of higher education institutions" in the 21st century.

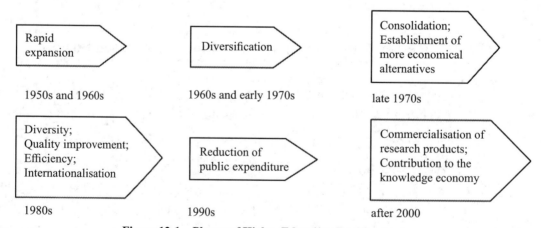

Figure 12-1　Phases of Higher Education Developments

Unit 12 Education & Social Development

Today's university is facing great strain and tension because of ongoing societal developments. Knowledge changed to a factor of production and theoretical knowledge gains more importance as source of innovation and basis for political decisions in highly industrialized societies. The Nobel Prize winner Joseph Stiglitz stated that knowledge is a global public good though the source of brainpower is limited by genetic distributions of talent and cultural disadvantages. The nature of education is bound to change and will become a continuing life-time affair for the professional and technical person. In this context, Daniel Bell articulated that we need especially postdoctoral universities where new knowledge and new techniques can be passed along.

The arrival of knowledge-based societies, of course, has a great importance according to the development of universities. One could say that they are the first institutions to benefit from this increasing usage of information. Universities of these days compete with other institutions, for instance, vocational colleges, research institutions and high-tech companies in popularity to cope with the increasing importance of knowledge. Universities cannot handle all these new forces and demands of the knowledge society which means that they are in an unstable situation and losing their position of high status and power. They have to be powerful and successful but loose at the same time their clear position (success vs. uncertainty). There is an intrinsic relationship between universities and knowledge societies, but the future consequences are not foreseeable. One sees a future of knowledge as strategic resource for universities. Others see a world of academic capitalism. Thus, academia goes together with the knowledge society where "competition with other institutions and a loss of the monopoly of universities" prevails (virtual universities, corporate universities, media organizations, consortia, strategic alliances, private and public institutions).

The new mode of knowledge production effects academic research and brings new opportunities because entrepreneurial activities emerge. It must be kept in mind, however, that the basic stable function of the university is to educate researchers and to generate the cultural norms of a society. Nevertheless, an epistemic dimension in this development of academic knowledge production to societal knowledge production brings new practices though also uncertainty for today's knowledge-based society. Good practices are needed from traditional science with "the heterogeneity of knowledge and the importance of new stakeholders" to combine either academic as well as economic functions of the academia.

Therefore, different mechanisms and practices of quality assurance are needed. A (internationally and nationally recognized) quality assurance system should be able to guarantee transparency and control of higher education programs and that diplomas and degrees of students are approved. Although international and national quality assurance agencies have been developed nearly all over the world, there are different approaches to ensure quality (internal or external procedures, accreditation vs. evaluations, quality audits etc.). While some countries established only one national agency (e.g. Finland), others have separate agencies with different responsibilities (e.g. Germany), which shows the political and cultural diversity of the countries all over the world. Furthermore, the initiative to establish international qualification frameworks helps small countries to set up a regional quality assurance system or assist different global quality assurance initiatives.

Tertiary education has to cope with lots of new challenges due to enormous changes (globalization, ICT, socio-political transformations, lifelong learning and knowledge-based society) but faces also new opportunities as playing the key role in today's society. Santiago et al. (2008) recommend some practical arrangements for a functioning quality assurance system:

- Avoid fragmentation of the quality assurance organizational structure
- Avoid excessive costs and burdens
- Improve quality information base
- Improve information dissemination

With these suggestions, current quality assurance systems, which vary among countries in their scope and emphasis, can be improved. Quality assurance schemes have to be developed as necessary instruments to adjust higher education institutions to the ongoing transformation processes. As the different systems are most of the time newly developed, they should be able to adapt to changes and try to act quickly to the needs of our knowledge-based society. Quality assurance in higher education is not fully developed but still under construction!

Notes:

1. **World War II (第二次世界大战):** World War II, or the Second World War, was a global military conflict lasting from 1939 to 1945, which involved most of the world's nations, including all of the great powers. Eventually, two opposing military alliances were formed: the Allies (同盟国) and the Axis (轴心国). It was the most widespread war in history, with more than 100 million military personnel mobilized. In a state of "total war", the major participants placed their entire economic, industrial, and scientific capabilities at the service of the war effort, erasing the distinction between civilian and military resources. Marked by

significant events involving the mass death of civilians, including the Holocaust（对犹太人的大屠杀） and the only use of nuclear weapons in warfare, it was the deadliest conflict in human history, resulting in 40 million to over 70 million fatalities. The war ended with the total victory of the Allies over Italy, Germany and Japan in 1945. World War II altered the political alignment and social structure of the world. The United Nations was established to foster international cooperation and prevent future conflicts. The Soviet Union and the United States emerged as rival superpowers, setting the stage for the Cold War, which lasted for the next 46 years. Meanwhile, the influence of European great powers started to decline, while the decolonization of Asia and Africa began. Most countries whose industries had been damaged moved towards economic recovery. Political integration, especially in Europe, emerged as an effort to stabilize postwar relations.

2. **Joseph Stiglitz (约瑟夫·斯蒂格利茨)**: Born February 9th, 1943, Stiglitz is an American economist and a professor at Columbia University. He is a recipient of the Nobel Memorial Prize in Economic Sciences (2001) and the John Bates Clark Medal (1979). He is also the former Senior Vice President and Chief Economist of the World Bank.

3. **Quality assurance (质量保证)**: Quality assurance, or QA for short, is the systematic monitoring and evaluation of the various aspects of a project, service or facility to maximize the probability that minimum standards of quality are being attained by the production process. QA cannot absolutely guarantee the production of quality products. Here QA refers to the guarantee of the higher education.

4. **Tertiary education (高等教育或第三级教育)**: Also referred to as third stage, third level, or post-secondary education. It is the educational level following the completion of a school providing a secondary education, such as a high school, secondary school, university-preparatory school. Higher education is taken to include undergraduate and postgraduate education, while vocational education and training beyond secondary education is known as further education in the United Kingdom, or continuing education in the United States. Colleges, universities, institutes of technology and polytechnics are the main institutions that provide tertiary education (sometimes known collectively as tertiary institutions). Tertiary education generally culminates in the receipt of certificates, diplomas, or academic degrees.

5. **ICT (信息通信技术)**: Also known as Information and Communication Technology. It is often used as an extended synonym for Information Technology (IT) but is usually a more general term that stresses the role of unified communications and the integration of telecommunications (telephone lines and wireless signals), intelligent building management systems and audio-

visual systems in modern information technology. ICT consists of all technical means used to handle information and aid communication, including computer and network hardware, communication middleware as well as necessary software. In other words, ICT consists of IT as well as telephony, broadcast media, all types of audio and video processing and transmission and network based control and monitoring functions.

New Words and Expressions:

1. exclusive [ik'sklu:siv]   *adj.*   独有的；排外的；专一的
     n.   独家新闻
2. tertiary ['tɜ:ʃəri]   *adj.*   第三的；第三位的；三代的
3. elite [ei'li:t]   *n.*   社会精英；掌权人物
4. articulate [ɑ:'tikjuleit]   *v.*   清晰地发（音）；明确有力地表达；用关节连接
     adj.   发音清晰的；口才好的
5. postdoctoral [ˌpəʊst'dɒktərəl]   *adj.*   博士后的
6. capitalism ['kæpitəlizəm]   *n.*   资本主义
7. monopoly [mə'nɒpəli]   *n.*   垄断；专卖权
8. epistemic [ˌepi'sti:mik]   *adj.*   知识的；认识的
9. accreditation [əˌkredi'teiʃn]   *n.*   达到标准；鉴定合格

Exercises:

I. Vocabulary.

Match the word in Column A to the correct definition in Column B.

Column A	Column B
1. exclusive	A. of or relating to knowledge or knowing
2. elite	B. belonging to or used by only one person or a group
3. articulate	C. to give official authorization to or approval of
4. capitalism	D. control by one company
5. accreditation	E. the most powerful, rich, or talented people within a particular group, place, or society
6. epistemic	F. an economic and political system in which property, business, and industry are owned by private individuals and not by the state

Unit 12 Education & Social Development

7. postdoctoral   G. third in order, third in importance, or at a third stage of development

8. monopoly   H. expressing oneself readily, clearly, or effectively

9. transparency   I. being beyond the doctoral level

10. tertiary   J. something transparent especially

II. Translate the following phrases into English.

知识社会 _____

阐明 _____

专有权 _____

第三级教育 _____

必然，必定 _____

高职院校，职业学校 _____

文化规范，文化准则 _____

质量保证，品质保证 _____

品质监察 _____

文化多样性 _____

适应 _____

III. Comprehension of the text.

Decide whether the following statements are true (T) or false (F) according to the passage.

1. In the 1970s, universities lost their exclusive right to provide higher education. Therefore, the term higher education is relatively new and became popular. (　)

2. Before World War II, university education was a domain of the elite. But after that, this situation changed dramatically. (　)

3. Although knowledge serves as a source of innovation and a basis for political decisions in highly industrialized societies, it has changed into a factor of production, and theoretical knowledge is given less importance. (　)

4. As Daniel Bell stated, postdoctoral universities are especially needed so that new knowledge and new techniques can be passed along. (　)

5. Universities can handle new forces like vocational colleges and demands of the knowledge society. In other words, universities are in a stable situation and strengthening their position of high status and power. (　)

6. The only function of the university is to generate the cultural norms of a society. (　)

7. Two dimensions should be guaranteed in a quality assurance system: one is the transparency and control of higher education programs, the other is the diplomas and degrees of students are approved. ( )
8. In terms of the quality assurance agency, all the countries have separate agencies with different responsibilities, which shows the political and cultural diversity of the countries all over the world. ( )
9. Tertiary education has to cope with lots of new challenges due to enormous changes but faces also new opportunities as playing the key role in today's society. ( )
10. In some countries, quality assurance in higher education is fully developed; while in other countries, it is still under construction. ( )

Supplementary Reading: The Global "Imagined Community"— International Education

What Is International Education?

International education is defined as "all educational initiatives that aim to build intercultural competency, knowledge of the international community, and a sense of global citizenship among students and education professionals". These educational initiatives include programs such as student and teacher exchanges, second-language learning, and educational cooperation between schools in different countries. International education provides personal benefits for students and teachers as well as benefits for host and provider countries.

The Role of International Education

In 2002 the researchers from the Centre for the Study of Global Governance at the London School of Economics argued that the growing practice of studying abroad may be one of the catalysts "of the emergence and spread of global community" because "students are major transmitters of knowledge and ideas, and interlocutors across cultures". According to the UNESCO Institute for Statistics, in 2007, more than 2.8 million university-level students were enrolled in educational institutions outside of their country of origin, nearly 1 million more than in 1999. In other words, with the support of various institutions, increasing numbers of students across the globe are, through their personal actions, creating one of the pillars of a global civil society.

Although there is some debate about the statistics, unfortunately, as many of us know, the

Unit 12 Education & Social Development

United States is lagging far behind and currently sends just 1.8 percent of the global average of students studying abroad for a semester or more abroad using UNESCO's criteria, while the number increases to about 4 percent using Open Doors criteria. National Association of Foreign Student Affairs (NAFSA) and other international education organizations, through their support for the *Simon Study Abroad Bill*, as well as other initiatives, are attempting to change that. But technical solutions will not be enough.

This implies that our programs should concretely provide students with the insights necessary to overcome ethnocentrism, to be reflective about the limits of national identity, and to provide critical perspectives on the activities of corporations and states. For example, at the Bachelor of Computer Applications (BCA) Abroad, we have taken several initiatives that are meant to enhance what Kaldor calls "a common consciousness of human society on a world scale". Thus, we have created a course, "The Global Conversation", which links our students and others throughout the world in academic discussions and online learning circles while taking a contextual approach that "connects the dots" between the myriad problems the human species currently faces around the globe.

We also organize two international student conferences each academic year that allow U.S., European, and other students to come together to discuss important global issues with noted experts. In the spring, we hold a conference in Strasbourg, France, focused on European–U.S. relations, which we initiated because we realized that when our students went to study sites in Europe, they were often shocked by the different perspectives held by European students on many of today's most important issues.

In the fall, we focus on divided societies in Derry/Londonderry, Northern Ireland, because helping students to understand the problematic nature of identity is essential to creating a more peaceful world. And finally, there's the annual Ron Moffatt Seminar for international education faculty and staff who are interested in the themes being discussed in this article.

When a student decides to study abroad, it suggests that to some extent he or she is prepared to experience social realities that may diverge from those home realities that too many never travel away from. One of our tasks as international educators is to enhance a student's experience of those other realities through program design. As I have argued in the volume edited by Ross Lewin: "Regardless of the type of program, we should be building in reflexivity—reflexivity about the culturally constructed nature of one's self, one's home society, and our understanding of the larger world." Central to that reflexive understanding of today's world is to understand how each of us is implicated in the maintenance of the nation-state system through our acceptance of

the "imagined community" of a specific nation.

As Benedict Anderson points out in the book of that name, the idea of "imagined communities" provided a key cultural and political element in the development of modern nations. "Imagined communities" have also been central to the reified identities that many people hold to dearly, and which are so often implicated in war and genocide. In contrast, what we increasingly need today is an imagined community at the global level in which our identities are, as Maalouf says, "the sum of all our allegiances" and within which "allegiance to the human community itself would become increasingly important"; in other words, a global community. Although one rarely, if ever, hears NAFSA described as the largest and most vibrant global civil community organization in the field of international education, it seems clear that we should become conscious of this, and in the process knowingly help to create that global "imagined community."

Unit 13　Educational Justice

Text A　Educational Justice in Schools

> 导读：在教育的起点、过程和结果诸阶段，在教育权利平等和教育机会均等等方面，在教育资源分配及教育质量达成等维度上，不因种族（民族）、性别、阶级（阶层）等诸多社会因素不同而产生教育领域内不公平现象，即能实现教育公平。教育公平包含三个层次：起点公平，确保人人都享有平等的受教育的权利和义务；过程公平，提供相对平等的受教育的机会和条件；结果公平，教育成功机会和教育效果的相对均等。教育公平内嵌于公平这一人类社会的普遍价值观，既是一种价值判断，又是一种价值选择与追求，是社会发展进程中人们对公平的向往理念在教育领域内的综合展现。随着时代的发展，教育公平的内涵越来越丰富、多元和多维，它通过实现教育的起点、区域、城乡、资源配置的公平，让每个人享受更高质量的教育，从而阻断贫困的代际传递。

What are the right normative grounds for evaluating education policy? I want to propose, briefly, four proper goals of education, and one distributive principle. The goals are as follows:

- Education should prepare children to become autonomous, self-governing individuals, capable of making good judgments about how to live their own lives, and to negotiate for themselves the complexity of modern life.

- Education should equip children with the skills and knowledge necessary for them to be effective participants in the economy, so that they can have a good range of options in the labor market, and have access to the income necessary to flourish in a market economy.

- Education should play a role in preparing children to be flourishing adults independently of their participation in the economy.

- Education should prepare children to be responsible and effective participants in political life—good citizens. It should do this both for their sakes, because a flourishing life is more secure if one is capable of making use of the rights of citizenship; and for the sake of others, because a flourishing life is more secure if others are capable of abiding by the duties of good citizenship.

The distributive principle is the principle of educational equality: The simple version says

that every child should have an equally good education. But what this means is obviously contested. When you compare children with similar talents, and similar levels of willingness to exert effort, it is pretty intuitive to say that educational equality is satisfied when they receive a similar level of educational resources. But consider Hattie, who is blind, and Sid, who is equally talented and hardworking, but sighted. In their case it seems intuitive that equality requires that more resources should be devoted to Hattie in particular, resources devoted to correcting fully for her disability. Consider an even more difficult case: Kenneth, who is highly talented, and Hugh, who has a serious cognitive disability. Again, it seems that Hugh should be granted more resources, but this time it is hard to see that they could correct for the disability, unless we were willing to disable Kenneth. I shall not resolve these difficulties here. The principle of educational equality has two straightforward implications. First, children with similar levels of ability and willingness to exert effort should face similar educational prospects, regardless of their social background, race, ethnicity, or sex. Second, those children with lower levels of ability should receive at least as many educational resources as those who are more able.

Since most of the ensuing discussion focuses on the principle of educational equality rather than the goals of education, I want to emphasize the importance of equality rather than improving the prospects of the least advantaged. The egalitarian theory within which my own view of educational justice is nested in fact emphasizes not equality, per se, but benefiting the least advantaged, and gives that principle priority over equality—so that when we have a choice between an equal distribution of a smaller pie and an unequal distribution of a larger pie in which all get more than under the equal distribution of the smaller pie, we choose inequality. If a tax proposal, for example, were to inhibit growth so that the worst off were even worse off, although more equally well off with others, that would be a bad thing for them, and for everyone else. But this general rule does not apply to all areas of life. The quality of someone's education has a real influence on their expected lifetime income, but its influence is dependent on the quality of his/her competitors' education.

Getting Sharon from only 2 up to 3 grade Cs does not do much good for her if we simultaneously get her nearest competitor Linda up from 3 to 4 grade Cs. The employer will still prefer Linda to Sharon. So merely raising the floor of achievement in education does not help the less advantaged in the pursuit of earnings in the labor market unless we simultaneously diminish the achievement gap. The size of the gap matters because of the particular connection education has to other, unequally distributed, goods. When I refer to "benefiting the least (or less) advantaged" in the context of education, then, I should be understood as being concerned with benefiting the least advantaged relative to others.

News Words and Expressions:

1. normative ['nɔːmətiv]	*adj.*	规范的；标准的
2. equip with		装配，配备，备有……
3. flourish ['flʌriʃ]	*v.*	繁荣，兴旺；茁壮成长
4. for the sake of		为了；为了……的利益
5. abide by		遵守……
6. intuitive [in'tjuːitiv]	*adj.*	直觉的；凭直觉获知的；（计算机软件等）使用简便的
7. egalitarian [iˌgæli'teəriən]	*adj.*	平等主义的
	n.	平等主义者
8. per se		本身；本质上
9. be worse off		处境较坏，情况恶化
10. be concerned with		涉及……；担心……

Exercises:

I. Choose the correct letter of A, B, C, or D.

1. What are the right normative grounds for evaluating education policy in the author's idea?

    A. Four proper goals of education.

    B. One distributive principle.

    C. Four goals of education and one distributive principle.

    D. Two distributive principles.

2. The followings are the goals of education except ____.

    A. Education should play a role in preparing children to be flourishing adults independently of their participation in the economy

    B. Education should prepare children to be responsible and effective participants in political life—good citizens

C. Education should equip children with the skills and knowledge necessary for them to be effective participants in the economy, so that they can have a good range of options in the labour market, and have access to the income necessary to flourish in a market economy

D. Everyone should have an equally education

3. What is the distributive principle of education?

A. Every child should have an equally good education.

B. Children should become autonomous, self-governing individuals, capable of making good judgments about how to live their own lives, and negotiate for themselves the complexity of modern life.

C. Children are full of the skills and knowledge necessary for them to be effective participants in the economy.

D. Children can have a good range of options in the labour market, and have access to the income necessary to flourish in the market economy.

4. The author mentioned the example of ____ to prove some difficulties in the principle of educational equality.

A. Hattie

B. Sid

C. Kenneth and Hugh

D. All of the above

5. Which is not the idea of the author?

A. We should emphasize the importance of equality rather than improving the prospects of the least advantaged.

B. Children with similar talents and similar levels of willingness always get the similar quality of education.

C. The quality of someone's education has an influence on their expected lifetime income which is dependent on the quality of his/her competitors' education.

D. Children with lower levels of ability should receive at least as many educational resources as those who are more able.

Unit 13 Educational Justice

II. Vocabulary.

Fill in the blanks with the most suitable words. Change the form when necessary.

equip	flourish	abide	egalitarian	intuitive
prority	exert	talented	emphasize	normative

1. He won both games without even seeming to _____ himself.
2. The plants _____ in the warm sun.
3. The boys _____ themselves with torches and rope, and set off.
4. He seemed to have a/an _____ awareness of how I felt.
5. Manufacturers are making safety a design _____.
6. You have to _____ by the referee's decision.
7. The social forces for service also exist some _____ issues.
8. The _____ artist carved an interesting decoration from this piece of tree root.
9. Our government tries to establish an _____ country.
10. It should be _____ that flying is a very safe way to travel.

III. Translate the following sentences into Chinese.

1. Education should prepare children to become autonomous, self-governing individuals, capable of making good judgments about how to live their own lives, and to negotiate for themselves the complexity of modern life.
2. Education should equip children with the skills and knowledge necessary for them to be effective participants in the economy, so that they can have a good range of options in the labor market, and have access to the income necessary to flourish in a market economy.
3. Education should play a role in preparing children to be flourishing adults independently of their participation in the economy.
4. Education should prepare children to be responsible and effective participants in political life—good citizens.
5. When you compare children with similar talents, and similar levels of willingness to exert effort, it is pretty intuitive to say that educational equality is satisfied when they receive a similar level of educational resources.

Text B Efficiency and Equity of Education

> **导读**：教育与培训政策的平等是民主化的一个重要内容，是指人们不受政治、经济、文化、民族、信仰、性别、地域等的限制，在法律上享有同等的受教育与受培训权利、在事实上具有同等的受教育和培训机会。而教育与培训政策的有效性是指教育与培训政策能完成活动和达到的结果的程度。教育的有效性与平等性时而互补互助，相辅相成；时而互不影响，各自发展；时而又给对方的发展造成不利影响。本文旨在探讨教育与培训政策的有效性与平等性的内涵以及两者之间的关系。

It was mentioned in the 2019 IMF (International Monetary Fund) Working Paper that education is critical to both individual well-being—through its impacts on human capital, employability, productivity, income and health—and overall economic growth. Given the effects of education on individual and economic development, the distribution of education is also crucial for societal inequality. So efficient education and training systems can create economic growth, and equitable systems can create social cohesion. Thus, it is not a surprise that European Union has realized the economic and social efficiency of education and training. This has been stressed by leading European economic advisors, and the European Union puts education and training at center stage in its agenda for jobs and growth. For example, the European Council concludes that "education and training are critical factors to develop the EU's long-term potential for competitiveness as well as for social cohesion".

While the definitions of equity and efficiency are elusive, it seems that most people agree to some variants close to the concept of equality of opportunity proposed by Roemer. The central idea of this concept is that inequality should be tolerated only if it is due to differences in effort, but not if it is due to circumstances which are beyond a person's control. Thus, equity would demand that a person's expected educational outcome should be a function only of his/her effort, but not of his/her circumstances, such as race, gender, or family background. The concept of efficiency is much more straightforward, representing a situation where a maximum aggregate outcome of the educational production process is obtained with given input or a given aggregate outcome with minimum input. Under this concept, an efficient situation is one which would be preferred by any individual who is ignorant of his/her position in society. In the calculus of applied welfare economics, equity and efficiency goals can be combined by maximizing welfare functions.

As many countries are facing large fiscal pressures from high levels of public debt and competing spending needs from infrastructure, health and social protection, they are becoming more and more cautious about their investments. However, promoting quality and equity in education often means increasing investment in education. In addition, achieving more equity in the design of education systems probably help to evade the need for intense redistributive policies at later ages, which are often viewed as obstacles to the creation of growth and jobs in Europe. So many governments tend to think that there is a trade-off that forces them to choose between efficiency and equity in their prioritizing.

In reality, the relationship between efficiency and equity in education and training systems may take different forms. In some cases, efficiency and equity may be independent from one another. In other cases, there may be trade-offs in the extent to which the two goals can be achieved. And in still other cases, there may be complementarities in the achievement of the two goals. Thus, certain policies may bring education and training systems closer to efficiency without having any impact on equity. Other policies may be highly equitable without affecting efficiency. Other policies may advance both efficiency and equity in a complementary way. And still other policies may show a trade-off by advancing either efficiency at the detriment of equity or equity at the detriment of efficiency. Therefore, efficient policies need not be inequitable, and equitable policies need not be inefficient.

But balancing equity and efficiency is not an easy task. It turns out current attempts to reach one or the other sometimes turn out to be both inefficient and inequitable. The IMF has pointed out that high priority must be given to improve education spending efficiency and equity, which can help improve overall education outcomes—essential for long term economic growth—with little adverse effect on fiscal sustainability. Taking Moldova as an example, the IMF has given specific recommendations for reforming the education system based on a survey and analysis. For example, to address the main inefficiencies in general primary and secondary education—the oversized school network and high employment, it suggested Moldova to lower employment after reducing teaching positions through consolidating the school network, increasing class size, or expanding teachers' working hours. And researchers found that the wage bill and basic maintenance and energy costs have absorbed an excessive share of public education spending, many school facilities are in urgent need of renovation and more investments are needed for study materials and equipment. Therefore, teacher training is suggested to be accelerated as teacher qualification is central to quality of education. This is particularly the case for schools that are most attended by disadvantaged students, and more resources to these schools will help improve both the overall quality of education and equality of opportunities by narrowing the outcome gap between advantaged and disadvantaged students.

Education is critical for individual well-being, economic development and social cohesion. The education sector, however, is facing important challenges in many countries. This includes the need to improve education outcomes and reduce inequality in an often fiscally constrained environment. Thus, improving the efficiency in the education sector will need to play a key role in achieving this objective. So countries should have a systematic approach to assess the efficiency and equity of public education spending, identify sources of inefficiencies and inequality, and formulate potential reform options.

Notes:

1. **IMF (International Monetary Fund)(国际货币基金组织):** The IMF is one of the international organizations established on 27th December 1945 in Washington, D.C., under the *International Monetary Fund Agreement*, with its headquarter in Washington, D.C. The IMF has three critical missions: furthering international monetary cooperation, encouraging the expansion of trade and economic growth, and discouraging policies that would harm prosperity. To fulfill these missions, IMF member countries work collaboratively with each other and with other international bodies.

2. **European Union (EU) (欧洲联盟):** European Union is an economic and political union of 27 member states which are located primarily in Europe. The EU traces its origins from the European Coal and Steel Community (ECSC) and the European Economic Community (EEC) formed by six countries in the 1950s. In the intervening years the EU has grown in size by the accession of new member states, and in power by the addition of policy areas to its remit. The *Maastricht Treaty* established the European Union under its current name in 1993. The last amendment to the constitutional basis of the EU, the *Treaty of Lisbon*, came into force in 2009.

3. **European Council (欧洲理事会):** European Council refers to the regular meetings of the heads of state or of government in the European Union. It comprises the heads of state or government of EU member states, along with its President and the President of the Commission. The High Representative takes part in its meetings, which are chaired by its

President.

4. Roemer (Buddy Roemer): Roemer is an American politician who served as the 52nd Governor of Louisiana, from 1988 to 1992. He was elected as a Democrat but switched to the Republican Party on March 11, 1991. Prior to serving as Governor, he was a member of the United States House of Representatives from 1981 to 1988.

New Words and Expressions:

1. employability [em,plɔɪ'bɪləti]	n.	可就业能力
2. cohesion [kəʊ'hi:ʒn]	n.	黏合；结合；凝聚性
3. circumstance ['sɜ:kəmstəns]	n.	条件；环境；境遇；经济状况；命运
4. well-being	n.	健康；安乐
5. straightforward [,streit'fɔ:wəd]	adj.	简单的；坦率的；率直的
6. trade-off		（在需要而又相互对立的两者间的）权衡；协调
7. elusive [i'lu:siv]	adj.	难找的；难以解释的；难以到达的
8. variant ['veriənt]	adj.	不同的；多样的
	n.	变种；变形
9. calculus ['kælkjələs]	n.	微积分
10. aggregate ['ægrigət, 'ægrigeit]	adj.	总数的；总计的
11. maximize ['mæksɪmaɪz]	v.	使增加到最大限度；充分利用
12. fiscal ['fɪskl]	adj.	财政的；国库的
13. complementary [,kɑ:mpli'mentri]	adj.	互补的；相互补足的
14. detriment ['detrimənt]	n.	损害；伤害
15. sustainability [sə,steɪnə'bɪləti]	n.	持续性；能维持性
16. maintenance ['meɪntənəns]	n.	维护，保养；维持，保持；（依法应负担的）生活费，抚养费

Exercises:

I. Choose the correct letter A, B, C or D.

1. _____ concludes that "education and training are critical factors to develop the EU's long-term potential for competitiveness as well as for social cohesion."

    A. European Union   B. European Council

C. Lisbon strategy D. European economic advisors

2. Efficient education and training systems can create economic growth, and equitable systems can create _____.

   A. economic prosperity B. jobs
   C. social cohesion D. economic prosperity and social cohesion

3. Achieving more equity in the design of education systems may help to _____ the need for intense redistributive policies at later ages.

   A. increase B. get out of
   C. admit D. avoid

4. It seems that most people could agree to some variant close to the concept of equality of opportunity proposed by _____.

   A. European Union B. European Council
   C. Roemer D. IMF

5. Equity demands that a person's expected educational outcome should be a function only of _____.

   A. his/her effort B. his/her background
   C. his/her circumstances D. his/her race

6. The following sentences can show that the relationship between efficiency and equity in education and training systems may take different forms except _____.

   A. Some policies may bring education and training systems closer to efficiency without having any impact on equity
   B. Some policies may show that efficiency and equity may be dependent on each other
   C. Some policies may be equitable without influencing on efficiency
   D. Some policies may advance both efficiency and equity in a complementary way

7. Taking _____ as an example, the IMF has given specific recommendations for reforming the education system based on a survey and analysis.

   A. Britain B. Switzerland
   C. Moldova D. Sweden

8. What is the central idea of Roemer's concept of equality of opportunity?

   A. Inequality should be tolerated only if it is due to differences in effort, but not if it is due to circumstances which are beyond a person's control.
   B. Equity would demand that a person's expected educational outcome should be a function only of his/her effort, but not of his/her circumstances, such as race, gender, or family

background.

C. The concept of efficiency is much more straightforward, representing a situation where a maximum aggregate outcome of the educational production process is obtained with given input or a given aggregate outcome with minimum input.

D. An efficient situation is one which would be preferred by any individual who is ignorant of his/her position in society.

9. What is the meaning of "elusive" in the second paragraph?
   A. Difficult to find.
   B. Difficult to achieve.
   C. Difficult to see.
   D. Difficult to describe.

10. In Moldova, the main inefficiencies in general primary and secondary education is _____.
    A. high salaries of teachers
    B. high employment
    C. the oversized school network
    D. both B and C

II. Vocabulary.

Fill in the blanks with the most suitable words. Change the form when necessary.

equitable	aggregate	evade	complementary	maximize
variant	elusive	detriment	calculus	straightforward

1. The meaning of the poem was somewhat _____.
2. The rate of growth of GNP will depend upon the rate of growth of _____ demand.
3. To improve the quality of life through work, two _____ strategies are necessary.
4. Gorky said: "Time is the most _____ judge."
5. There are wide regional _____ in house prices.
6. In order to maximize profit, the firm would seek to _____ output.
7. The system itself is perfectly _____.
8. These difficulties have been overcome without _____ to performance.
9. _____ is a branch of advanced mathematics which deals with variable quantities.
10. By his own admission, he _____ paying taxes as a Florida real-estate speculator.

III. Comprehension of the text.

Decide whether the following statements are true (T) or false (F) according to the passage.

1. The definitions of equity and efficiency are elusive. ( )
2. Given the effects of education on social cohesion, the distribution of education is crucial for societal inequality. ( )

3. The IMF has pointed out that high priority must be given to improving education spending efficiency and equity, which can help improve overall education outcomes. ( )
4. There are many accepted definitions of equity so that most people cannot agree to the concept proposed by Roemer. ( )
5. In the calculus of applied welfare economics, equity and efficiency goals can be combined by maximizing welfare functions. ( )

Supplementary Reading: Educational Policy, Housing Policy and Social Justice

Education, housing policy and systemic injustice are linked together in contemporary Britain. I follow this general preamble with a concrete example. A close friend was for many years a vicar within a tough housing estate in the north of England, and during that time I got to know the region quite well. Some twenty thousand people lived closely together, many of them in subsidized housing. Local crime rate was high, and the regional schools, especially at the secondary level, had major problems with respect to truancy, exclusion and educational standards. Many of the teachers, given the overall situation, did an amazingly good job. But it is pretty obvious that, by and large, the children were disadvantaged—in comparison with, say, the state schools that my own children went to (in the local village and a nearby comprehensive) within the part of Cambridge shire in which I live.

Perhaps a more telling comparison is between the housing estate referred to and the city of St John's, Newfoundland, where I lived for twenty-nine years. Here the housing for those economically disadvantaged is not concentrated in one or two large estates, but is spread out in smaller concentrations in different parts of the city. The largest concentrations of public housing in St John's are in areas that each contains approximately 200 dwellings. The average number of occupants in these dwellings is 2.5, so that each of these areas house roughly 500 persons, and of course, many fewer children.

The result of this system is that most schools have a share of children from economically and socially challenged backgrounds. Unlike the example from the north of England, this means that children from deprived backgrounds are much more likely to be in a school in which a good educational level is possible, and—at the same time—children from more privileged backgrounds are much more likely to rub shoulders with children who came from a very different background.

Unit 13 Educational Justice

There is a sharing of both pain and gain. Such mixing, in my view, is highly desirable for all concerned, children, teachers and parents. The situation is also helped by the fact that a far smaller proportion of economically well-off families in Newfoundland send their children to private schools than in Britain. As a result, the average state school is more socially balanced.

Perhaps I have somewhat idealized the situation in St John's, but my principal point can still be made, namely that, in practice, we cannot separate educational policy from housing policy, and that both of these are intimately related to social justice—by which I mean the attempt to give every child a reasonably fair chance of a good education. The reasons for this claim are easy to see. Unless children are to be bussed from one region to another, concentrations of people who are economically deprived are closely related to matters such as lack of motivation and lack of parental supervision.

In these circumstances I am amazed at how well some schools cope with the difficulties. Nevertheless, it is apparent that—looking at Britain as a whole—we live in a hugely unjust society in which, within the state sector, children in some areas have a fair chance of a good education and others very little. One can always find occasional exceptions—those who by heroic personal drive or heroic local teachers have survived against the odds—but such happy outcomes should not be used to avoid the issue of social inequality. One of the likely reactions to my claim, and the implication that we ought to do something about it—for example, by adopting a housing system that is closer to the example of St John's than to the northern estate referred to—is that a major change of this kind is impractical. Indeed, in the short run, it is. But surely with matters such as educational reform and housing reform we must take the long view, and resist political programs that only look to winning the next election—an outlook that is unlikely to go beyond about five years. Every year there are opportunities to rebuild some areas and most years there are new developments. I am pleading that in all such cases, there should be a deliberate policy of mixed housing, with relatively small concentrations of housing for the disadvantaged—perhaps—of a size that would not take up more than twenty per cent of places in the local primary school. There should be a balance between at least four kinds of property: three or four bedroom detached houses likely to be used by the so-called professional classes; three bedroom houses for the traditional "artisan" class; social housing; bungalows or apartments suitable for the elderly. Given such a policy, my claim is that the educational problems in many of the worst schools would gradually be eased. There would still be an element of injustice, because the state system can never adequately compensate for poor parenting, but at least there would be a realistic chance of every child attending a school in which they could discover the joys of learning.

Unit 14　Educational System & Educational Law

Text A　E-learning in Modern Educational System

> **导读**：随着信息时代的发展与互联网的进步，教育行业也得到了很大的发展：教育理念不断创新，传统的教学模式越来越与学生以及市场的要求相脱节，网络的普及使得教学工作面临迫切的转型。在此背景下，网络教学应运而生。网络教学（E-learning）又称数字学习，也译电子学习，是指在一定教学理论和思想指导下，应用多媒体和互联网技术，通过师、生、媒体等多边、多向互动和对多种媒体教学信息的收集、传输、处理、共享来实现教学目标的一种教学模式。网络教学包括讲授式、演示式、探索式、讨论式、信息收集整理式等教学模式，具有开放性、交互性、共享性等特点。网络教学打破了传统教学在时空上的局限，易于拓宽学生的知识面，使得学业评价更加公开、公平、公正，并且有利于推广研究性学习。2020年，随着新冠疫情在全球范围的蔓延，网络教学成为疫情防控期间全球教育的不二选择，为保障教育教学活动的正常开展立下了汗马功劳。在此特定背景下，全面开展网络教学对于各类学校而言已经从"可选项"变为了"必选项"，推动"互联网+"技术的网络教学正从"新鲜感"向"新常态"转变。

　　The term "e-learning" has been in existence since October 1999 when it was used during a Computer-based Training (CBT) Systems seminar in Los Angeles. Together with the terms "online learning" and "virtual learning", this word was meant to qualify a way to learn based on the use of new technologies allowing access to online, interactive and sometimes personalized training through the Internet or other electronic media (intranet, extranet, interactive TV, CD-ROM, and so on), so as to provide students with new opportunities to maximize their success and select the best options for their education, location, learning style, and mode of learning content delivery. E-learning has many advantages over traditional learning in the classroom. Primarily, the pace of e-learning is tailored to the learner. Then, the costs are usually lower, without time and space limitations. Also, the material is easier to maintain. A good alternative to regular e-learning is blended learning which is a combination of traditional and e-learning. This form of learning involves combining traditional classroom lectures with occasional teaching using some form of

Unit 14 Educational System & Educational Law

tutoring systems or systems for e-learning.

Interestingly, the principles behind e-learning and early forms of e-learning existed even in the 19th century. Long before the appearance of the Internet, distance courses on particular subjects were being offered to students from different countries. Isaac Pitman, a qualified teacher, taught the pupils shorthand via correspondence in the 1840s. In fact, Pitman was sent completed assignments by his students via the mail system and (s)he would then send them more work to be finished. The first testing machine, allowing students to test their knowledge, was invented in 1924. In 1954, B. F. Skinner, a Harvard Professor, invented the "teaching machine". This machine enabled schools to administer programed instruction to the students.

Also, learning, a process of achieving certain competences, can be defined as a dynamical combination of cognitive and meta-cognitive skills, knowledge and understanding, as well as the development of social skills and growth in ethical values. The target of every educational program should be to enable its participants to have an optimal balance in developing all the above. E-learning enhances the quality of educational process by enabling the practice of new roles in the process of learning. In addition, during this process, lifelong learning technologies are used. There are different forms of e-learning: (1) ICT; (2) mixed learning as a combination of classroom teaching and teaching over the system; and (3) learning at distance. When choosing a form of e-learning, one should bear in mind the type of the course it should be applied to as well as the needs and possibilities of students and professors. E-learning should not be seen as an alternative educational system but as an enhancement of the existing one.

Today, we are faced with a new generation of students, and the aberrational characteristics present among them in comparison with the older generations are only going to be more emphasized with the upcoming ones. The new generations of students are capable of fast information adoption and multitasking, and they call for a random access to information ("anytime, anywhere"), as they are accustomed to Google-like informational systems and multiple media operating. They expect to be rewarded at all time. Past educational systems were based on the idea of delivering the knowledge to students who accepted the given knowledge in a passive manner. Professors played the role as keepers of the knowledge. Through e-learning, a new educational environment can be set and an environment can be constructed in the direction of interaction, processing information, researching and problem-solving. The students are asked to actively get involved, and often work in teams. The role of the professor is to design the methods of learning and help the students develop their talents and capabilities. Meanwhile, adaptation in e-learning has generated tremendous interest among researchers in computer-based education. As a consequence, two key terms appeared: adaptivity and adaptability. Adaptivity is such kind of behaviour where the user triggers some actions in the system that guides the learning process, i.e., modifies e-learning lessons using different parameters and a set of pre-defined rules. Adaptability is such kind of behaviour where the user makes changes and takes decisions on the learning process, meaning a possibility for learners to personalize an e-learning lesson by themselves.

To sum up, e-learning, an emerging and rapidly growing area, has a potential to transform existing teaching strategies, learning environments, educational activities, and technology in a classroom, with the aim of acquiring knowledge, constructing personal meaning, and growing from the learning experience.

Notes:

1. **E-learning (网络学习):** E-learning comprises all forms of electronically supported learning and teaching. The information and communication systems, whether networked or not, serve as specific media to implement the learning process. It is essentially the computer and network-enabled transfer of skills and knowledge. E-learning applications and processes include Web-based learning, computer-based learning, virtual classroom opportunities and digital collaboration. Content is delivered via the Internet, intranet/extranet, audio or video tape, satellite TV, and CD-ROM.

2. **Blended Learning (混合式学习):** The idea of blended learning is that some students can benefit from doing part of their learning in a digital environment, and part of it face to face. The benefits of blended learning include the fact that many students can learn best independently, on their own time frame, and via interface with digital technology. At the same time, learning done in this virtual way is often best consolidated by in-person interactions. In many ways, blended learning combines the best of both worlds.

Unit 14 Educational System & Educational Law

News Words and Expressions:

1. extranet ['ekstrənet]	n.	外联网	
2. primarily [praɪ'merəli]	adv.	主要地；根本地	
3. correspondence [ˌkɒrə'spɒndəns]	n.	来往信件；通信；相关；相似	
4. competence ['kɔmpitəns]	n.	能力；胜任；（法庭、机构或人的）权限	
5. dynamical [daɪ'næmɪkəl]	adj.	动力学的；有生气的；有力的	
6. tremendous [trə'mendəs]	adj.	巨大的；极大的；极好的；精彩的	
7. in accordance with		依照；依据	
8. be accustomed to		习惯于	

Exercises:

I. Read the text and answer the following questions.

1. What is the topic or subject being discussed?
2. What is the definition of "learning" in the passage?
3. What are the benefits of e-learning?
4. What's the difference between adaptivity and adaptability?

II. Choose the correct letter A, B, C or D.

1. The principles behind e-learning and early forms of e-learning existed in the ____.
   A. 18th century   B. 19th century
   C. 20th century   D. 21th century

2. What was the function of "teaching machine" invented by B. F. Skinner?
   A. Administering programed instruction.   B. Testing students' knowledge.
   C. Providing unlimited opportunities.   D. Developing certain skill sets.

3. The writer mentioned ____ ways for e-learning.
   A. two   B. three   C. four   D. five

4. The new generations of students are good at ____.
   A. fast information adoption
   B. multitasking
   C. Google-like informational systems and multiple media operating
   D. All of the above

III. Comprehension of the text.

Decide whether the following statements are true (T) or false (F) according to the passage.

1. Two key terms adaptivity and adaptability appeared in the application of e-learning. ( )
2. When choosing a form of e-learning, we should take the type of the course, and the needs as well as possibilities of students and professors into consideration. ( )
3. E-learning should be seen as an alternative educational system. ( )
4. Lifelong learning technologies are used in the e-learning. ( )

Text B Legislation and Equality in Basic Education

导读：随着世界经济和社会的进步越来越依靠知识、技术、技能和能力，人力资源将成为国家在全球市场生存中的决定因素。在这种新的社会历史条件下，让所有儿童、青年和成人的基本学习需要真正得到满足，是世界各国旨在缩小差距、促进社会全面进步的一个必要手段。因此，基础教育的意义和作用受到了高度的关注，它要满足全民的基本学习需求，要求世界各国在现行基础教育服务范围内，保障每一个体的基本权利。不同于高等教育，基础教育在保障基础公平、维护起点公平上起着尤为重要的作用，是提高国民素质、实现国家富强的基础，因此基础教育的平等问题也备受关注：对于个人而言，获得平等的接受基础教育的机会，为个人的发展奠定了重要基础；对于国家而言，基础教育平等有助于国家基础劳动力素质的培养，是一个国家发展的重要基石。

Despite its different meanings and manifestations, the principle of equality has been used to confront social inequalities in a variety of stratified societies and cultures. While the United Nations is striving for universal primary education for children across the globe by 2015, educational inequality persists and has become a significant challenge for educational policy-makers, scholars, and practitioners worldwide. With reference to compulsory schooling legislation, in China, law is used in policy-making as a pragmatic instrument to address specific educational problems, and as a last resort, holds governments of various levels accountable for improving education. In doing so, law can be a device of social justice to promote equality in education by serving as an important mechanism to check and balance the state's power regarding its obligations toward providing basic education, redistributing public resources, reducing disparities, and promoting equality in compulsory schooling. However, using legislation to

Unit 14 Educational System & Educational Law

promote equity in basic education is constrained by economic conditions and other extra-legal factors. Effecting change requires favorable economic, social, and cultural conditions, as well as the cooperation of those who interpret and enforce the law.

Many sociological and educational studies have discussed the relation between equality and education. For example, Horton and Hunt (1984) argued that in modern society, people are given status or rewards according to their merits, which are often measured by results of schooling, and in turn can affect individuals' life chances. Dahrendorf (1975) considered education as an important vehicle of social mobility in a stratified society and equal educational opportunity as a basic right of every person. Levin (1976) expanded the meaning of educational equality to include: equality of educational access, equality of educational participation, equality of educational results, and equality of educational effects on life chances. Equality of opportunity within education, as Bilton, Bonnett, Jones et al (2002) argued, needs to be ensured so that opportunities for success in school are the same for everyone with similar abilities, regardless of sex, ethnicity, and socio-economic background. Iannelli and Paterson (2007) concluded, however, that the social project of "using education to equalize life chances has been a failure". They even argued that education "cannot be used, on its own, to eradicate social inequalities, and is relatively powerless to counter the middle-class strengths of effective networks, self-confident aspirations and sheer wealth".

Despite the debate, the provision of basic education for all with a minimum period of schooling is still believed to be a vital means for reducing inequality within and between societies. Since World War II, the UN has advocated a rights-based approach to basic education. In the *Universal Declaration of Human Rights*, the UN declared that "everyone has the right to education" and that education shall be "free" and "compulsory", at least during the elementary and fundamental stages. This right can empower individuals to achieve "the goals of personal autonomy and efficacy" and enable them to determine the course of their lives.

In response to these global aspirations, many countries have adopted strategies to provide basic education for all. Of these strategies, compulsory schooling legislation is a particularly common one. Legislation can compel the state to provide eligible children with free basic

education for a minimum period of, for example, six or nine years and compel parents to send their children to school. As a result, despite such problems as gender disparity, the number of children in the world enrolled in primary school increased by 6% to 688 million from 1999 to 2005, and the number of children out of school dropped from 96 million in 1999 to 72 million in 2005. However, providing and legislating compulsory schooling does not necessarily mean the complete eradication of educational inequalities in compulsory schooling. Many studies have shown that inequality in school education continues to exist in many forms. As noted by Coleman, Jencks, Levin, and Ballantine, they include: inequalities in educational input and output, and educational opportunity and life chances for children of different social groups, for boys and girls, and for local and non-local students. Inequality of students' academic performance can be caused by many factors, such as cultural practices, social class, family background, ethnicity, gender, and sexuality. Using legislation as a means to institutionalize equality in basic education is part of an international trend of increasing reliance on legislation to bring about social change.

Notes:

1. **Basic education (基础教育):** Basic education refers to the whole range of educational activities taking place in various settings (formal, non-formal and informal) that aims to meet basic learning needs. According to the International Standard Classification of Education (ISCED), basic education comprises primary education (first stage of basic education) and lower secondary education (second stage). In countries (developing countries in particular), basic education often includes also pre-primary education and/or adult literacy programs.

2. *Universal Declaration of Human Rights* **(UDHR) (世界人权宣言):** *Universal Declaration of Human Rights* is a declaration adopted by the United Nations General Assembly on 10 December 1948. The declaration arose directly from the experience of the Second World War and represents the first global expression of rights to which all human beings are inherently

Unit 14 Educational System & Educational Law

entitled. It consists of 30 articles which have been elaborated in subsequent international treaties, regional human rights instruments, national constitutions and laws.

News Words and Expressions:

1. manifestation [ˌmænifeˈsteiʃn]	n.	表现；显示；（幽灵的）显现
2. stratified [ˈstrætifaid]	adj.	分层的；形成阶层的；分为不同等级的
3. pragmatic [præɡˈmætik]	adj.	实际的；实用主义的
4. mechanism [ˈmekənizəm]	n.	方法；（生物体内的）机制；机械装置
5. disparity [diˈspærəti]	n.	（尤指因不公正对待起的）不同；不一致；不等
6. provision [prəˈviʒn]	n.	（法律文件的）规定，条款；提供
7. efficacy [ˈefikəsi]	n.	功效；效力
8. autonomy [ɔːˈtɒnəmi]	n.	自主；自主权；自治
9. eligible [ˈelidʒəbl]	adj.	有资格的；具备条件的；合适的
10. accountable [əˈkaʊntəbl]	adj.	负有责任的；有说明义务的
11. with reference to		关于（等于in reference to）

Exercises:

I. Choose the meaning of the following words used in the passage based on the context.

1. Manifestation

   A. A very clear sign that a particular situation or feeling exists.

   B. The act of appearing or becoming clear.

   C. The appearance of a ghost or a sign of its presence.

   D. Evidence.

2. Stratified

   A. Various.　　B. Having several layers of earth, rock, etc.

   C. Having different social classes.　　D. Useful or right.

3. Pragmatic

   A. Concerned with the study of scientific ideas.

   B. Solving problems in a sensible rather than by having fixed ideas or theories.

   C. Based on carefully organized methods.

   D. Related to the style of a piece of writing or art.

4. Disparity

   A. Change.
   B. Variation.
   C. Equal pay, rights, or power.
   D. A difference connected with unfair treatment.

5. Eradicate

   A. To forget.
   B. To destroy or get rid of something.
   C. To build.
   D. To understand.

6. Autonomy

   A. Freedom to govern a region, country without being controlled by anyone else.

   B. The ability to make your own decisions without being influenced by anyone else.

   C. A person who behaves like a machine, without thinking or feeling anything.

   D. A machine that moves without human control.

7. Efficacy

   A. The quality of being able to produce the result that was intended.

   B. A figure made of wood, paper, stone that looks like a person.

   C. The physical or mental energy that is needed to do something.

   D. An attempt to do something.

8. Aspiration

   A. The sound of air blowing out that happens when some consonants are pronounced.

   B. Someone who hopes to get a position of importance or honor.

   C. A strong desire to have or achieve something.

   D. A way of speaking or behaving.

9. Eligible

   A. Very beautiful and graceful.
   B. Clever and simple.
   C. Upset and unhappy.
   D. Qualified for or allowed or worthy of being chosen.

10. Institutionalize

    A. To make something systematize.

    B. Cause to be admitted.

    C. To officially tell somebody what to do.

    D. To inform somebody about something.

II. Comprehension of the text.

Decide whether the following statements are true or false according to the passage.

1. The United Nations has already solved the problem of primary education for children across

Unit 14 Educational System & Educational Law

the globe. ( )
2. Using legislation to promote equity in basic education is only constrained by economic conditions. ( )
3. Levin considered education as an important vehicle of social mobility in a stratified society and equal educational opportunity as a basic right of every person. ( )
4. Iannelli and Paterson argued that education cannot be used, on its own, to eradicate social inequalities, and is relatively powerless to counter the middle-class strengths of effective networks, self-confident aspirations and sheer wealth. ( )
5. Providing and legislating compulsory schooling means the complete eradication of educational inequalities in compulsory schooling. ( )

III. Translate the following sentences into Chinese.

1. While the United Nations is striving for universal primary education for children across the globe by 2015, educational inequality persists and has become a significant challenge for educational policy-makers, scholars, and practitioners worldwide.
2. With reference to compulsory schooling legislation, in China, law is used in policy-making as a pragmatic instrument to address specific educational problems, and as a last resort, holds governments of various levels accountable for improving education.
3. Equality of opportunity within education, as Bilton argued, needs to be ensured so that opportunities for success in school are the same for everyone with similar abilities, regardless of sex, ethnicity, and socio-economic background.
4. In the *Universal Declaration of Human Rights*, the UN declared that "everyone has the right to education" and that education shall be "free" and "compulsory", at least during the elementary and fundamental stages.
5. As a result, despite such problems as gender disparity, the number of children in the world enrolled in primary school increased by 6% to 688 million from 1999 to 2005, and the number of children out of school dropped from 96 million in 1999 to 72 million in 2005.

Supplementary Reading: Major Continuities and Changes in the *Compulsory Education Law*

Since national educational systems were first organized in the 18th century, legislation has been used to initiate and enforce various educational policies. One of the earliest types of education law-making was compulsory schooling legislation. Today over 170 countries use legal means to protect children's rights to access compulsory schooling for a minimum period. Despite being a late-comer, in 1986 China enacted the *Compulsory Education Law of the People's Republic of China* and began to provide 9 years of compulsory schooling. However, the law was significantly revised.

The *Compulsory Education Law of the People's Republic of China* was expanded from 18 articles of about 1800 words to 63 articles of over 7000 words. Further, content analysis of the *Compulsory Education Law of the People's Republic of China* (1986 Edition) and the *Compulsory Education Law of the People's Republic of China* (2018 Revision) reveals continuities and changes. The law continues to defend the rights of children to access basic education. Through the revised law the National People's Congress (NPC) of the People's Republic of China attempts to force the state administration to become more accountable for implementing and enforcing its basic education policies and measures.

The law was revised at the 22nd Session of the Standing Committee of the 10th NPC in 2006, and then amended for the second time according to the "Decision on Revising Five Laws of the People's Republic of China" passed at the 7th Session of the Standing Committee of the 13th NPC on December 29, 2018. Similar to the 1986 edition, the 2018 version continues to defend citizens' rights to access compulsory schooling by keeping five major policy principles of basic education for all. First, the revised law acknowledges the importance of the fundamental function of education in training for the socialist cause the constructors and successors in ideals, morality, knowledge and discipline. Second, the revised law reiterates the principle of equal opportunity for eligible children over age 6 (or 7 in areas with less developed conditions) to receive 9 years of

Unit 14 Educational System & Educational Law

compulsory schooling. The revised law re-emphasizes the nondiscriminatory nature of admission to basic education for all regardless of a student's physical condition, gender, ethnicity, religion and socio-economic status. The revised law also adds a new provision to protect the right of juveniles to receive basic education. Third, to ensure such equal opportunity, the revised law continues to stipulate a policy of examination-free admission by catchment area in the place of their parents' or guardians' household registration. And the catchment area refers to schools within 3 km of the student's residence, rather than the nearest school. Fourth, parents or guardians are legally obliged to send their eligible children to school. Fifth, child labor remains illegal.

Unlike the 1986 edition, which was concerned primarily with the quantity and efficiency of compulsory schooling, the 2018 version deals more with the quality and fairness of basic education, which also stipulates a series of legislative changes with a view to remedy the legal loopholes of the old version and address new concerns and problems arising from social and educational changes since the 1980s. These problems include: the effects of examinations on teaching and learning, widespread fee abuses, lack of a mechanism to ensure investment in basic education and an increase in disparity. The first problem is related to the quality of education, whereas the other three are more related to issues of equality in compulsory schooling. A very pressing problem in compulsory schooling legislation that drew the NPC's law-makers' attention is increasing the concern about students' heavy workload and the quality of their education. After many state measures failed to address these concerns, law-makers were invited to decide on the interests of various stakeholders concerning student workload and to promote quality education.

Unit 15　Educator & Educational Thoughts

Text A　Disciples of Confucius

> 导读：孔子（前551—前479）是我国古代伟大的思想家和教育家，儒家学派创始人，世界最著名的文化名人之一。孔子首次提出"有教无类"的教育思想，认为世界上所有人都享有受教育的权利。他认为教师在教书育人的过程中应该"诲人不倦""循循善诱""因材施教"；认为学生应该有好的学习方法，如"举一反三""温故而知新"；学习还要结合思考——"学而不思则罔，思而不学则殆"，好学——"三人行必有我师"；学习态度要端正。孔子的教育思想，至今仍然有重要的启发和教育意义。

Confucius' teachings were later turned into an elaborate set of rules and practices by his numerous disciples and followers who organized his teachings into the *Analects of Confucius*. Confucius' disciples and his only grandson, Zisi, continued his philosophical school after his death. These efforts spread Confucian ideals to students who then became officials in many of the royal courts in China, thereby giving Confucianism the first wide-scale test of its dogma.

Two of Confucius' most famous later followers emphasized radically different aspects of his teachings. In the centuries after his death, Mencius and Xun Zi (荀子) both composed important teachings elaborating in different ways on the fundamental ideas associated with Confucius. Mencius articulated the innate goodness in human beings as a source of the ethical intuitions that guided people towards rén (仁), yì (义), and lǐ (礼), while Xun Zi underscored the realistic and materialistic aspects of Confucian thought, stressing that morality was inculcated in society through tradition and in individuals through training. In time, their writings, together with the *Analects of Confucius* and other core texts came to constitute the philosophical corpus of Confucianism.

This realignment in Confucian thought was parallel to the development of Legalism, which saw filial piety as self-interest but not a useful tool for a ruler to create an effective state. A disagreement between these two political philosophies came to a head in 221 BC when the Qin state conquered all of China. Li Ssu, Prime Minister of the Qin Dynasty convinced Qin Shi

Huang to abandon the Confucians' recommendation of awarding fiefs akin to the Zhou Dynasty before them which he saw as counter to the Legalistic idea of centralizing the state around the ruler. When the Confucian advisers pressed their point, Li Ssu had many Confucian scholars killed and their books burned—considered a huge blow to the philosophy and Chinese scholarship.

Under the succeeding Han Dynasty and Tang Dynasty, Confucian ideas gained even more widespread prominence. During the Song Dynasty, the scholar Zhu Xi added ideas from Daoism and Buddhism into Confucianism. In his life, Zhu Xi was largely ignored, but not long after his death his ideas became the new orthodox view of what Confucian texts actually meant. Modern historians view Zhu Xi as having created something rather different, and call his way of thinking Neo-Confucianism. Neo-Confucianism held sway in China, Korea, and Vietnam until the 19th century.

The works of Confucius were translated into European languages through the agency of Jesuit scholars stationed in China. Matteo Ricci started to report on the thoughts of Confucius, and father Prospero Intorcetta published the life and works of Confucius into Latin in 1687. It is thought that such works had considerable importance on European thinkers of the period, particularly among the Deists and other philosophical groups of the Enlightenment who were interested by the integration of the system of morality of Confucius into Western civilization.

Notes:

1. **Mencius (孟子)**: Mencius, also known by his birth name Meng Ke or Ko, was born in the State of Zou. He was a Chinese philosopher who was arguably the most famous Confucian after Confucius himself.
2. **Xun Zi (荀子)**: Xun Zi was a Chinese Confucian philosopher who lived during the Warring States Period and contributed to one of the Hundred Schools of Thought. Xun Zi believed man's inborn tendencies need to be curbed through education and ritual, counter to Mencius'

view that man is innately good. He believed that ethical norms had been invented to rectify mankind.

3. **Legalism (法家):** Legalism is a Classical Chinese philosophy that emphasizes the need for order above all other human concerns.

4. **Matteo Ricci (利玛窦):** Matteo Ricci was an Italian Jesuit priest, and one of the founding figures of the Jesuit China Mission, as it existed in the 17th—18th centuries. His current title is Servant of God.

5. **Li Ssu (李斯):** Li Ssu was the influential Prime Minister of the feudal state and later of the dynasty of Qin, between 246 BC and 208 BC. A famous Legalist, he was also a notable calligrapher. Li Ssu served under two rulers: Qin Shi Huang, king of Qin and later First Emperor of China—and his son, Qin Er Shi. A powerful minister, he was central to the state's policies, including those on military conquest, draconian centralization of state control, standardization of weights, measures and the written script, and persecution of Confucianism and opponents of Legalism. His methods of administration of China are seen by some as an early form of totalitarianism.

6. **Zhu Xi (朱熹):** Zhu Xi was a Song Dynasty Confucian scholar who became the leading figure of the School of Principle and the most influential rationalist Neo-Confucian in China. His contribution to Chinese philosophy included his assigning special significance to the *Analects of Confucius*, the *Mencius*, the *Great Learning*, and the *Doctrine of the Mean*, his emphasis on the investigation of things, and the synthesis of all fundamental Confucian.

7. **Deists (自然神论者):** Deists are a partial list of people who have the belief in a God based on natural religion only, or belief in religious truths discovered by people through a process of reasoning, independent of any revelation through scripture or prophets. They have been selected for their influence on Deism, or for their fame in other areas.

New Words and Expressions:

1. analects ['ænəlekts] n. 文选；论集
2. dogma ['dɒgmə] n. 教条；教理；信条
3. underscore [ˌʌndə'skɔː, 'ʌndəskɔː] vt. 强调；划线于……下
4. inculcate ['inkʌlkeit, in'kʌl-] vt. 教育；谆谆教诲；教授；反复灌输
5. realignment [ˌriːə'lainmənt] n. 重新排列；重新组合；改组
6. filial ['filjəl] adj. 孝顺的；子女的，当作子女的

Unit 15   Educator & Educational Thoughts

7. orthodox ['ɔːθədɔks]   *adj.*   正统的；传统的；惯常的
8. deist ['diːist]   *n.*   自然神论者；自然神论信仰者

Exercises:

I. Choose the correct letter A, B, C, or D.

1. _____ continued Confucius' philosophical school after Confucius' death.
   A. His followers
   B. His followers and his only grandson
   C. His followers and his disciples
   D. His disciples and his only grandson

2. _____ who composed important teachings elaborating in different ways on the fundamental ideas associated with Confucius were two of Confucius' most famous later followers.
   A. Xun Zi and Zisi
   B. Xun Zi and Mencius
   C. Mencius and Zisi
   D. Zisi and Zhu Xi

3. _____ convinced Qin Shi Huang to abandon the Confucians' recommendation of awarding fiefs.
   A. Li Ssu.
   B. Zhu Xi.
   C. Legalist.
   D. Zisi.

4. Which dynasty did not accept Confucian thought?
   A. Han Dynasty.
   B. Tang Dynasty.
   C. Qin Dynasty.
   D. Song Dynasty.

5. _____ started to report on the thoughts of Confucius, and _____ published the life and works of Confucius into Latin in 1687.
   A. Jesuit scholars; Matteo Ricci
   B. Jesuit scholars; Prospero Intorcetta
   C. Prospero Intorcetta; Matteo Ricci
   D. Matteo Ricci; Prospero Intorcetta

II. Vocabulary.

Fill in the blanks with the most suitable words. Change the form when necessary.

| underscore | inculcate | constitute | conquer | orthodox |
| dogma | filial | attack | articulate | |

1. The numbers _____ a trend that has occurred in previous economic downturns.
2. Her staff find her bossy and _____.
3. The _____ Thanksgiving dinner includes turkey and pumpkin pie.

4. The village had been _____ by the French air force.

5. She tries very hard to _____ traditional values into her students.

6. Now I've tried to _____ exactly what I felt to be the truth.

7. The 50 states _____ the USA.

8. Qing Ming Festival is a way that Chinese show _____ piety.

9. The Normans _____ England in 1066.

III. Read the text and answer the following questions.

1. What did Xun Zi stress according to Confucian thought?

2. What did Li Ssu do to abandon Confucian thought?

3. Whose thought called Neo-Confucianism was famous among China, Korea and Vietnam until 19th century?

4. How was Confucian thought famous among the European?

5. What is the main idea of this passage?

Text B   Educational Thought and Teaching

> 导读：教育思想是指人们对人类特有的教育活动现象的一种理解和认识，是人们在一定社会时代背景下，通过教育实践活动形成的对教育现象、教育问题的观念意识层面的理解和认识。教育思想具有实践性、多样性、历史性、社会性、继承性、可借鉴性、预见性和前瞻性的特征，并渗透在教育活动的各个环节、各个方面、各个领域，直接或间接地对人们的教育实践活动起着一定的作用。教育思想有助于人们理智地把握教育现实，使人们依据一定的教育思想从事教育实践；有助于人们认清教育工作中的成绩和弊端，使教育工作更有起色；有助于人们合理地预测未来，勾画教育发展的蓝图。

The oriental world contains the two oldest and, if they could be juxtaposed, the two basic theories of education. In Indian philosophies, we find strong elements of deep concentration and a focus on internal values. In the teachings of Chinese philosophies there appears an equally strong theme of preparation for life of activity on Earth. Every subsequent theory embodies in some measure man's explorations in these two directions.

The teachings emanating from India were and are a majestic illustration of a whole range

Unit 15 Educator & Educational Thoughts

of oriental philosophies which regard education as a means through which men can prepare themselves for life. One of the central conceptions of this education is duty, the capacity to uphold and support the laws of moral conduct within and without one. Human desires, the quest for satisfaction of material needs, the thirst for fulfillment of the senses are the obstacles with which men must contend in their search for a balanced life. Education thus is a process of inculcating self-discipline, so that the mind and the body can be freed from excessive concern for material pursuits. To this aim of self-mastery, other aims are subordinated. Inward-directedness, self-introspection, and contemplation are the ends of schooling.

The teaching coming from China stressed the opposite tradition in education. At its center lies the wholehearted dedication to life and the proprieties of daily living. Men like Confucius focus on moral and ethical teachings. They have often busied themselves with the salvaging and re-edition of sacred Chinese scriptures. But for the Chinese, the focus is on practical and ethical living. The more immediate concern of man is life. "While you don't know about life, what can you know about death." For Confucius and his future countless followers, the class of Chinese literati, who through his precepts became the class of officials in China, the virtuous life, decorum in mores and manners, service and responsibility toward others, were the canons of the system. Education was to be completely dedicated to these canons. It thus became a means to inculcate good precepts, and a way to pass on ancient wisdom. Teaching by example, by immersing oneself in the cultural heritage of the age became the model of good living and good pedagogy.

Both the value-centered and the earth-centered teachings resulted in practice in systems of formal education in which children were forced to memorize ancient writings by repetition and by rote, while older students apprenticed or clustered informally around their teachers. Oriental education allowed much room for mystic or intellectualized approach to living. More practical preparation was less conspicuous or imparted on a family basis.

Western educational practices owe a great deal to Plato and Aristotle. The teachings of these two philosophers are best-known parts of development of Greek thought and practice in education. The early Greek cosmologists were concerned with the nature of existence and with man's relationship to the universe. On the other hand, concern with the cosmos did not prevent the Greeks from developing a scientific philosophy which arose alongside with the rationalistic conception of man as the center of knowledge. The Greek philosophy recognized that the aim of education is to sensitize man both to the infinity, and to the business of social life on earth. The model to which all educational processes were destined to lead was "man beautiful and virtuous". Greek education remained for all times a model of activity of man as an idealistic and thinking, but also rational and political being adjusting himself through reason to social and spiritual levels of life. Plato and Aristotle left provocative social proposals in *Republic* and *Politics* respectively; but they also pointed the way to eternal verities, the logos.

One of the several outstanding Roman thinkers, Quintilian concentrated on elaborating a system of education based on oratory as a means to restore the moral virtues. Quintilian emphasized both moral values and "actual practice and experience of life", a natural interest in a nation whose claim to fame lay not only in the powers of intellectual concentration but also in military prowess and administrative skill. Part of Quintilian's tragedy was that he advocated eloquence and republican virtue at the time when it could no longer serve public good, but it could only be used by careerists and sycophants around the imperial throne. His precise pedagogical devices were thus deprived of the vigorous goals, in the service of which they could have been used in an earlier age.

With Aquinas, the dichotomy between practical and theoretical education loses its overwhelming significance. Several years later, schools such as those influenced by Hermann Francke continued to flourish, retaining an idealistic dimension. But in the broadest sense man surrenders his curiosity and quest of the unknown to the overriding certainty that life on earth must be seriously cultivated.

Notes:

1. **UNESCO (United Nations Educational, Scientific, and Cultural Organization) (联合国教育、科学及文化组织):** UNESCO is a specialized agency of the United Nations established on 16 November 1945. Its stated purpose is to contribute to peace and security by promoting international collaboration through education, science, and culture in order to further universal respect for justice, the rule of law, and the human rights along with fundamental freedoms proclaimed in the UN Charter. It is the heir of the League of Nations' International Commission

Unit 15 Educator & Educational Thoughts

on Intellectual Cooperation.

2. Aristotle (亚里士多德): Aristotle was a Greek philosopher, a student of Plato and teacher of Alexander the Great. His writings cover many subjects, including physics, metaphysics, poetry, theater, music, logic, rhetoric, linguistics, politics, government, ethics, biology, and zoology. Together with Plato and Socrates, Aristotle is one of the most important founding figures in Western philosophy. Aristotle's writings were the first to create a comprehensive system of Western philosophy, encompassing morality and aesthetics, logic and science, politics and metaphysics.

3. Thomas Aquinas (托马斯·阿奎纳): Aquinas was an Italian Dominican priest of the Catholic Church, and an immensely influential philosopher and theologian in the tradition of scholasticism, known as Doctor Angelicus, Doctor Communis, or Doctor Universalis. He was the foremost classical proponent of natural theology, and the father of Thomism. His influence on Western thought is considerable, and much of modern philosophy was conceived as a reaction against, or as an agreement with his ideas, particularly in the areas of ethics, natural law and political theory.

New Words and Expressions:

1. juxtapose [ˌdʒʌkstə'pəʊz]	v.		把……并列；把……并置
2. emanate from	v.		发源于；从……发出
3. majestic [mə'dʒestik]	adj.		威严的；雄伟的
4. decorum [di'kɔːrəm]	n.		端庄稳重；恪守礼仪
5. apprentice [ə'prentis]	n.		学徒；徒弟
	v.		使某人当（某人的）学徒
6. cluster ['klʌstə]	v.		群聚；聚集
	n.		（人或动物的）群，团，组
7. infinity [in'finəti]	n.		无穷；无限；无限远的点
8. provocative [prə'vɒkətiv]	adj.		煽动性的；挑衅的；引诱的
9. eloquence ['eləkwəns]	n.		口才；雄辩
10. sycophant ['sikəfænt]	n.		谄媚者

教育学专业英语

Exercises:

I. Choose the correct letter of A, B, C, or D.

1. What is the meaning of "juxtapose" in the first paragraph?

   A. To give some examples.　　B. To put things together.

   C. To compare the things.　　D. To make things different.

2. What is the meaning of "illustration" in the second paragraph?

   A. An example.　　B. A picture.

   C. An article.　　D. A book.

3. The teachings emanating from India regard education as _____.

   A. duty

   B. a process of inculcating self-discipline

   C. the life of the spirit

   D. a means through which men can prepare themselves for life

4. The role of education as a process of inculcating self-discipline is _____.

   A. for human desires　　B. for the life of the spirit

   C. for human duty　　D. for the mind and the body

5. Teaching by example, by immersing oneself in the cultural heritage of the age became the model of _____.

   A. good living　　B. good pedagogy

   C. good spirit　　D. good living and good pedagogy

6. Western educational practices owe a great deal to _____.

   A. Plato and Aristotle　　B. Plato and Socrates

   C. Alexander and Socrates　　D. Alexander and Aristotle

7. Which of the following statements is not true according to the Greek thought?

   A. The early Greek cosmologists were concerned with the nature of existence and with man's relationship to the universe.

   B. The concern with the cosmos prevented the Greeks from developing a scientific philosophy which arose alongside with the rationalistic conception of man as the center of knowledge.

   C. The Greek philosophy recognized that the aim of education is to sensitize man both to the infinity, and to the business of social life on earth.

   D. Greek education remained for all times a model of activity of man as an idealistic and thinking, but also rational and political being adjusting himself through reason to social and spiritual levels of life.

Unit 15 Educator & Educational Thoughts

8. Which of the following statements is not true of Quintilian?
   A. He concentrated on elaborating a system of education based on oratory as a means to restore the moral virtues.
   B. His tragedy was that he advocated eloquence and republican virtue at the time when it could no longer serve public good, but it could only be used by careerists and sycophants around the imperial throne.
   C. He emphasized both moral values and "actual practice and experience of life", a natural interest in a nation whose claim to fame lay only in the powers of intellectual concentration.
   D. His precise pedagogical devices were deprived of the vigorous goals, in the service of which they could have been used in an earlier age.
9. What is the meaning of "surrender" in the last paragraph?
   A. To stop fighting.   B. To give.
   C. To control.   D. To give up.

II. Comprehension of the text.

Decide whether the following statements are true (T) or false (F) according to the passage.

1. Human desires, the quest for satisfaction of material needs, the thirst for fulfillment of the senses—these are the obstacles with which men must contend in their search for a balanced life. ( )
2. Education became a means to inculcate good precepts, and a way to pass on ancient wisdom. ( )
3. Both the value-centered and the earth-centered teaching resulted in practice in systems of formal education in which children were forced to memorize by writing. ( )
4. That more practical preparation was less conspicuous or imparted on a family basis was the reason why the education of Asia was affected. ( )
5. The teachings of Plato and Aquinas are best-known parts of development of Greek thought and practice in education. ( )

III. Translate the following sentences into Chinese.

1. Education is a process of inculcating self discipline, so that the mind and the body can be freed from excessive concern for material pursuits.
2. Both the value-centered and the earth-centered teachings resulted in practice in systems of formal education in which children were forced to memorize ancient writings by repetition and

by rote, while older students apprenticed or clustered informally around their teachers.
3. The Greek philosophy recognized that the aim of education is to sensitize man both to the infinity, and to the business of social life on earth.
4. His precise pedagogical devices were thus deprived of the vigorous goals, in the service of which they could have been used in an earlier age.
5. In the broadest sense man surrenders his curiosity and quest of the unknown to the overriding certainty that life on earth must be seriously cultivated.

Supplementary Reading: Frederick James Gould: Education Inspired by Humanity's Story

Born into the impoverished lower middle-class family in 1855, Frederick James Gould worked as a teacher between 1871 and 1896. Later, he left teaching and moved to Leicester where he was elected to the school board in 1900. After leaving Leicester in 1910, he became active in large number of educational associations and continued to write and publish on educational matters at a phenomenal rate until his death on 6 April 1938. Two of his close associates, E. M. White, a lecturer on Civics, and F. H. Hayward, a one-time schools inspector, then compiled a selection of his later writings under the title of *The Last Days of a Great Educationist*. His prolific output and his lifelong, tenacious and pioneering championing of moral education and educational reform probably merit this eponymous praise.

There is no denying that Gould placed a very high emphasis on the power of education to change people's lives for the better. In 1891 he wrote a Utopian novel, *The Agnostic Isle*, in which the improved ordering of society was directly attributed to the education provided for the citizens. Gould placed moral education at the forefront of all his thoughts on education and summarized the essential components of any good moral education system under four headings, i.e., order, beauty, service and progress, a list that barely changed during the course of his life. By order he did not mean discipline but rather the striving for an essential and natural order by the universe and all that lay therein, including human society. In 1899, he produced an outline syllabus to affect this overall scheme. Children, he argued, should be taught lessons based round moral themes rather than traditionally defined subjects. These new lessons would feature the concepts of self-respect and self-control, truthfulness, kindness, work and duty, mutual dependence, justice and cooperation, nature, and, lastly, art.

Unit 15　Educator & Educational Thoughts

　　Furthermore, he advocated teaching through the use of stories that could be read to the children and which concluded with an obvious moral that Gould recommended be elicited from them. He produced 15 books of such tales during his life. The titles of the chapters in the series of four books Gould produced around the turn of the century called *Children's Moral Lessons* are indicative of this overall approach. Also, in a *Labor Prophet* article of 1893, he had sketched out the broad parameters of how these lessons ought to be taught and further suggested that the children in socialist Sunday schools be divided into two groups, juniors and seniors, roughly on age lines, that classes begin at 3.00 p.m. with a socialist hymn and that lessons were as far as possible illustrated with pictures or, even better, magic lantern slides. Within this style of lessons Gould had very definite opinions on how his stories should be used to achieve his aims. He held out against what he called "lazy moralists", that is to say teachers who might have believed that simply presenting children with a good tale with a moral to learn at the end would ensure that the moral was adopted by its young audience. This type of activity, he argued, tended to present the children with a series of negative instructions, a list of "don'ts" and was, moreover, extremely boring. Instead, Gould advocated a dramatic presentation using props and blackboard sketches to set the scene from which the truth would emerge "naturally and spontaneously".

　　In his 1900 publication *Moral Instruction*, he laid out his general approach to methodology in the classroom: "Education must allow for more conduct and less lecturing, and the conduct must be transformed into neighborly conduct." To achieve this neighborliness, he advocated exercises in four aspects of civic life. First, there was what he called "social alertness". This consisted of personal and environmental cleanliness, respect for public order, and an understanding of one's civic duties such as voting. Second, there was ordered recreation as opposed to a mere romp. Third, excursions were to be arranged to places that gave concrete examples of the organic nature of social life such as cathedrals, castles, local authority buildings, harbors, lighthouses, mines and factories. And lastly, the practice of charitable works and visits to the less fortunate was to be encouraged.

References

1. Abidin, R. R. & Kmetz, C. A. (1997). "Teacher-student interactions as predicted by teaching stress and the perceived quality of the student-teacher relationship." Research presented at the Annual Meeting of the National Association of School Psychologists, Anaheim, CA.

2. Bardhan, P. & Mookherjee, D. (2000). Capture and governance at the local and national levels. *American Economic Review,* 90(2), 135–139.

3. Bardhan, P. & Mookherjee, D. (2006). Decentralization and accountability in infrastructure delivery in developing countries. *Economic Journal,* 116(1), 101–127.

4. Bardhan, P. (2002). Decentralization of governance and development. *Journal of Economic Perspectives,* 16(4), 185–205.

5. Bilton, T., Bonnett, K., Jones, P., Lawson, T., Skinner, D., Stanworth, M., Webster, A. (2002). *Introductory Sociology.* 4th ed. Basingstoke: Palgrave Macmillan.

6. Bindhu, R. & Kumar. L. (2007). Problem-based learning: What and how do students learn? *Med Educ*, 16(3), 235-266.

7. Bowlby, J. (1988). On knowing what you are not supposed to know and feeling what you are not supposed to feel. In *A Secure Base*: *Parent-child Attachment and Healthy Human Development*. New York: In Basic Books, 99–118.

8. Brophy, J. & Good, T. (1974). *Teacher-student Relationships: Causes and Consequences*. New York: Holt, Rinehart and Winston.

9. Bru, E. B., Boyesen, M., Munthe, E. & Roland, E. (1998). Perceived social support at school and emotional and musculoskeletal complaints among Norwegian 8th grade students. *Scandinavian Journal of Educational Research*, 42, 339–356.

10. Calvin, John. (1995). *Institutes of the Christian Religion: 1536 Edition*. Grand Rapids: Associated Publishers and Authors.

11. Campbell, R. J., Kyriakides, L., Muijs, R. D. & Robinson, W. (2003). Differential teacher effectiveness: Towards a model for research and teacher appraisal. *Oxford Review of Education*, 29(3), 347–362.

12. Carr, M. (1990). The role of context and development from a lifespan perspective. In W. Schneider & F. E. Weinert (eds.). *Interactions among Aptitudes, Strategies, and Knowledge in*

References

Cognitive Performance. New York: Springer Verlag, 222–231.

13. Carr, M. (2000). "Challenges to young girls' strategy use." Invited presentation as a part of a WME symposium at the Annual Meeting of the National Council of Teachers of Mathematics, Chicago.

14. Dahrendorf, R. (1975). *The New Liberty: Survival and Justice in A Changing World.* London: Routledge & Kegan Paul.

15. Dawes, Milton. (2005). On time-binding consciousness. *ETC: A Review of General Semantics,* 62(3).

16. Day, C., Elliot, B. & Kington, A. (2005). Reform, standards and teacher identity: Challenges of sustaining commitment. *Journal of Teaching and Teacher Education,* 21, 563–577.

17. De Grauwe, A. (2005). Improving the quality of education through school-based management: learning from international experiences. *Review of Education,* 51, 269–287.

18. Fisher, D. L. & Cresswell, J. (1999). Relationships between the principal's interpersonal behaviour and the school environment. *International Studies in Educational Administration,* 27, 29–44.

19. Giroux, Henry A. (1992). *Border Crossings: Cultural Workers and the Politics of Education.* New York: Routledge.

20. Goldworthy, R., Schwartz, N., Barab, S. & Landa, A. (2007). Evaluation of a collaborative multimedia conflict resolution curriculum. *Education Technology Research and Development,* 55(6).

21. Goodlad, J. (1990). *Teachers for Our Nation's Schools.* San Francisco: Jossey-Bass.

22. Guneyli, A. & Aslan, C. (2009). Evaluation of Turkish prospective teacher's attitudes towards teaching profession. *Procedia Social and Behavioral Sciences,* 1, 313-319.

23. Hanushek, Eric A. & Woessmann, L. (2007). The role of education quality for economic growth. In *World Bank Policy Research Working Paper, Number 4122.* Washington D.C.: World Bank.

24. Hartup, W. W. (1996). The company they keep: friendships and their developmental significance. *Child Development,* 67, 1–13.

25. Hauck, Ben. (2007). A tangible experience of time-binding. *ETC: A Review of General Semantics,* 64(1).

26. Hayakawa, S. I. (2001). The aims and tasks of general semantics: implications of the time-binding theory (part I). *ETC: A Review of General Semantics,* 58(1).

27. Hayakawa, S. I. (2004). Ethics of time-binding. *ETC: A Review of General Semantics,* 61(4).

28. Horton, P. B. & Hunt, C. L. (1984). *Sociology*. Auckland, NZ: McGraw-Hill-Hu.

29. Iannelli, C. & Paterson, L. (2007). Education and social mobility in Scotland. *Research in Social Stratification and Mobility,* 25(3), 219–232.

30. Jackson, P., Boostrom, R. & Hansen, D. (1993). *The Moral Life of Schools*. San Francisco: Jossey-Bass.

31. Kearney, P., Plax, T. G., Hays, L. R. & Ivey, M. J. (1991). College teacher misbehaviors: What students don't like about what teachers say or do. *Communication Quarterly*, 39, 309–324.

32. Korzybski, Alfred. (1950). *Manhood of Humanity*. 2nd ed. Lakeville, CT: International Non-Aristotelian Library; Institute of General Semantics.

33. Kreitner, R. & Kinicki, A. (2007). *Organizational Behavior*. Arizona: McGraw-Hill Ryerson.

34. Levin, H. M. (1976). Educational opportunity and social inequality in western Europe. *Social Problems,* 24(2), 148–172.

35. Luther, Martin. (1967). A sermon on keeping children in school. In *Luther's Works, Volume 46: Christian in Society III*, 207–258.

36. Luther, Martin. (2018). Letter to the German rulers. In John William Perrin. *The History of Compulsory Education in New England*. Sheridan, WY: Creative Media Partners, LLC.

37. Madsen, K. & Cassidy, J. W. (2005). The effect of focus of attention and teaching experience on perceptions of teaching effectiveness and student learning. *Journal of Research in Music Education*, 53(3), 222–233.

38. Mancini, V. H., Wuest, D. A., Vantine, W. K. & Clark, E. K. (1984). The use of instruction and supervision in interaction analysis on burned out physical educators: Its effects on teaching behaviors, level of burn out, and students' academic learning time. *Journal of Teaching in Physical Education*, 3(2), 29–46.

39. Mark, M. (2001). Evaluation's future: furor, futile, or fertile? *The American Journal of Evaluation*, 22, 457–479.

40. McGee, Michael Calvin. (1990). Text, context, and the fragmentation of contemporary culture. *Western Journal of Communication*, 54(3).

41. Meador, D. (2013). Virtual reality for collaborative E-learning. *Computers & Education*, 50(4), 286-305.

42. Moss, C. M. & Brookhart, S. M. (2009). *Advancing Formative Assessment in Every Classroom: A Guide for Instructional Leaders*. Alexandria, VA: ASCD.

43. Petty, R. & Cacioppo, J. T. (1986). The elaboration likelihood model of persuasion. In L.

Berkowitz (ed.). *Advances in Experimental Social Psychology Vol. 19*. New York: Academic Press, 123–205.

44. Pianta, R. C., Steinberg, M. & Rollins, K. (1995). The first two years of school: Teacher-child relationships and deflections in children's classroom adjustment. *Development and Psychopathology*, 7, 295–312.

45. Rafferty, T. (2003). School climate and teachers' attitudes toward upward in secondary schools. *American Secondary Education*, 31(2), 49–70.

46. Rose, M. (2005). *Lives on the Boundary*. New York: Penguin Books.

47. Ryan, F. J., Sweeder, J. J. & Bednar, M. R. (1998). Technology and the moral sense: Re-wiring moral education. *Document presented on the Novena Conference: Society for Information Technology & Teacher Education International Conference*. Washington D.C.: Site 98.

48. Santiago, P., Tremblay, K., Basri, E. & Arnal, E. (2008). Tertiary education for the knowledge society. *OECD Thematic Review of Tertiary Education: Synthesis Report, vol. 2*. Paris: OECD.

49. Sava, F. A. (2001). Causes and effects of teacher conflict-inducing attitudes towards pupils: A path analysis model. *Journal of Teaching and Teacher Education*, 18, 1007–1021.

50. Sockett, H. (1993). *The Moral Base for Teacher Professionalism*. New York: Teachers College Press, Columbia University.

51. Stiggins, R. J., Arter, J. A., Chappuis, J., & Chappuis, S. (2009). *Classroom Assessment for Learning: Doing It Right—Using It Well*. Columbus, OH: Allyn and Bacon.

52. Stronge, J. H., Ward, T. J. & Grant, L. W. (2011). What makes good teachers good? A cross-case analysis of the connection between teacher effectiveness and student achievement. *Journal of Teacher Education*, 62(4), 339–355.

53. Turnbull, B. & Mee, J. (2003). Teacher perspectives of school management teams. *Educational Research and Evaluation*, 9(4), 373–389.

54. Weinberg, Harry L. (1959). *Levels of Knowing and Existence*. New York: Harper & Row.

55. Williams, M. & Burden, R. (1997). *Psychology for Language Teachers: A Social Constructivist Approach*. Cambridge, UK: Cambridge University Press.

56. Zimmerman, B. J. (2001). Theories of self-regulated learning and academic achievement: An overview and analysis. In B. J. Zimmerman & D. H. Schunk (eds.). *Self-regulated Learning and Academic Achievement: Theoretical Perspectives*. Mahwah, NJ: Erlbaum, 1–65.

57. 霍小光、吴晶、施雨岑. (2016). 教师节，听听习总书记怎么说. http://www.xinhuanet.

com/politics/2016-09/10/c_1119544092.htm. 2024年8月3日访问.

58. 习近平. (2022). 高举中国特色社会主义伟大旗帜　为全面建设社会主义现代化国家而团结奋斗——在中国共产党第二十次全国代表大会上的报告. https://www.gov.cn/xinwen/2022-10/25/content_5721685.htm. 2024年8月3日访问.

59. 新华社. (2018). 习近平出席全国教育大会并发表重要讲话. https://www.gov.cn/xinwen/2018-09/10/content_5320835.htm?tdsourcetag=s_pctim_aiomsg&wd=&eqid=bc6374bb00083eb9000000026491070a. 2024年1月1日访问.

教育学专业英语

尊敬的老师：

您好！

本书练习题配有参考答案，请通过邮件联系责任编辑索取。同时，为了方便您更好地使用本教材，获得最佳教学效果，我们特向使用该书作为教材的教师赠送本教材配套电子资料。如有需要，请完整填写"教师联系表"并加盖所在单位系（院）公章，免费向出版社索取。

北京大学出版社

教 师 联 系 表

教材名称		教育学专业英语			
姓名：	性别：		职务：		职称：
E-mail：		联系电话：		邮政编码：	
供职学校：		所在院系：			（章）
学校地址：					
教学科目与年级：		班级人数：			
通信地址：					

填写完毕后，请将此表邮寄给我们，我们将为您免费寄送本教材配套资料，谢谢！

北京市海淀区成府路 205 号
北京大学出版社外语编辑部　吴宇森
邮政编码：100871
电子邮箱：wuyusen@pup.cn

外语编辑部电话：010-62759634
邮 购 部 电话：010-62534449
市场营销部电话：010-62750672